HACKING COLLEGE

HACKING COLLEGE

*Why the Major Doesn't Matter—
and What Really Does*

NED SCOTT LAFF *and*
SCOTT CARLSON

JOHNS HOPKINS UNIVERSITY PRESS | *Baltimore*

© 2025 Johns Hopkins University Press
All rights reserved. Published 2025
Printed in the United States of America on acid-free paper
2 4 6 8 9 7 5 3 1

Johns Hopkins University Press
2715 North Charles Street
Baltimore, Maryland 21218
www.press.jhu.edu

Library of Congress Cataloging-in-Publication Data

Names: Laff, Ned Scott, author. | Carlson, Scott, author.
Title: Hacking college : why the major doesn't matter—and what really does / Ned Scott Laff and Scott Carlson.
Description: Baltimore : Johns Hopkins University Press, 2025. | Includes bibliographical references and index.
Identifiers: LCCN 2024033276 | ISBN 9781421450759 (hardcover) | ISBN 9781421450766 (ebook)
Subjects: LCSH: Education, Higher—Aims and objectives—United States. | Universities and colleges—United States—Administration. | Academic achievement—United States. | College majors—United States.
Classification: LCC LA227.4 .L35 2024 | DDC 378.73—dc23/eng/20240821
LC record available at https://lccn.loc.gov/2024033276

A catalog record for this book is available from the British Library.

Special discounts are available for bulk purchases of this book. For more information, please contact Special Sales at specialsales@jh.edu.

*To the kids in our lives,
Rachel, Becky, Elly,
Jack, Hudson,*

and Sasha

CONTENTS

INTRODUCTION. *Scott Carlson* 1

1. The Blank Spaces 15
2. The Curricular Maze 43
3. The Wicked Problem 71
4. The Hidden Job Market 98
5. The Liberal Arts and Field of Study 122
6. The Need for Hacking 152
7. Visible Students and Agile Institutions 178

Acknowledgments 203
Notes 205
Index 217

HACKING COLLEGE

INTRODUCTION

(Don't skip this.)

Scott Carlson

IN MAY 2023, DURING THE LAST WEEK OF CLASSES in the spring semester, Ned Laff and I drove from Chicago to Springfield, Illinois, to visit the campus of Lincoln Land Community College. I was writing a *Chronicle of Higher Education* story about the problems that students encounter when transferring from a two-year to a four-year institution and the unnecessary bureaucratic barriers and misdirection they hit along the way, a theme we were exploring for this book. During our research, Ned had noticed that the University of Illinois at Springfield numbered its courses in a way that would almost ensure that a student transferring there from a community college—including its main feeder school, Lincoln Land—would lose credits. Having worked on these issues at colleges for decades, Ned had an eye and ear for the details that only an insider would catch, so I asked him to tag along on the reporting trip and sit in on the interviews.[1]

The college administrators we met did what you would expect—they talked up a new transfer agreement and initiatives in student coaching, and they touted their successes. But on any campus, students are usually able to offer a clearer picture of what's really going on. When we talked with some of Lincoln Land's students about the guidance they had gotten at the college, we could see the factors that might well cause students to stumble as they plodded along in their academic journeys.

In the commons building at Lincoln Land, we sat down with four students: Paul, Cordelia, Eric, and Giles. None of these students was first-generation; they came from families where their parents had college educations, some of them with multiple degrees. All had a sense of what had called them to college, and most believed they had majors in mind that would launch them into careers.

Paul said he was planning to transfer to Illinois State University, to study either graphic design or marketing—the latter being a major suggested by his father because he thought it was in demand. But Paul did not seem to have a clear sense of what marketing was. He thought it was the same as advertising, and he did not see how graphic design, advertising, and marketing could come together in a degree plan that fit his academic strengths.

Cordelia was interested in art and in helping people and was taking advice she had gotten from her mother. "She's like, you can just combine them and do art therapy—like, it's an actual thing," Cordelia said. "But I don't really know how to pursue that, other than look for schools that have majors and apply to them." Cordelia's advisor, called a "success coach" by the college, would check in with her now and then by text but had never offered any advice on how to pursue art therapy or how to find people working in the profession. "It's not any super-specific help."

Eric, a freshman, said he had "an intense fascination" with the art, objects, and architecture of the Victorian period and claimed he could accurately date old houses by looking at their design. "I'm an antiquarian," he said. "I could probably work in a museum's archive because I'm so fascinated with touching little objects of history." His history professor and friends in the antiquarian community had suggested he talk about his interests with people working for historical societies and the Illinois State Museum. "I plan to volunteer over there, if I can, and maybe get to know them a bit more and maybe make more connections over time. But that's kind of the only thing I know to do." Because of its connections to Abraham Lincoln and historical tourism, Springfield has a hidden job world related to architectural preservation and nineteenth-century reenactment—a world Eric knew was there but didn't know how to tap into.

Giles, who had just finished his term as a student trustee, had concentrated on English at Lincoln Land. But he wanted to transfer into global studies at the University of Illinois at Springfield to pursue international law and become a diplomat for the country of Georgia, where he had visited when he was younger and had found the people, the language, and the culture fascinating. But no one had advised him on how to focus his studies on the history, politics, and languages of the Caucasus region nor how to find upper-division and graduate programs that might open up job opportunities in Eastern Europe and West Asia. Although his college was less than eight miles from the state capitol, no one had suggested that he visit the legislative and lobbying offices downtown that deal with international trade, immigration, and cultural exchange for the State of Illinois. And he had not been directed toward research opportunities among the consulates and international trade organizations three hours north, in Chicago.

When we met with these four students, Ned ran through some of the principles we cover in *Hacking College*: how to think about disciplines and majors more broadly, how to identify faculty members and off-campus experts by their fields of study, and how to make contact with people and to open up opportunities—all straightforward strategies in making a path from college to career. "Has anyone on this campus talked to you about anything like this?" Ned asked the group at one point.

"Never," replied Giles.

That's no surprise. In fact, it's one of the reasons Ned and I got together in the first place.

In early 2018, after I had written a long *Chronicle* report about the "future of work" and college career centers, I followed it up with a series of stories about apprenticeship programs, the impact of artificial intelligence, and the confusing routes from graduation to a job. In response to my article about job outcomes for liberal-arts students,[2]

I got an email message from one Ned Laff, who was finishing out his career at Governors State University, located south of Chicago, and who wanted to talk. "What if liberal-arts departments and colleges simply had to rethink how to 'connect the dots' differently without actually changing anything on their campuses?" Ned wrote. "The answer is not in career services. The pathway to workable solutions lies in the intersection between students' 'hidden intellectualism' and the 'hidden job market,' which career services are not set up to explore."

I made a mental note to call Ned, then soon forgot about it. Six months later, after I wrote a story about underemployment, Ned wrote again with the same message. "I do wish we had time to sit and really talk," he implored. This time, I called him. We had a good conversation about the inner workings of colleges and the problems students have in navigating the undergraduate maze. I knew there was something there but needed more time to investigate it—and I was already slated to write several long *Chronicle* reports in the near future.[3] I promised to call Ned the next time I was in Chicago.

Finally, in February 2020, I went to Chicago to see a friend and agreed to meet up with Ned at the Evanston Public Library. We talked for a couple of hours, before walking down the street to a bar, where we got lunch and talked for a few hours more. Ned hammered on a point that day: Why couldn't colleges do a better job of guiding students out of undergraduate programs and into careers? Evidence of their failures was all around us, in the underemployment rate and the common stories about college graduates who struggle to launch. Many of the problems, he argued that afternoon, had to do with the bureaucratic focus on "guiding" students to degree completion with a singular focus on the major. The major is a myth, Ned contended—another institutional structure that tends to blind students to the relationship between the college curriculum and their own personal interests as legitimate areas of academic study.

Instead, he advocated looking at the undergraduate degree as a Field of Study, a method that offered a wider lens on the college experience, unifying the degree's disparate pieces and connecting those pieces to the work world beyond college. Field of Study, as he used the term, models how faculty pursue their own research.[4] There are no generic faculty, as each professor is a field-of-study specialist, working on problems from a multidisciplinary perspective. If students started thinking this way too, they could see how to connect their interests to their studies and take ownership of their college education.

I told Ned that I thought this is what academic advising was supposed to do already. But Ned had long been frustrated by the transactional conversations typical of much academic advising, and he likened traditional advising of students to leading livestock through a slaughterhouse. Students could see how ineffective those conversations were but didn't have the context and know-how to change their situation.

Around the time Ned first reached out to me, Governors State conducted a snapshot survey of 395 students, comparing their interactions in conventional advising with the conversations they later had with peer mentors trained in the Field of Study process. The students, largely first-generation and low-income, had two common reactions: "Why didn't somebody talk to me about this before?" and "This would have changed what I am doing in college." In their responses to the survey, whose results were published by the American Association of Colleges and Universities in 2018, many students struggled to explain what they were trying to accomplish with their undergraduate degree or how their college plans could lead to a personally satisfying outcome, whether to a job or to graduate school.[5]

I found the Field of Study approach interesting, but I was still skeptical. I realized that I had never looked closely at academic advising and its impact on student success and careers, and Ned challenged me to observe some advising in person. So, in the last weeks before the pandemic closed campuses, I sat in on advising sessions at half a dozen institutions of different types. What I witnessed in those sessions—and what I have seen and heard since—made me think that Ned had hit the mark.

One of the first advising appointments I observed stunned me: A nineteen-year-old woman met with her advisor and said she had picked a major in political science because she wanted to be president of the United States one day. The advisor breezed right past that nugget of information and pushed the student to pick a minor, settle on a foreign language (which was required by her major), and fill in the rest of her requirements on the degree audit. There was no discussion of what she might do for a living before she became commander in chief, why she was picking African studies as a minor (she thought it might help her with global negotiations as president someday), or what she would do with Swahili, the language she chose because it seemed to pair with a minor in African studies. It was simply check, check, check.[6]

Few of the advising sessions I attended matched this degree of malpractice, but almost all were merely transactional, focused on pushing students through the system. And many of the conversations and encounters I have had in the years since have confirmed that the transactional interaction is common, if students are lucky enough to get even that much attention. Over the course of writing this book, Ned and I talked to dozens of students at various colleges—including institutions that publicized their college-to-career initiatives—who were having trouble making sense of their undergraduate education. In some cases, we started coaching them.

One student had been part of both the Posse Foundation and Chicago Scholars and had attended an elite university that used the "life design" approach to career development, yet he had spent his college career switching through majors that seemed marketable but had little connection to his passion and talents in videography. He freely admitted that he had no interest in his current major in urban studies and had chosen it only because it would allow him to graduate in four years and avoid debt. When this student had asked his faculty advisor how to find a career after graduation, the professor said that it was a tough job market out there and that his own kid was having trouble landing work. The professor told the student that, like his own kid, he might have to work at a bar for a while until he figures it out.

After watching interactions like these, I wrote "A Crusade against Terrible Advising," which tallied the shortcomings of conventional advising and mentioned alternative approaches that tried to help students make more informed decisions about their courses, such as "appreciative advising," developed at Florida Atlantic University. The article also featured students who had worked with Ned and undertaken the Field of Study process discussed in this book.

"Terrible Advising" was one of the more popular articles on the *Chronicle*'s website that year and generated some discussion with publishers about a possible book on advising. On paper, Ned and I made a good pairing as coauthors: Ned, the insider, had worked closely with students for more than thirty-five years at a variety of public and private institutions in curriculum development, interdisciplinary majors, general education, student advising and success, and experiential-learning programs. I, the outsider, had logged more than twenty years at the *Chronicle of Higher Education*, writing lately about the transition from college to career, the cost and value of a degree, higher-education finance, the connections between institutions and communities, and higher education's effect on inequality.

When Ned and I got together again to talk about a book project, we found that we did not want to write only about advising. We were interested in writing about the narratives, structures, and underlying institutional motivations that set up students to complete what Ned, in our first meeting, had called "empty college degrees." An empty college degree—consisting of a reputedly useful major and a smattering of unrelated courses on a transcript—leads students to underemployment or to stop out altogether; what's more, it drives the national conversation questioning the value of higher education.

The title for the book emerged organically. Early in the project, Ned, who is a Trekkie, made regular references to the Kobayashi Maru, a bit of *Star Trek* lore mentioned in *The Wrath of Khan*. James T. Kirk, once faced with an unwinnable test at Starfleet Academy, hacked into the computer to change the parameters of the test to allow him to win. Students, Ned argued, had to do the same in higher education. Later we found the work of the technologist Bruce Schneier, who saw hacking across society and culture as a tool to change individual fortunes and society as a whole. When I mentioned the book's thematic threads to my friend and *Chronicle* colleague Goldie Blumenstyk—as well as our struggle to come up with a title that reflected the book's tension between asking the system to change versus working the existing system—she had one of her characteristic lightbulb moments: "How about *Hacking College*?"

The problem of empty college degrees is a major theme in chapters 1 and 2. Chapter 1 focuses on the misperceptions that students and parents have about how college connects to careers, which are stoked by the media's relaying of myths about having the "right major," attending the "best school," and winning the plum job. Discussions about empty college degrees have been around for decades, with generations of students confused about how to fill in the "blank spaces" in their undergraduate plans.

Throughout this book, we use a handful of key terms in making our case for Field of Study, and here is an opportunity to introduce the first of them: **blank spaces** can be seen if you look at any degree audit. They are the electives and other open choices that compose most of the undergraduate degree—spaces that students have to figure out how to fill, a crucial but underappreciated aspect of college.

In chapter 2, we discuss how solving the conundrum of blank spaces runs aground on some of the structures and vested interests of higher-education institutions. We raise the problem of students who come to college without the background needed to clearly explain their intellectual interests and who wind up getting tracked into programs that do not fit their goals or academic strengths. We argue that instead of seeing blank spaces as a stumbling block or burden, they are actually a means for students to explore their "hidden intellectualism" and "vocational purpose" in creating a meaningful and marketable undergraduate degree.

The term **hidden intellectualism** comes from Gerald Graff, a professor of English and education at the University of Illinois at Chicago, in his book *Clueless in Academe: How Schooling Obscures the Life of the Mind*.[7] Graff argues that the interests students bring to college from their everyday lives—baseball, motorcycles, Bible Belt religion—are legitimate areas of study and that engaging their hidden intellectualism is key to helping students see the connections between their interests and the intellectual resources on a campus. Importantly, Graff asserts that students arrive on campus as "latent" intellectuals already possessing these motivating interests. The challenge, we argue, is that students have trouble connecting that latent intellectualism to the structure of the curriculum and to a potential career path.

Vocational purpose comes from the idea of vocation, or one's calling. Students learn to translate their hidden intellectualism into a career trajectory. This is where they see their interests, skills, and talents binding with a personal sense of purpose in the vast world of work.

In chapter 3, we begin discussing the Field of Study approach in detail, shifting the emphasis away from the major and toward teaching students how to use the blank spaces to create a more integrated, multidisciplinary education. Through Field of Study, students learn to translate their vocational purpose, their sense of *why*, into an undergraduate program of study that addresses a real-world "wicked problem." A **wicked problem** is a fuzzy, complicated, pressing, and perhaps unsolvable human predicament requiring a multidisciplinary approach—and taking any approach to a wicked problem depends on how you define it. A student's own college career represents a personal wicked problem: How can the student translate their vocational purpose and sense of why into an integrated undergraduate experience?

In chapter 4, we examine the tension between following a major with a purported high return on investment and choosing to follow an interest or feed a passion. We argue that students can fulfill both goals if they think broadly about the "hidden job market." The **hidden job market** is traditionally defined as those jobs that aren't advertised and are acquired through connections, but in this book, we expand that definition to include the granularity of positions that exist in any world of work; these are the many ancillary or adjacent jobs that people may not know by name but are out there to find. A student can discover multiple career paths that fit a hidden intellectualism or vocational purpose if taught to see the breadth of the hidden job market.

In chapter 5, we take our discussion in a slightly different direction. The assumption that "major equals job" not only misleads students, but it has also been disastrous for liberal-arts colleges and departments. Taking our alternative approach to advising that incorporates hidden intellectualism, vocational purpose, a wicked problem, and the hidden job market could transform the conversation about the value of the liberal arts—and thereby help academics and administrators rebuild enrollments in disciplines typically written off as "nonvocational."

Any savvy reader will recognize elements of Field of Study in other college-to-career methods, and to be sure, there's nothing new about problem-based multidisciplinarity in higher education. Our iteration comes out of the Individual Plans of Study (IPS) program at the University of Illinois at Urbana-Champaign, where Ned worked in the late 1970s and early 1980s while he was completing his doctorate. Undergraduate colleges and universities at the time were experimenting with interdisciplinary initiatives in an attempt to be more agile. It was easier to allow the students, under faculty guidance, to take advantage of new combinations of courses across the university than it would have been to restructure entrenched departments and launch new academic programs.[8]

Roland "Rollie" Holmes, an assistant dean of the College of Liberal Arts and Sciences, created the vision for the program: to provide an avenue for students whose interests lay outside the scope of existing majors. To be admitted, students had to prepare a proposal that explained the rationale of their degree plan, including how different course clusters fit together; how they would integrate experiential-learning opportunities; and where they might find career opportunities. Two faculty advisors had to sign off on the plan. IPS had a tight enrollment cap, to block students from misusing the program to avoid course requirements. Only a small percentage of the students who approached IPS were allowed to move forward with a proposal.

But IPS had a broader impact, as it helped even mainstream majors. When students applying to the program were turned down, Ned and other mentors learned that they could still apply the principles of IPS to help those students design integrated undergraduate experiences from within traditional majors. Later, friends of those students would amble into the IPS office to get help crafting their own undergraduate program.

Holmes made a lasting impression on Ned. One night after work, Ned remarked to Holmes that it seemed like most of the students who emerged from college successfully just happened to run into the right advisor or serendipitously encountered a crucial piece of information that paved their way to graduation or a good first job.

"You're starting to get it," Holmes replied. "It's not supposed to be about luck."

This book is filled with stories of students who got lucky, in a sense, because they stumbled across people who engaged them in a different kind of conversation and taught them a process to hack the college game. All of the students profiled in this book are real, and all but one (Carla, whose example comes from a conference workshop) were interviewed for the book. In some instances, we have used the student's full name. Others requested privacy but allowed us to use a first name or pseudonym.

Their stories function as case studies in the chapters by exemplifying how the principles of Field of Study played out in real students' lives. For instance, three such cases in chapter 6 emphasize that *how* you do college may be more important than *where* you do college. To make any college path successful, a student has to hack the many procedures and structures that exist within any institution.

Books in the college-to-career genre often tell the stories of go-getter students who successfully navigated their way into a job and a comfortable life, but those stories often leave out key details of how those students *created* their luck; and in any case, those students often came from a privileged background and attended a name-brand institution, factors that provide huge advantages. The students in this book are different, as they came from lower-income backgrounds and entered schools not among the elite. We tell their stories in detail to show *how* they used the Field of Study method to understand the granularity of their desired work world, to leverage the educational resources on and off their campus, and to build out their social and cultural capital—a skill set they can call on again and again in life.

The terms "social capital" and "cultural capital" are mentioned frequently in this book. Both come from Pierre Bourdieu, a French sociologist who discussed how each can confer resources and advantages that can lead to an individual's success.[9] Much of the discussion about student success and college-to-career focuses on how students can acquire **social capital**—that is, how students can expand their professional and social networks while pursuing their undergraduate degree.

But that discussion doesn't always give **cultural capital** its due, as it provides a foundation for building social capital and social mobility. It is an underacknowledged asset of the college experience. Cultural capital includes the competencies, knowledge, and skills a person acquires simply from the environment in which they live. Cultural capital can grow with exposure to new cultures and new environments and, in doing so, can open up a broader sense of possibilities, particularly for students from lower-income backgrounds. Someone can have a wealth of cultural capital in one environment and be bereft of it in another, because its value fluctuates just like any currency when crossing borders.

Cultural capital is the primordial goo that hidden intellectualism emerges from. A key part of Field of Study focuses on helping students identify the cultural capital they already have and then build on it. This is how Shay, in chapter 3, uses her knowledge of and enthusiasm for spoken-word performance to create opportunities, experiences, and connections in Washington, DC, thus changing the trajectory of her social mobility. And, as you will see in almost all of the students' stories, that growth in social and cultural capital drives a growing belief in themselves.

When you are writing a book, people often ask, "Who's your audience?" Given that our publisher, Johns Hopkins University Press, regularly issues books aimed at decision makers in higher education, you'd think our primary audience would be associate provosts of undergraduate studies, deans of colleges, directors of student success, and the like. For that reason, in chapter 7, we share some thoughts about how a Field of Study approach could be field-tested at a learning institution that currently practices a conventional approach to academic advising. Some aspects and perspectives from Field of Study could be adapted for career centers and advising approaches that colleges are already using. The technological solutions popular today—data analytics and early-alert systems that flag floundering undergraduates—are valuable, yet they only go so far in remedying the problem of empty degrees. What students really need is to have a different kind of conversation about their college career.

All the same, we are realists. Colleges are slow to change, and the Field of Study frame challenges many embedded bureaucratic interests and processes. What's more, it comes at a time when administrators are reluctant to rock the boat in higher education.

Knowing this, we wrote this book as a kind of manifesto of educational populism, to be read by anyone seeking to understand how students get lost in college and how to provide solutions for them from the bottom up. We hope to empower anyone—a faculty member, a resident-life coordinator, a high-school counselor, a Division III coach—to have conversations with students that can change their trajectories. Most important, perhaps, an inquisitive student or a parent could get ahold of this book and find in it a way to start hacking college.

When Ned and I had conversations with students, as we did that day in the commons building at Lincoln Land, I saw them light up, as they started to realize how they could connect their dreams and aspirations to college and a life after. "Can you write down those things he told me?" Eric said to Giles, but Giles said he didn't have his phone with him. Cordelia, though, had already pulled out her phone to record tips about how to research art-therapy programs and offered to record details for both Eric and Giles too. Paul, sitting off to the side, scribbled in a notepad. After about half an hour, our interview was over, and we shook hands with the students and walked out to the parking lot.

Many of the conversations we had with students ended on a melancholy note. After all, there are still so many out there looking for a lucky break and so many who are invisible on campus—like Paul, Cordelia, Eric, and Giles. We knew that when we left them, they would be, once again, on their own.

1

The Blank Spaces

OVER TIME, MANY STUDENTS START TO BELIEVE that getting an education is merely about clearing hurdles. Isaiah Moore had cleared his share before he strode into Ned's office at Governors State University in 2018, furious that he had to jump over yet another hurdle: a "pointless" science requirement that had nothing to do with his aspiration to be a Chicago city alderman or a congressman from Illinois.

The story of how Isaiah began to unpack the meaning of his college education starts with that pointless science requirement.

In many ways, Isaiah was just a regular kid from the South Side of Chicago, with advantages compared to some of his peers. His mom, a single parent, had gone to college and nurtured his ambition to change his community. She pushed Isaiah into Air Force Academy High School, one of the few magnet programs in Chicago's public schools designed for college preparation. He worked hard and did well, landing in the top 10 percent of his class.

Through a chance conversation with a peer at school, he found out about Chicago Scholars, a foundation that mentors students from underserved communities, helping them get in and succeed at college. He applied, interviewed, and was accepted to the program that year—

another hurdle cleared. He hoped the foundation would help him get into a competitive college that would lead to Chicago City Hall after graduation.

But Chicago Scholars left many of the decisions up to Isaiah. His mentor asked him to come up with a short list of institutions where he could pursue studies for his political aspirations: University of Illinois at Urbana-Champaign, the University of Illinois at Chicago, DePaul University, and, Isaiah's first choice, Morehouse College (which, in the end, was too expensive and too far from home). Isaiah ultimately chose DePaul, after a fun "admissions overnight" that was mostly devoted to social life at the university and set up to woo newly admitted students. Even with the scholarship DePaul offered him, he and his mother both took out loans to cover his first year.

Isaiah declared a major in political science—after all, "politics" is right there in the name of the major, he reasoned—but he got little help from Chicago Scholars and his advisor at DePaul. No one asked Isaiah substantive questions about his goals or helped him dig into the curriculum to explore what was available on campus. He liked his courses in political science at DePaul, but he couldn't see how they would usher him into the gritty world of Chicago politics.

Over time, the hurdles started getting higher. The pace of DePaul's ten-week quarters was challenging; Isaiah kept up academically, but he started to fall behind financially. His aid package was lowered his sophomore year, and he and his mother borrowed yet more money to make up the deficit. Worried that he would shackle his mother and himself to a pile of debt, with little sense of how the DePaul degree would lead to a real job in politics, he transferred to one of the cheapest institutions in the city, a place he once toured as a high-school student and vowed he would never attend: that was Governors State University, where he met Ned.

There Isaiah sat during an orientation session for incoming transfer students, slumped in his chair, disappointed with where he had landed after all the sacrifice. Surely, he thought, this marginal state institution could not launch him as well as DePaul or Morehouse. But in a session on Field of Study, Ned told Isaiah, and the rest of the assembly, that Governors State, or almost any other institution for that matter, has everything a student needs to go anywhere and do anything—if, that is, students learn to think deeply about how they are weaving together the pieces of their undergraduate education.

Something about that message stuck with Isaiah and led him to follow Ned back to his office. He had just learned from an advisor that he had to sign up for a life-science course to complete his general-education requirements. To Isaiah, the course was just another hurdle and more wasted money, and it seemed to have zero connection to Chicago politics.

"Why do I have to take this lousy course?" he blurted out as he walked through the door. "I am never going to use it."

Why We Wrote This Book

Isaiah's question, so familiar to those who work with students, captures the mess students face in trying to tie college to their personal interests and aspirations for a career. Rather than getting help in aligning their ambition with a course of study, they are often given a formula, one amplified by the media: the "right" major equals the "right" job, especially if you are at the "right" college. But most students don't see why—or are never taught how—they should combine the major, electives, on- and off-campus experiences, and assorted general-education requirements into a cohesive whole.

Instead, many students come to believe that college itself is just another pointless hurdle before reaching the job market. They see hiring managers using the undergraduate degree as nothing more an applicant filter. Some hiring managers, by setting the college degree as a minimum requirement, inadvertently reinforce its role as a mere signal. And with students focused on the idea that an employer is just looking for someone "with a degree" or is looking for the "right major," they pay less attention to whether they have knitted together the appropriate skills needed for a profession or a job sector. It's no wonder, then, that multiple surveys indicate that employers are unhappy with the lacking skill sets that graduates bring to their first job.

The problem starts with the message that students and parents hear from the media and policy wonks, from the College Scorecard, from high-school counselors, and from colleges themselves: the major is the central focus of a college education, the thing that defines a college experience, and the key factor in getting a good return on investment from college. So, many students grit their teeth and continue the hurdle-jumping they started well before high school. They slog through general education and the rest of the peripheral requirements with as little effort as possible, and they focus on completing the requirements for a "job-relevant" major, with the belief they are headed down a career pathway.

As a result, those students do not know what they are doing in a particular class they chose and sometimes have no solid sense of why they picked a particular major or institution. Most critical of all, they do not understand how their studies in general education, in a major, and in electives and minors can add up to an undergraduate experience that integrates with their educational, professional, and personal goals. Moreover, too many students do not know how to take advantage of the rich curricular and learning opportunities that colleges provide outside the classroom, in programs and offices all over campus. This confusion is an underlying reason why so many students change majors, transfer schools, fall behind, or stop out—some of the critical problems that higher education struggles to address.

Even many students who walk across a stage to take a diploma have graduated with an "empty college degree"—a major that sounds like a job, with a smattering of disconnected courses on a transcript, yet few relevant experiences that channeled their college learning. As a result, many wind up underemployed, which drives parents, employers, and policymakers to question the value of an undergraduate education.

There's a better way to address the problem, and it's about reframing how we look at obvious pieces that make up a college education and about showing students how they can create an integrated and meaningful college experience. But to understand why students need different conversations to help them think differently about their undergraduate experiences, we have to look first at how parents and students get these misperceptions to begin with.

The Mixed Messages We Send

It's easy to understand the pressures that parents and students—especially those from historically underserved families—feel about pursuing a college education. The media is rife with articles about the rising costs of attending college, the problems with financial aid and student debt, and the perils of choosing the "wrong major" or the "wrong school." Many of today's students—more often first-generation, nonwhite, and low-income—face an array of financial and job-market pressures, starting with the ever-rising cost of attendance. They also feel the widening wealth gap and the "stickiness" at the extremes of socioeconomic strata: Children born in the top quintile of wealth are likely to stay there, just as children born in the bottom quintile will likely never crawl out. Children born in the middle three quintiles, economists say, have varying chances of going in either direction. And education, parents and students are told, will improve one's odds of moving up.[1]

That's because more jobs today require advanced training and substantial critical-thinking skills, with the advent of new technologies that enable automation, digitalization, and artificial intelligence. Middle-skills jobs, which once provided graduates with good entry-level career pathways, are being replaced by technologies that can perform routine tasks at the core of those occupations; therefore, entry-level jobs, which are now frequently outsourced, don't necessarily lead to advancement within a company.[2] As a result, the "hazy" route to a career that often characterized the job search for college graduates of the twentieth century is narrowing and more difficult to navigate now. These trends seem to be creating a kind of hourglass workforce, with non-routine cognitive careers at the top and repetitive manual labor at the bottom. With the nation's attention trained on that growing wealth gap, parents and students understand these trends intuitively, if not explicitly.

The financial stakes in a college degree have only risen with the emphasis that policymakers have placed on attaining postsecondary credentials for the job market. Since the early 1980s, the public school system has shifted its orientation to college for all, de-emphasizing pathways in the trades and other vocational routes. Employers have responded to these trends, too, making the college degree a prerequisite to a job interview, even for positions that rarely required college training in the past.[3] That tacit requirement reflects a growing disparity in pay: the wage premium for a college degree has doubled since the 1970s, not because college graduates earn so much more than they used to—their wages are in fact flat—but because workers with only a high-school diploma now earn so much less.[4]

Amid all of this, parents and students are hit by stories of college graduates being underprepared for the job market, laden with college debt, and underemployed in a job that may not require a bachelor's degree.[5]

So, no wonder many parents and students want a clear formula—a ranking of institutions, a list of marketable majors—to ensure that college doesn't lead to a job as a barista or bartender. Because we live in a world obsessed with data, the education system has become a data machine, churning out metrics for governments and accreditation agencies. There's no shortage of media outlets, think tanks, analysts, and businesses seeking to process and profit from those numbers to provide facile rankings and lists, oriented on money and return on investment. The outcome: rankings of colleges whose graduates enjoy the highest starting salaries and lists of majors tied to high-paying careers versus those that ostensibly lead to poor employment prospects.

For instance, Third Way, a left-center think tank, developed the "Price to Earnings Premium" (PEP), a rating of how long it takes students to recoup college costs, based on the wage premium those students should get with a college degree. The PEP rating relies on the wages earned by graduates of particular programs at specific colleges, using data pulled from the nascent College Scorecard, with only a few years of data available.[6] Perhaps in time, the scorecard will offer an accurate sense of the programs that consistently launch students successfully into the job market, but for now the data is a black box. We don't know why students in majors at some colleges earned more than students in similar majors at other institutions, whether they remained ahead of their peers over the long run, nor whether these students—financially successful or not—are in fulfilling careers and living comfortable, active, and inquisitive lives.[7]

The problem of leaning on big data about majors is that it's like a check-engine light. It might indicate there's a problem, but you have to get under the hood to find out what's really going on.

You can see this limitation in *Five Rules of the College and Career Game*, a 2018 report from Georgetown University's Center on Education and the Workforce. The report is aimed at addressing the "growing buyer's remorse" among students and the "lack of information about degrees and the careers they could lead to," noting that 51 percent of college graduates would choose a different degree path if they could do college over. "Students deserve to know what they are paying for," the report says.[8]

However much they deserve it, parents and students still might not know what they are paying for after reading the report. Some of its broad conclusions are clear—engineering majors make more money than education majors, no surprise—but a lot of variation lurks in the ranges of possible salaries. According to the report, arts and humanities majors in the 75 percent earning bracket make significantly more money than engineering majors in the 25 percent earning bracket.

Maybe, then, the major is not as important as everyone seems to think. The data doesn't tell us what made some fine-arts majors, English majors, or philosophy majors more successful than some graduates in engineering, nor why some engineering majors didn't rank higher in the earnings brackets. Did some humanities majors get the right advice, skills, and connections from their college experience to plot a path to a good-paying career? Or were they just lucky or perhaps born into socioeconomic or cultural advantage?

With these ambiguities, the report's seemingly contradictory "five rules" could confuse a parent or student who wants a formula to beat the college-to-career game. The five rules tell us that education levels matter and more is better (rule 1) but also that less education can be worth more (rule 4). The major can be more important than one's level of education (rule 2), but it does not control anyone's financial destiny because of the great variation in earnings for any particular major (rule 3). And of course, there is the perennial comment that humanities and liberal-arts majors will never catch up to the highest-earning majors (rule 5)—yet many humanities majors clearly do exceptionally well in life.

A pack of journalists and pundits also analyze the transition from college to career, offering a lot of cautionary tales but, in the end, reinforcing the fixation on college name brands and majors. For instance, in *There Is Life after College: What Parents and Students Should Know about Navigating School to Prepare for the Jobs of Tomorrow*, Jeffrey J. Selingo invented labels for categories of students—"sprinters, wanderers, and stragglers"—that seem to correlate highly with background wealth, choice of school, and even career aspirations. In his book, the sprinter goes to Georgetown and works at Pricewaterhouse-Coopers, while the straggler is an adult student at a two-year institution who wants to be a woodworker after several false starts at college—without much perspective provided on whether the sprinter knows where she's sprinting to or whether the straggler is actually on his own right track. The wanderer in the middle, a communications student from the University of Mary Washington, isn't really wandering. Selingo says she discovered "too late" in her undergraduate career that her institution does not have a major in journalism, her career goal, but in truth you don't need to major in journalism to become a reporter, magazine writer, or editor, particularly at a university situated only an hour outside media-saturated Washington, DC. For wandering and straggling students who fail to cobble together a cohesive undergraduate degree for the job market, Selingo offers a band-aid solution favored by the "disruptor" crowd: spend yet more money on private-sector add-ons, in the form of bootcamps, badges, and microcredentials, which tend to focus on tech, big finance, and start-ups.[9]

Taking an optimistic tone, George Anders tries to reassure arts and humanities majors (and their parents) that they will find a career in *You Can Do Anything: The Surprising Power of a "Useless" Liberal Arts Education*, yet many of his examples are drawn from students who went to elite colleges, out of reach to many students and their parents. Yes, you can study nineteenth-century French art at the University of Chicago and later go on to work for a top firm, like Morningstar or Google. But that's not a playbook available to most students.[10]

The 2017 College Student Survey by Gallup, a polling company, and Strada, an education foundation, found that two-thirds of students weren't confident that they were amassing the skills needed to succeed in the workforce, and half weren't sure that their major would lead to a good job. The Gallup-Strada survey noted that students often rely on friends and family for advice about colleges and majors, and less on career services or academic advising.[11] (Perhaps this is because those campus offices often have their shortcomings, something we cover in chapter 2.)

Some suggest that students may suffer from having just too much to choose from. People may hear the compliant that Isaiah expressed—about having to take a lousy, useless course—and conclude that colleges should diminish or do away with the distraction of the general-education requirement and get on with the business of the major. That notion has been the impetus behind the creation of guided pathways and the discussion of three-year degrees, under the logic that institutions should assist students in narrowing their choices to those routes that faculty and administrators believe reflect student career interests.[12]

This problem, though, of students graduating with what we call empty college degrees—resulting from their inability to make sense of their college education and leading to employers bemoaning the incompetency of those graduates—has been acknowledged for decades. In 1985, the American Association of Colleges (AAC), the precursor to the American Association of Colleges and Universities (AAC&U), published *Integrity in the College Curriculum: A Report to the Academic Community*. "The major in most colleges is little more than a gathering of courses taken in one department, lacking structure and depth ... where the essential message embedded in all the fancy prose is: pick eight of the following." The "following," the authors noted, after studying college curricula across the country, was simply lists of two dozen or more courses. General education, AAC argued, reflected this same lack of cohesion, representing "more of a marketplace philosophy than a common set of expectations."[13]

In the report, AAC shared a letter from the American Economic Association, commenting that "we know preciously little about what the economics major is or does for students" and that "it is unlikely, whatever the major or institution, that the average graduating senior had 'any integrated sense of his major discipline and its links to other fields of inquiry.'" The business community, according to AAC, complained of recruiting graduates not ready to take the next steps after graduation.

In 1995, in an article in *Liberal Education*, Carole Geary Schneider, then president of AAC&U, reflected on *Integrity in the College Curriculum*, disappointed that little about the situation had changed. As Schneider characterized it, college graduates' transcripts often resembled a cafeteria menu, lacking coherence and integration. She characterized the problem as a college curriculum turned into a marketplace of new courses, new subjects of study, new disciplines brokered by faculty through their research. Undergraduate programs, she argued, have become a confusing array of courses, concentrations, and course requirements for students. (*Liberal Education* reprinted Schneider's article in 2014.)[14]

Looking at the Blank Spaces

The red flags raised by the surveys on college-student readiness, the reports by academic organizations, and the accounts in the media get at the symptoms and consequences of the problem but not at its core: Helping students find success in college is not about cutting down the curriculum to offer less-confusing choices or about directing students to extracurricular badges or certificates that will offer "job-relevant" skills. It's certainly not about finding a major associated with a high median salary or one that will ostensibly lead to employment, just because it carries a name that sounds like a job.

Getting a college education should be about undertaking a Field of Study, a much more expansive lens on the undergraduate experience than the typical obsession with the major. The Field of Study approach focuses on a multidisciplinary wicked problem of genuine personal interest to a student, one stemming from the student's hidden intellectualism or vocational purpose and unifying the components of their undergraduate experience.

Based on decades of our having conversations with low-income and first-generation students, we have seen that most of them arrive at college with an incipient idea of what they want to do with their lives—they just may not come with social and cultural capital enough to explain that idea or picture how that idea exists in the professional world. And these students largely do not have the college literacy needed to make use of the vast array of learning resources available to blaze a path to that world. Most students are not undecided; they are simply undeclared—because they don't yet see where their interests fit into the various majors offered in the academic catalog.

Under a Field of Study approach, those inchoate ideas are validated. Any desired life pursuit could be real, existing in the hidden job market. Through Field of Study, students must test their ideas about that life pursuit by engaging with people in the world outside academe and then must use the entirety of the college curriculum and resources to explore that interest.

Prior to walking into the Center for the Junior Year at Governors State University, Isaiah had never been engaged in a deep conversation about the nature of college learning, the possibilities on campus, the challenge of assembling those pieces into a coherent course of study, and how to link all of that to his aspirations for after college. He knew where he wanted his undergraduate career to lead—into politics of the City of Chicago—but he believed that a big chunk of his college experience had nothing to do with that. The system had taught him to check off the boxes of general education and electives in order to move on to the "important" work of the major.

The conventional major-oriented approach, which most students encounter, works like blinders that obscure the possibilities present in the college experience. Yes, higher-education institutions offer a dizzying variety of courses, programs, and concentrations; this is the nature of agile institutions, which constantly produce new knowledge and translate that knowledge into learning opportunities on campus. In the hands of students who understand why they are on a college campus and how to take advantage of those learning opportunities, this wide range is a gold mine. For those who do not come with this understanding, the breadth of offerings often becomes a liability that leads to empty college degrees, to transcripts that look like the cafeteria menu that Schneider described.

We want to redefine the problem to concentrate on how students learn to negotiate their choices among the "blank spaces" in their degree programs and on how they can turn those spaces into assets that pave the way to a satisfying career and good life. Most of the typical undergraduate degree is composed of these blank spaces, and the challenge for every student lies in how to fill them meaningfully. The undergraduate experience has four basic components: general education, major requirements, minors or electives, and on- and off-campus experiential learning—all of it full of blank space.

Here is our sketch of the big picture of the baccalaureate with its blank spaces.

General education, in most cases, requires only two compulsory courses among the foundational skills: composition I and composition II. To satisfy the requirements for quantitative literacy, the knowledge domains (such as the fine arts, the natural sciences, or the humanities), and global learning and diversity, students pick from lists of courses under each category. For students who have chosen a major, a few of those blank spaces may be taken up by required courses. For those who are still "undecided," they are often simply told to explore or are referred to a survey course to get a sense of what a major is all about. (In reality, such introductory courses rarely give students a clue of the depth and granularity of knowledge they could find in a major.)

Majors are usually not so different from general education. Most require only three or four core courses. The rest consists of category areas, with courses listed under each area, along with a number of elective hours required to complete the major. All are blank spaces to be filled.

Many minors require only one or two specific courses and then offer a list of courses for students to choose from—yet more blank spaces to be filled. If a student has no minor and is filling the last third of the hours needed for graduation with electives, it's a free-for-all.

Experiential learning and co-curricular activities also represent sets of open-ended options. Alas, many students believe they don't have the time or money to pursue these external opportunities, don't know how to find experiences if they aren't advertised, or aren't always sure how to connect outside-the-classroom experiences to what they want to do.

What students face, then, is the paradox of choice: with so many possibilities, they struggle to make decisions about courses and activities that will resonate with their hidden intellectualism, their vocational purpose, and their life goals. Too many students face these choices on their own, and they make easy calls, picking courses that fit their schedules, that have popular professors, or that will not tax them academically.[15]

This conglomeration of unrelated, insubstantial courses—the outcome of merely clearing hurdles—is what leads students to complete empty college degrees.

This state of affairs might seem obvious to some people, particularly those who see frustrated, wandering students during advising sessions or faculty office hours every week, if they see those students at all. We have come to accept that students enter college confused about how it all works, and many in the college community tacitly assume that most students will muddle through—even perhaps believing that the muddling through is part of the process, something that separates the tenacious from those who aren't "cut out" for college.

The reality, though, is that students like Isaiah, who have every ability to succeed and launch well from college, are never taught how to use these blank spaces and opportunities to hack the college game: to connect their studies to their aspirations, to learn how to choose among the options granted to them purposefully, and to find the ground-floor doors into meaningful careers and lives. Helping students learn to fill in these blanks well certainly goes beyond the hype around choosing a major. It requires a different kind of conversation from the ones that students will typically encounter.

Isaiah's Lesson

Isaiah got lucky. In storming into the Center for the Junior Year, Isaiah didn't realize he would have an opportunity to re-examine how he approached his undergraduate experience. In that moment, when he started to unpack his interests and align them with his college track, with the help of someone who understood how to play the college game, Isaiah was learning a valuable lesson in how to fill in the blanks.

Isaiah had a distinct advantage compared to many other students, whether at elite schools or less-selective colleges, in that he had a clear sense of his hidden intellectualism and vocational purpose: to work in Chicago city politics. But Isaiah lacked the social and cultural capital, and the fundamental information about the world of politics, to begin to clarify the roles he might want to play.

From the beginning, Isaiah was dependent on the advice from Chicago Scholars, high-school counselors, and college admissions representatives, all of whom generally press a matriculating student to pick a major as soon as possible—and usually aren't thinking about a student's college career or aspirations beyond the first semester. Many people in these roles also aren't usually thinking holistically about the nature of the college curriculum and the breadth of learning opportunities across campus that could help students clarify their vocational aim. DePaul, for example, has a program in public policy that could have connected Isaiah to Chicago city politics, fitting his interests much better than political science. But Isaiah never heard about it.

When Isaiah mentioned his interests, he had gotten a typical knee-jerk response at DePaul, focused on the major and an easy career crosswalk: an interest in politics means he should go into political science, a major-equals-job mentality, with no consideration for the learning opportunities in the blank spaces or in experiences available on and off campus.

This kind of linear thinking is endemic across higher education. Consider this simple question: What major should a premed student declare? If biology or chemistry are at the top of your list, then you might be falling into that trap of straight-line thinking. In fact, medical schools and the medical profession have always wanted people from a range of backgrounds, and with the exception of MD-PhD programs, there are no required majors listed for any medical school. You can major in French, business administration, computer science, fine arts, or even (to answer the linear thinking displayed in *Dead Poets Society*) Shakespeare and poetry, and still become a doctor.[16] It's not about the major but about how students use the blank spaces to design their pathways. It is about planning a Field of Study.

The first step in a Field of Study process is to help students clarify their hidden intellectualism and vocational purpose. When Isaiah told his advisors and mentors that he was interested in city politics, someone should have said, "I don't know what you mean by that. Could you explain it to me?" Because "city politics" could mean dealing with public finance and economic development, setting up green spaces, addressing food or health disparities, negotiating between police and communities, improving media relations, maintaining streets and sanitation, and more. Just laying this out raises multiple possibilities for how to plan an undergraduate experience that would lead into city politics. And those possibilities depend on how students define their hidden intellectualism and vocational purpose, and then fill in the blanks.

Isaiah wanted to get his hands dirty in trying to improve underserved neighborhoods. But he hadn't had the conversations he needed to flesh this out while he was at DePaul. Instead, he was tracked into a political-science major, advised what the requirements were, and scheduled for his first quarter—and this is where Isaiah started running into trouble. He found that his political-science program introduced students to political theories and how to use those theories to analyze political events, movements, and the relationships between nation-states, not on the day-to-day details of what it takes to make a city run.

After Isaiah transferred from DePaul to Governors State, he still had no conversation about his vocational purpose; his courses and credit hours were simply slotted to meet the general-education and political-science requirements at his new school. It was when he sat down to talk about his latest hurdle—that lousy science course at Governors State—that he got his first sense of how to think with a Field of Study frame of mind.

After clarifying his interests and vocational purpose, he was able to fill in the blanks more intentionally. When Isaiah pondered what science course he should take, he had to grapple with a deeper question: "What do I want to do in city politics?" Essentially, what was his angle, his "why"? Isaiah wanted to make changes that would help people in his neighborhood, but his notion of what he wanted to do was still murky. This opened the door for a teachable moment, to begin to clarify for himself not simply what problems he wanted to solve but also what that might entail for his learning experience in college. To spur some thoughts, Ned played Isaiah a news clip about a mishandled smokestack implosion in a Chicago Latinx community, which covered the community with a cloud of toxic dust that exacerbated the already poor health conditions in the neighborhood. The city had an active role in the demolition, approving permits and overseeing the work.

Now when considering the question "What does it mean to get involved in city politics?" Isaiah saw a complex urban, civic, and environmental-health issue: a "wicked problem" to figure out, with no simple answers. His original question—"What science course should I take?"—was now easier to answer: one in environmental studies. But more important, he developed his own sense of *why* he was taking a life-science course, how it would fit into the professional plan he was developing for himself, and how the course would integrate with his vocational purpose. (Of course, students often want simple answers, and initially Isaiah was no different, asking his advisors to help him pick an easy general-education science course that would give him a good grade. But that undermines the learning experience involved in discovering one's own answer.)

The next stage of the Field of Study process involves entering the world outside academe to find out more—a stage we call the "research investigative inquiry." Isaiah was prepped with a strategy for setting up interviews with his local congressional officers, city alderpersons, and others named in the news clip. He was also prepped with a set of questions designed to learn what those officials have to go through to deal with environmental-health problems and what they need to have in their background to do that. Lastly, an important step, Isaiah set up a follow-up appointment in the Center for the Junior Year to share what he discovered from his investigation.

Isaiah returned in three weeks. By then, he had spoken with staff members in two alderpersons' offices and with people on the city staff of a congressperson whose district covered the area highlighted in the news broadcasts. This process taught him moxie. His calls to these officials initially went unanswered, but Isaiah eventually put on a suit and walked into their offices, asking to talk with people.

He discovered that city politics is messy and vast. The issue of economic investment in communities of color touches on public finance, equity in private investment, health-care disparities, affordable housing, business development, urban violence, equity in the school system, and more. Through these conversations, Isaiah began to clarify the areas in city politics that matched his interest and started to see how he could fill in the blank spaces meaningfully to design a purposeful undergraduate experience. Isaiah was building out his cultural capital.

He also came back with a glimpse into the world of his "hidden job market," the many positions in the workforce that are not listed on job boards, are frequently overlooked by career centers and other counselors, and are not even on the radar of most students and their parents. People working in city politics include not just the representatives holding offices but also their staff members who cover various areas of expertise. Those staffers interact with other people, who lobby, inform, or protest the city government on a range of issues. These are just some of the ways people make a living and make a difference in the realm of city politics—a range that students like Isaiah rarely consider, if they even know exists.

During his interviews, as planned under the research investigative inquiry, Isaiah asked city staff members about opportunities for experiential learning. By the end of the process, Isaiah had talked himself into an internship in the office of Representative Bobby Rush, the congressman from his home district.

From there, his undergraduate career took off, once Isaiah was connected to a new confidence that the Field of Study process had unlocked. He could see how the college-to-career game was played and where he could find opportunities for personal entrepreneurism. He learned that some staff members in congressional offices weren't organized, didn't know the issues, or didn't bother to connect with or respond to the public. "They weren't worth anything at all," he recalls today, and that's when Isaiah started to realize just how much he could bring to any environment like this. As he built out his cultural capital, his vistas of personal possibilities started to expand; he could see new opportunities out in the world and how he might take advantage of them.

Through the Field of Study process, Isaiah began to construct social networks that opened new possibilities and pathways. When he heard that he could apply for a semester of study at the Washington Center—working and learning in the nation's capital alongside students who usually come from elite privates and flagship publics—he jumped at the chance and won a spot, along with financial support.

That led Isaiah, a kid from the South Side of Chicago, to a new sense of validation that was motivating. "I would walk out of my luxury apartment, within walking distance from the Capitol, with my head high and my suit on, just thinking that every possibility in the world was mine," he says. "I realized I can make a difference in people's lives in big and small ways, and it gave me the confidence to do grad school."

Isaiah used his experience and the Field of Study frame to plot his next step. This time, there would be no guessing. He learned to look for faculty in graduate programs whose academic interests were close to his own field of study. He found a program in the University of Illinois at Chicago's College of Urban Planning and Policy, designed to deal with urban issues through a relationship with the city, which would continue building out Isaiah's social network. Through the program, he realized that education could play an important part in changing a community's future, so he used his network to land a position at St. Leo High School, dedicated to developing leaders among young African American men. In his teaching and mentorship position, Isaiah sees an opportunity to improve communities in Chicago, while also laying the groundwork for a political campaign in the next five to ten years.

"All those kids are going to be voters real soon," says Isaiah, noting that their parents, also potential voters and donors to a campaign, will come to see him as someone who cares. "This is an opportunity to work with people who live in this district."

Isaiah learned how to test his ideas in the real world. In doing so, he saw how the different components of his undergraduate education could integrate with his vocational purpose. And all of this started from a conversation about a lousy general-education requirement. That conversation, and short ones that followed, set Isaiah on the path to reframing his college experience and changing how he approached his general-education courses, his major, and his experiential opportunities.

These conversations took no more time than a standard advising or career-development appointment. But for students with backgrounds like Isaiah's, these kinds of interactions are critical.

The Significance of Filling in the Blanks

Confusion on the path from college to career is common among students, rich and poor. Even privileged students don't always see how to tie their interests and goals to the vast array of learning opportunities in college nor how to design those into meaningful and marketable undergraduate experiences. But students from wealthy backgrounds more often have family and friends who can stress-test a college plan and career aspiration and provide connections and resources that can make meaning out of the confusing relationship among general education, the major, and the rest of the course hours a student needs to complete a degree.

In short, many wealthy families have the resources to hack the game of college to get the desired outcome in life. From birth, students from those families gain a range of experiences from their environment that provide them with the cultural capital needed to see the vistas that Isaiah never could, and they also come with the social connections associated with that cultural capital that open opportunities.

In the already-mentioned *There Is Life after College*, Selingo provides an interesting take on this, as he explores the problem of students graduating from college unprepared for the "real world of work" (his, like many other books in this college-to-career genre, tends to focus on only a few areas, like tech, finance, big data, and start-ups). Published in 2016, the book opens with Selingo on a train ride: He joined a group of students from elite colleges, "riding the rails" from San Francisco to Washington, DC, as part of the Millennial Trains Project, yet another program intended to lead recent graduates to self-discovery and some sense of what they want to do with their degrees and lives. At night, students would hear from guest lecturers, including Selingo. While on the stretch from Chicago to Pittsburgh, Selingo had a conversation with two young women, Cameron Hardesty and Jessica Straus, who had majored in English at Davidson College and proved to be an impetus for his book.[17]

"Davidson is the kind of small liberal arts college that prides itself on providing students with broad foundational skills," Selingo says, "but it is not a place that trains you for a narrowly tailored job. You can't major in sports management, physical therapy, or video game design at Davidson, for instance."

Jessica Straus seems to agree with him: "It didn't prepare me at all for the real world," she says. Selingo points out that Straus was quick to note that her courses "didn't encourage her to translate classroom learning into explicit know-how sought by employers today," although, through Davidson, she did pursue a dream to study abroad in Cambridge and work in a Barcelona art gallery. Cameron Hardesty had gone to Spain as well. The pair of women knew various classmates who were "working odd jobs in New York City as executive assistants," an outcome Selingo paints as a failure to launch. "The college degree is becoming the new high school diploma," Hardesty complained—in other words, just another hurdle.

With some condescension, Selingo notes that these women—part of "a generation raised by hovering helicopter parents," with resumes burnished by extracurriculars—had all the advantages in the world. "If these recent graduates were struggling, what about those who didn't have their pedigrees?"

Selingo wants to crack this nut to provide students with strategies that will help them better navigate the transition from college to career and land on their feet. But his account contains a number of disconnects: Doesn't working in an art gallery provide a student with a sense of the real world of work? Couldn't a college that provides a vast array of learning opportunities, both on and off campus, prepare a student to work in sports management, video-game design, or physical therapy? Instead Selingo rolls out a familiar litany: students pass through the assembly line of advising, focusing on "tactical issues," such as degree audits and course prerequisites and the like. And, as does everyone else out there, Selingo focuses on the major but doesn't describe how students can become agile learners.

Davidson may not have majors in sports management, video-game design, or physical therapy (which, we should note, is a graduate program anyway). But students at Davidson can absolutely use the blank spaces to prepare themselves to work in sports management or the video-game industry or to assemble a compelling application to a physical-therapy graduate program—even while declaring a major in an undervalued liberal-arts discipline. The learning opportunities are there. The key is learning how to fill in the blanks.

In fact, Cameron Hardesty used experiential learning, a skill in finding mentors, and her pedigree to do just that in her own life and career—she just did it after her graduation from Davidson. Around the time of the train ride, Hardesty was using her skills as an English major in various public-relations jobs in Washington, DC. But, like many recent graduates in the job market, she wasn't happy with her direction. She decided to move back to Spain after her study-abroad experience to reset her career. She taught English there for a year, while she became fluent in Spanish. During her time in Spain, a friend connected her to a global public-relations firm.

When she returned to the States, she started working in digital public affairs for various firms and agencies in Washington. With her ability to use social media bilingually and a contact from a former job, she landed a digital strategy position in public affairs at the White House Office for Drug Policy under the Obama administration.

At the White House, she clarified her hidden intellectualism and vocational purpose, and she found her hidden job market in the world of flowers. "I love flowers. Always have," she writes in her bio on the website for Poppy, an online flower company.[18] While at the White House, she volunteered to work with Laura Dowling, the White House's chief floral designer. She gathered skills and made contacts, including the husband of a friend who hired her as a spokesperson and head of products at UrbanStems, an online floral and gifting company. There, she gained skills in product development, data analysis, and supply-chain management.

In 2019, she became the founder and CEO of Poppy, which now draws on her complete skill set. Her competencies in media and public relations, digital strategy, supply-chain management, product development, and even Spanish (with her flower suppliers located in Central and South America) are now invaluable to her vocational purpose and her once-hidden job world, the floral industry. Her education at Davidson—somewhat denigrated in Selingo's account—has taken on a different hue in recent years. "A big reason why I'm successful in startup life is because of my liberal-arts education at Davidson College, which taught me how to synthesize vast amounts of information into understandable points and communicate them clearly," she told *Forbes* in a 2017 profile. (In 2022, after a successful fundraising round, she hired her friend from the train ride, Jessica Straus, as her chief operating officer.)[19]

Interestingly, the path that Hardesty took is similar to the path Isaiah found through the Field of Study method, with a critical difference: Hardesty was able to take advantage of the social and cultural capital that she brought from her background to create opportunities for herself, which eventually led to a career that meshed with her vocational purpose. In order to level the playing field for Isaiah, he had to be taught how to make connections among his experience, his schooling, and his hidden intellectualism—and how to tie these elements to the hidden job market.

At American colleges and universities, most students never find mentors who engage them in conversations about how to pursue their goals and dreams and how to craft an undergraduate experience to realize those dreams.

"Too often, students approach potential mentoring opportunities as merely transactional—seeking an adviser's approval for course registration, for example—rather than engaging in bigger questions about intellectual interests and about life and career goals," writes Leo M. Lambert, the former president of Elon University, in an editorial for Gallup. "Mentoring relationships are a form of social capital. I suspect that students with college-educated parents and those from higher socioeconomic backgrounds come to college with more experience in mining this type of social capital—a big leg up on their peers." Those students can mine that social capital because they come with a lot of cultural capital that helps them make the connections and drives meaning behind the relationships they form.[20]

It Has Always Been about Conversations

Higher education is awash with books and reports that purport to solve major challenges affecting undergraduate education. They are written by university presidents, education scholars, policy analysts, or journalists who study or observe the problem, rather than "work the problem"; that is, the authors often don't work closely with students. Perhaps understandably, their solutions to high dropout rates, rampant debt, underemployment, inequality, and other issues vexing colleges are mostly top-down: shift curriculum from seat time to competency, require experiential learning, create guided pathways, merge and close programs, and emphasize "career-connected learning" to meet what *they assume* are workforce needs—without actually asking students what *their* needs are.

Top-down solutions have a place. But there's a reason why college leaders commonly compare their institutions to battleships, massive operations difficult to turn in new directions. In higher education, top-down solutions are often hampered by conflicting interests on campus—and yet, they still might not reflect the best interests of students. What's more, new programs and strategies are usually subject to the whims of college leaders; when those leaders leave, the "solutions" often leave with them.

This book illuminates a foundational educational experience—something that happens when students really open up and talk to people on campus about their curiosities and goals. These conversations are not about creating a new program or a career pathway, or building a new career center or student-success center. What drives the success of any of these top-down initiatives—or what could drive student success with no new initiative at all, only existing resources—is improving the quality of the conversations that students have on campus. Through these conversations, students learn to define their hidden intellectualism, see that hidden intellectualism in the hidden job market, build their cultural capital, and learn how to fill in the blanks.

Teaching and mentorship have forever hinged on human connection and conversation. The relationships between students and their instructors have always been key to effective learning. It's a dynamic highlighted in psychological studies of the classroom, in sentimental movies about great teachers, in the mythologized image of Socrates sitting under a tree with pupils.

In the successful modern college experience, that dynamic is hinted at everywhere, documented in studies of higher education over decades. In *Making the Most of College: Students Speak Their Minds*, Richard J. Light describes how advisors and mentors, in asking "unexpected questions" tailored to individual students, can help a young person discover a vocational calling and their passion. "A great college education depends upon human relationships," he writes, an "obvious idea" that many students and educators overlook.[21]

Gerald Graff, in *Clueless in Academe: How Schooling Obscures the Life of the Mind*, notes that "academic intellectual culture is a conversation rather than a mere inventory of texts, facts, ideas, and methods" and that part of any advisor or instructor's job is to help students see the connections between the world of academe and their personal interests—or, as Graff characterizes it, students' "hidden intellectualism."[22]

That dynamic is also present in widely publicized findings, from Gallup and other organizations, showing that students who have success in life encountered professors or mentors at college who seemed to care about them, who made learning exciting, who helped them find experiential-learning opportunities, and who encouraged them to pursue personal goals and dreams.[23]

But the dynamic that Light, Graff, and Gallup discuss is not pervasive across students' experiences on any college campus. The goal of this book is to show people how to make it so.

The Field of Study conversations with Isaiah display the pillars of what we will discuss through the rest of the chapters of this book. These conversations are pedagogical and grounded in questions that challenge students to discover for themselves the "why" behind their undergraduate experiences. The Field of Study method asks them to carry that *why* through a series of steps:

- The *why* is grounded in having students first clarify their hidden intellectualism and vocational purpose. Vocational purpose and hidden intellectualism are the thing that students feel genuinely drawn to. It's not good enough for a student to sit down and say, "I want to be a mental-health professional." A clarifying question should be "Who do you want to work with, and why?" A student who wants to work with adolescents would pursue a different path than a student who wants to work with veterans with post-traumatic stress disorder. And students should feel that any kind of vocational purpose is valid—because the possibilities on campus and in life are vast. If a student wants to address lung health through the world of bicycles, or nurture talent development in public art, or build a metaverse like the OASIS from *Ready Player One*, those pursuits are all valid starting places.

- Students are then tasked to identify the people on and off campus who are already doing what they want to do. In corners on campus or in the hidden job market, they're out there.

- Students are next assigned a research investigative inquiry, and equipped with question prompts, to meet with people in their hidden job market to learn about the skill sets, knowledge, and hands-on experience they need to acquire.

- Once they return from their research inquiry, students are asked to translate what they discovered into learning opportunities on- *and* off-campus. The results are often surprising to them—and to us. Students learn to explore areas on campus they normally would not look into.

- With this information in hand, students begin to design their undergraduate studies. Here, they start to see the importance of the blank spaces, which become the vehicle for integrating their learning across the curriculum. They see the difference between tracking through a major and designing their Field of Study.

— This curricular designing trains students to use the skills of academic inquiry to explore the text that is their lives. As with all good academic inquiry, students learn to test their thinking continually throughout their undergraduate careers. This means that students are learning how to chart their own course through life, regardless of how their interests or the job market may change. And they learn how to create social networks and build their cultural capital so they can continue to test their planning for the real world. Essentially, they become agile learners.

Whether students want to begin a career trajectory immediately after earning a bachelor's degree, or decide to pursue graduate or professional studies or even to transfer to another college, the purpose of the process is the same: to clarify the *why* behind what they hope to do.

If we want students to leave college with a degree that is not only marketable, but personally meaningful, we need to focus on the blank spaces. They allow students to weave curricular categories into a tapestry that make up an integrated undergraduate experience. When conversations draw out students' hidden intellectualism and identify how they can take advantage of the blank spaces, general education takes on more importance, electives become critical components (instead of simply slots to fill), and their majors emerge organically. As we'll explain in the chapters ahead, students also find blank spaces in the hidden job market all around them, and in pursuing experiential learning in these environments, they see how abstract classroom content fits with hands-on practices in the real world. Along the way, students learn college literacy and how to hack the college game—a skill particularly useful for first-generation and historically underserved students.

In the end, when students learn how to see their college experience through the lenses of their interests and life goals, the breadth of the college curriculum begins to take on a relevance that they had not experienced before. In a sense, it is these students, not the faculty or administrators, who are building the curriculum, and they are doing it for themselves. In the process, the students begin to break down the silos and see the entire college campus as a learning resource that is theirs to take advantage of.

This book emerged from the stories of students who trusted the process and engaged in these conversations at various types of colleges: big research universities, regional public colleges, small private colleges, and two-year institutions. These are not stories about wealthy and well-connected students at elite schools but rather stories about students who hit potholes, who were drifting, and who came to college underprepared. Still, they defied what the predictive algorithms and personal backgrounds would suggest about their chances for success.

Once a student learns how to navigate the college environment with their newfound sense of purpose, that student begins to show their peers and advisors what's possible in the hidden job market. This book offers a journey through which students can teach us, if we talk to them and listen closely to their answers.

2

The Curricular Maze

CARLA IS ABOUT TO START her second year of college, majoring in marketing, and in danger of stopping out. How would you help her succeed?

Carla's story is a case study—one presented by Ned to a roomful of vice presidents of undergraduate affairs, deans of academic affairs, department chairs, and other administrators at a 2017 conference for Thrive Chicago. Thrive, a MacArthur Foundation grantee, is a citywide collective focused in part on fostering college access and developing programs to improve degree completion among Chicago's underserved students. Carla was one of those students, and the point of the presentation was to test how administrators would respond to her dilemma.[1]

At a crossroads, Carla had arrived at a transfer day program at a university near her home, one of many programs held at the institution each semester to build relationships with prospective community-college transfer students. The day's agenda was simple: highlight academic programs and resources to support student success and meet with potential transfers to discuss their progress in their community colleges' guided pathways programs—and how they would fit into one of the university's majors upon transferring.

Carla was worried about her ability to transfer and brought questions to the program. She had graduated from high school in a largely Latinx school district, and her primary language at home was Spanish. Her parents, who were undocumented immigrants, worked blue-collar jobs to support Carla and her siblings. Carla's performance in high school had been above average, but not outstanding—in part because she worked to support expenses at home and helped raise her younger siblings.

Carla told her high-school counselor about her interest in "spreading the word" for organizations. Her counselor recommended that she pursue a business degree with a major in marketing. (High-school counselors often want to guide students from low-income or immigrant backgrounds into majors that ostensibly lead to high-paying fields.)

After high school, Carla opted to enroll at a community college to save money. On her application, she checked off marketing as her academic and vocational interest, and she was tracked into the college's guided pathway for business.

Right away, Carla ran into academic roadblocks. She was struggling in algebra, but she had bigger hurdles ahead: requirements in the business core include more advanced mathematics courses like business calculus, accounting, and business statistics. Soon she realized that catching up on math would extend her time at the community college, straining the financial resources within her family. She worried she was on a path to stopping out.

At the transfer day program, she described her challenges and asked her advisors how she could graduate in a timely way and still pursue her interests. What Carla discovered—and what we will describe throughout the chapter—was that the solution was something unexpected.

We discussed in chapter 1 how students bring to college misperceptions about the significance of majors and minors, how they are taught to diminish the importance of general education, and how they misunderstand the relationship between college studies and on-ramps to the job market. As students arrive at college, those myths and misperceptions aren't necessarily corrected. In fact, many of the structures at a typical college exacerbate some of the wrong turns a student might make in pursuing a meaningful and marketable degree.

That's because the organizational structures within a college are often built to support the bureaucracy of the institution, not necessarily the students' best interests. To change that focus, institutions would have to challenge some embedded agendas and mindsets—for example, that some majors (like biology or chemistry) automatically lead to certain career fields (like medicine). That rote mindset not only benefits enrollments for those departments, but it also makes student guidance an easy rubber-stamping process. To seriously address the problems that students face, college leaders will have to rethink the ways that students are tracked through the system— although doing so could open up political problems for themselves, which might be a reason why success rates in higher education seem to be stuck where they are.

The Myth of the Academic Major

Prior to arriving at college, students receive emphatic but often misleading messages from parents, high-school counselors, data hounds, and the media about the importance of the major and its relationship to career outcomes. In many ways, colleges complicitly reinforce these perceptions from the moment that students talk with admissions, leading the most vulnerable students deeper into a mess of creating empty college degrees.

This happens in part because some administrators, staff, and faculty members believe the same myths about majors and careers that the general public does but also because institutions (or aspects of them) are trying to protect their self-interests and don't want to alter the organizational structure. If students were to learn that a "practical" major on campus does not guarantee a good shot at a desired career outcome, or that some common career paths might be found in areas of campus not considered career-relevant, that would challenge the conventional wisdom that majors lead to jobs, which could upend a whole host of things, from departmental enrollments to institutional budget allocations.

Within institutions, the major retains the same stature and emphasis that students, parents, and the media place on it. Majors emerged in the late nineteenth and early twentieth centuries merely as an organizing feature of the curriculum, as knowledge expanded and became more specialized. Prior to the emergence of majors, an undergraduate curriculum consisted of nearly all the courses offered by the institution, a truly liberal education. Majors offered students the choice of concentrating on a particular discipline (English, history, philosophy, natural sciences, and so on) to learn its practices, values, and canons, while still retaining aspects of liberal education through general education and electives.[2]

The emergence of majors, in time, influenced the college organizational structure as well. Academic departments started to coalesce around the disciplines, bringing about political rivalries and competition for students and resources. That rivalry and resource competition has become especially acute today, in an environment where institutional budgets are strained, the number of late-teenage collegegoers is in decline, and academic departments are being asked to prove their worth to the institution or else face diminishment or closure after a program audit. Many colleges (and parents) have embraced a notion that students should pick a major as soon as possible—even on the college application—on the logic that students who have an early direction are likely to graduate within four years,[3] although research has contradicted that assumption.[4]

You can find 1,200 major options in the *Book of Majors 2018*, published by the College Board, along with lists of the most likely career outcomes for the top 201 majors. Top-line career outcomes for American literature, for example: "high-school teacher; journalist; editor; college professor." The book notes that literature majors can work in any career requiring "strong research skills"—like investment banking, for example—but it doesn't offer clues on *how to navigate* into those careers.[5]

This is the backdrop when students like Carla step onto campus. The choice of a major is often based on uninformed assumptions held by students like Carla and the people advising them—most commonly, that major equals job. That simplistic calculation, influenced by lists of majors ranked by salary potential, has led to the rise of some departments and colleges (business, computer science, engineering) and the decline of others (foreign languages, humanities, and social sciences, to a great extent). That pull toward reportedly profitable majors creates its own momentum: departments with popular, highly enrolled majors can command more resources and prominent spaces on campus; this in turn helps them attract yet more students to their programs. Departments in decline, meanwhile, enter a death spiral, losing the resources they need to keep faculty and make course offerings current, putting them in danger when program reviews come around. At many colleges, even the *perception* of the practicality and profitability of a particular major can influence whether it survives an institutional program review.

Understandably, a student like Carla—who is facing down the most stressful decision of her college career, one that will potentially carry life consequences—might well think conventionally when choosing a major, perhaps following "group think" into one of those popular and prominent majors. If a student does not see a connection to what she wants to do on the menu of majors, she might assume she cannot pursue that personal interest or vocational calling on campus. What's more, she might struggle to see her path in college because of the way institutions segment and silo their individual academic departments, even their various colleges of business, engineering, or liberal arts.

In fact, major does not equal job, and except for the most prescribed (often licensed) occupations, most employers care more about the skills an applicant can demonstrate than what major he or she chose in college. Increasingly, corporations, government agencies, and nongovernmental organizations are dealing with global challenges and "wicked problems" that require complementary, intersecting skills that go beyond the confines of the major. In business literature, the so-called T-shaped professional, a person who can go deep in one discipline but also range across related areas, has emerged as an ideal hire.[6]

Within the siloed college environment, professors themselves rarely even adhere to the borders of their own discipline, likely having interests that cross departments and sometimes colleges. Here's an obvious example: faculty who bring together engineering, computer science, and medicine into bioengineering. A less obvious one: faculty who bring together race and ethnic studies, medicine, and public health to address the cultural factors that lead to an uneven distribution and use of health care. Professors know that other disciplines inform their own research, and they seek out faculty from other disciplines with shared research interests. Such is the underlying rationale for having interdisciplinary research centers.

This expansive notion of a university—as a networked environment supporting professors' individualized and cross-disciplinary curiosity—does not usually filter down to the conversations that students have with faculty about how to design their undergraduate studies. Students primarily learn to recognize faculty members by their academic departments, which coincide with majors. One faculty member's individual research interests might become apparent to those few students who work closely with that professor on a senior thesis or capstone project, but most students rarely get a good sense of the breadth of specialties, interests, and personal obsessions of their professors.

Faculty members create their identities in academe by field of study, not by major. They provide the model for how students themselves should create their undergraduate program, showing them how to fill in the blank spaces.[7]

A student's hidden intellectualism and vocational purpose can be as interdisciplinary, even as specific, as the research interest of any faculty member. When students begin to define and explore their hidden intellectualism and vocational purpose—largely through a research investigative inquiry, when they go out to talk to people in the world of their hidden job market—they start to see the relevance of disciplines outside their major. Students interested in marketing and data analytics see how sociology, for example, sheds light on the social dynamics that can influence public responses to an advertising campaign. Economics can be a crucial program for premed students seeking to understand the costs of delivering health care. Students in wealth management and investment programs see how women's studies can help them address wealth disparities.

When students design their undergraduate programs this way, they tie the activities of the real world to the learning opportunities divvied up by majors on campus. It's not the college organizational structure that should guide students through the undergraduate program; it's the problems they each are solving as they start to unpack their interests and see the relevance of other majors, programs, and routes through their fields of study.

Of course, to start thinking this way, students crucially need conversations and guidance to unpack the college experience. But what passes for sound advice and mentorship in college generally isn't sufficient—a problem long known by observers of student success. In some sectors of higher education, the response has focused less on improving that advice and more on limiting choices.

Guided Pathways and the Need for Conversations

Redesigning America's Community Colleges: A Clearer Path to Student Success laid out many of the same problems we outlined in chapter 1: students are overwhelmed by the options in pursuing postsecondary education, and the authors argue that "nowhere are the features—and disadvantages—of the cafeteria model more apparent that in the design of community college degrees and certificates."[8]

Thomas R. Bailey, Shanna Smith Jaggars, and Davis Jenkins—the book's authors, all from the Community College Research Center (CCRC) at Columbia University—noted that two-year institutions had been designed to offer courses across a broad array of subject areas, to maximize access for students with any interest. Today, that range of programming at community colleges spans everything from certificate programs in automotive technology and cosmetology to academic preparation for transferring to four-year colleges and universities. This is a wealth of educational opportunities, often offered affordably (or even free) to students from all socioeconomic backgrounds. Students who learn how to navigate the curriculum could chart a course to nearly any career destination.

The problem is that students at these two-year institutions face "a complex and often bewildering choice of courses and programs," CCRC's researchers said. "The typical student is overwhelmed by the many choices available, resulting in poor program or course selection decisions, which in turn cost time and money, and likely lead many students to drop out in frustration."[9]

Naturally, this kind of confusion should lead colleges to provide mentorship and advice from staff and faculty members, along with other support to help students figure out how to get a relevant two-year degree or certificate or to transfer to a suitable four-year institution. Students could get unparalleled benefits from staff members and mentors who engage them in meaningful conversations about their interests and career goals. CCRC's researchers claim that an academic advisor is "the most important resource" to students who are trying to chart a course to graduation and life goals, including a career.

That claim notwithstanding, the researchers then pointed to various ways that the rushed and disconnected intake, advising, and support functions at the average "cafeteria college" undermined the postsecondary goals of students at two-year schools. Many schools brought students in with little information about their talents and interests and then quickly pushed them through orientation and enrollment into their first-term courses. Limited budgets prevented institutions from adding bodies to the advising staff, leaving advisors with unworkable caseloads (nearly 800 to 1,200 students per advisor at some institutions) and a range of other responsibilities in addition to guiding students. On top of this, the researchers noted that many students (nearly 40 percent at the outset) either did not seek out advising services or got conflicting or meager advice when they did. So students often relied on self-advising through the college website, which could be outdated, leading them to become even more lost. With different support functions working in isolation across the cafeteria college, "students must rely mostly on themselves."

Redesigning America's Community Colleges advocated a different approach: "guided pathways," a model based on research in behavioral economics, organizational effectiveness, learning theory, and a handful of pilot programs at leading two-year institutions. In terms of student supports, the authors argued that colleges should beef up advising services, set up technology that allows colleges to monitor students' progress, and hone student-success courses to focus on information that helps students connect the curriculum to their life goals.[10]

But even with more supports, the curriculum remained an amorphous smorgasbord of options in the minds of many students, so Bailey, Jaggars, and Jenkins offered a solution: if the options facing students are bewildering, then structure the options in a way that might help them make more informed choices. The book influenced the creation of "meta-majors" within guided pathways, academic tracks that are ostensibly designed to help students focus on career-relevant programs that *colleges believe* align with their students' interests. The idea is that students could link to a meta-major on a college's website (such as business, public and human services, science and technology, or health sciences) and find curricular plans that outline the requirements under the academic programs listed there (such as accounting, sociology, or biology). Undecided students could use the meta-majors to explore the college's list of career opportunities linked to each particular program and see how those programs might line up with their ambitions for what they want to do with their lives.

Guided pathways have been adopted at scores of two- and even four-year institutions. But it's not clear that the framework has brought the type of clarity that Bailey, Jaggars, and Jenkins had hoped for. For starters, at many community colleges, the meta-majors are merely a different way of organizing degree tracks and certificates. For example, here are the meta-majors at Skyline College, a two-year institution in San Bruno, California: Arts, Languages & Communication; Business, Entrepreneurship & Management; Science, Technology & Health; and Society & Education.[11] These meta-majors merely re-label the existing college structure, and they are not so different from the programs organized by academic divisions at, say, Naugatuck Valley Community College in Waterbury, Connecticut: Liberal Arts/Behavioral and Social Sciences; Business; Science, Technology, Engineering and Math; and Allied Health, Nursing and Physical Education.[12]

Whether colleges choose to divide up their offerings by meta-majors, guided pathways, or divisions, students are still given lists upon lists of programs, required courses, and blank spaces to be filled in. Guided pathways, then, present the same problems of choice that bedevil students at any institution, while offering the illusion that students who are under a guided pathway are on a clear route to a career. In some cases, particularly in career-oriented programs such as nursing, computer science, or accounting, this *may* be true. But for students who have not clarified their goals and aspirations, the usual difficulties arise: they are tracked into programs that may not align with their hidden intellectualism or vocational purpose, and this misalignment is an underlying reason why students change programs or stop out.

Let's look at an example of guided pathways at Skyline College and try to navigate it. Pretend you're a nineteen-year-old aspiring journalist, hoping to transfer to a state institution in a couple of years.

Journalism-for-transfer falls under the Arts, Languages & Communication meta-major category, along with programs in art, dance, filmmaking, literature, music, and, oddly, cosmetology (which is also found under the business meta-major). On a page designed to help orient students at Skyline, the college describes its meta-majors in broad, generic terms. The Arts, Languages & Communication description, for instance, paints a picture of the type of student who would thrive in that meta-major: "Creativity and communication are your strengths. You enjoy connecting with people through language—

written, verbal or both—and you like reaching out to bring people together. You express yourself freely, whether it's through language, art, film, theater or media and you know that art, in every form, is one of the best ways to explore new ideas and points of view."[13]

In the end, these meta-majors still sort programs into different sets of silos. Do the courses that would train an effective journalist reside neatly in a communications-oriented meta-major? It depends on what someone would want to do with journalism.

A journalism student could easily fit under the Society & Education meta-major, where journalism isn't mentioned: "You're interested in the organizations, laws, politics, interactions, and social bonds that make our planet such a rich and diverse place—and you're always craving to learn more. Studying human behavior, culture and identity excite you. You have an intellectual spirit, and you enjoy sharing that with others because you understand the importance of doing your part within your interconnected community."

A student pursuing journalism, quite frankly, could find vocational interest in journalism under any of the meta-majors at Skyline. Journalists cover issues in business, politics, communities, the arts, sports, education, science and technology, and they tell their stories through a variety of media, like long narrative pieces, spots on television or radio, or posts on TikTok or other social media. Each of these subject areas and media platforms requires different kinds of contextual backgrounds and training.

Who's to say, though, that a student interested in journalism should pursue the journalism program in the first place? Journalists are more than just writers; they find their corner in journalism by becoming subject-matter experts. A student might want to pursue their hidden intellectualism in their love of cars and someday write for *Motor Trend* or *Car & Driver* or work in public relations for Ford or Audi. Does that student still belong in a journalism program? Perhaps that student might find a better home under the Science, Technology & Health meta-major at Skyline College, which includes automotive technology. Or that student could simply complete a generic associate of arts degree by filling in the blanks on the degree audit with courses from journalism and automotive technology. It all depends on the student—and students need meaningful conversations to unpack these interests and connect them to the curriculum.

Organizing academic programs under meta-majors represents the same inward-looking perspective that colleges already use to describe their programs. It just establishes a different set of silos by prioritizing the relationships between these programs within the confines of a college's internal organization. It does not help students discover how multidisciplinary learning translates into opportunities in the hidden job market. After all, the majority of jobs are of this kind, including those positions at small- to medium-sized employers mostly overlooked or unseen by colleges.

Our nineteen-year-old finds in the journalism-for-transfer pathway the paradox of choice that confuses every student when they are trying to design a meaningful undergraduate experience. That journalism pathway at Skyline requires three core courses, then asks students to choose three courses from a list of eleven options that include economics, statistics, political science, logic, photography, and argumentation, some of which could count for general education. The requirements in journalism add up to about nineteen hours; our nineteen-year-old will have to pick another forty-one credit hours to complete general-education requirements and elective hours for an associate degree or to transfer.

If our nineteen-year-old fills these blank spaces haphazardly, as many students do, she may still wind up with the empty, cafeteria-style degree that guided pathways were meant to avoid.

This raises another concern as well: whether the clustering of programs under any kind of division, silo, or meta-major allows for the multidisciplinary preparation any student needs for the hidden job market.

For example, Skyline has listed psychology under Society & Education. Why isn't psychology under Science, Technology & Health? After all, many students pursue psychology because they want to get into a profession focused on improving people's mental health. But psychology could also be relevant to Business, Entrepreneurship & Management because psychology combined with management points toward the field of organizational psychology.

What if a student had an interest in health professions and started his college career at Skyline with the intention of pursuing a graduate degree in physical therapy or applying to a physician assistant program or perhaps even attending medical school? These career paths are not reflected in *any* of the meta-majors, but all the relevant courses and learning opportunities are on Skyline's campus—they are just scattered across the meta-majors. To make this more confusing, there is no standard and required major in higher education that a student needs to declare to pursue any of these graduate tracks in health sciences. For instance, a student could major in communications, business, or sociology and still pursue health fields—in doing so, adding to his job-market value by bringing more coveted T-shaped skills to a health profession. We could imagine scenarios like these across the academic programs and the meta-majors for almost any career path.

In part, this is why organizations like EAB have noted that despite "the wealth of available resources (and funding) from foundations and various organizations like Complete College America and the American Association of Community Colleges, campus leaders still struggle to describe exactly what success looks like" when guided pathways are implemented.[14] There is more to a meaningful undergraduate education than merely completing degree requirements.

Six years after the release of *Redesigning America's Community Colleges*, Jenkins and colleagues at CCRC reported on the evolution of guided pathways and where colleges might have misinterpreted their intentions. "Guided pathways was never about limiting options," they wrote, while acknowledging that many people had interpreted it that way. Guided pathways were supposed to help students "enter a high-opportunity program" that leads directly to a good career or to a promising transfer to a four-year institution. "Colleges should backward-map all programs, starting with good jobs in fields of economic importance to their communities," the follow-up report said. "Guided pathways reforms will not advance equity if they merely lead to increased completion of college credentials per se; they will only do so if they enable underserved students to complete programs aligned with their career and educational interests and aspirations."[15]

But once again, it's the colleges that are mapping the pathways to "good jobs" as they define them—even though it's not clear that colleges could be aware of, or even map to, most of the job possibilities and career routes in the vast world of work. A student might want to work in the economically important world of health care, but that field includes many possibilities and permutations, some of which don't even involve health-care delivery. Indeed, Jenkins and colleagues pointed out that many colleges were getting "hung up on trying to create perfect maps for every student situation." More students, they said, needed to have conversations about their interests and strengths to create individualized educational plans.[16]

In offering the illusion of a preformed trajectory, guided pathways and meta-majors could discourage students (and their institutions) from having the essential conversations needed to clarify why students are in college, what they are aiming for, whether they even understand the meta-major they have chosen, and how their course choices fit with their vocational purpose and the hidden job market. For people who have experience with higher education and the job market, this is difficult enough to navigate; for your average nineteen-year-old, it can be so daunting that they stumble and leave college altogether.

The Case Study of Carla

Let's return to the case study offered at the Thrive conference. Carla—based on her interest in "spreading the word," which she assumed was marketing—had been tracked into a guided pathway for business. Still struggling with algebra, and with business calculus and micro- and macroeconomics on the horizon, Carla faced the possibility of having to repeat algebra to raise her grades in order to meet the required grade point average to complete the business core. Yet repeating courses would put her at risk of not making standard academic progress toward her degree, imperiling her financial aid. She juggled these stresses along with her thirty-hour-a-week job.

Carla's story is common. What ideas would the administrators gathered for Thrive have for helping her? After all, this group of department chairs, deans, and vice presidents had been involved in designing majors and pathways, and all conveyed an interest in helping low-income students succeed.

The group offered a number of conventional suggestions for Carla. They first focused on her high-school preparation and suggested that she could sign up for tutoring through student support, where she might also connect with success coaches or peer mentors who could check up with her biweekly. They suggested that Carla, who struggled to meet her bills every month, could consider working fewer hours or even try switching to a work-study job on campus. To lighten the load during the semester, they thought, Carla could meet with advising to find a way to put off some of her course hours until summer session. To do that, she would also have to meet with financial aid to avoid financial-aid probation and keep pace with standard academic progress.

What if Carla's high-school preparation was not in truth the root cause of her academic difficulties? Remember, Carla had an interest in "spreading the word." Maybe, like so many students, she was pursuing the wrong major, one that did not play to her academic strengths or her genuine professional interests.

In fact, when Carla had met with mentors at the Center for the Junior Year at Governors State, they posed the usual opening question that underlies a Field of Study approach: "We have no idea what you mean when you say *marketing*. Could you explain it to us?" What the mentors learned from Carla, when she started describing in detail what she aspired to do, did not sound like marketing. She was interested in social media, and one of her challenges was that there was no major in social media on her campus. Carla believed that "marketing" is another term for "advertising," or merely informing people about products and services.

So, when pressed to declare a major on her community-college application, Carla had chosen marketing, and the people on campus, from admissions to advising, had assumed she knew what she was doing. They merely monitored her progress through the degree audit—like so many other students, following a track but not one leading where they wanted to go. At the point where those students start running into academic difficulties, they *might* have the conversations needed to clarify their hidden intellectualism and vocational purpose, understand the college structure, and plan an academic program that works for them. If, that is, they don't just disappear from campus.

Ned shared with the gathering at Thrive what Carla had told the mentors: her real interest was in how to make the best use of Pinterest, Instagram, Facebook, and other platforms. But since there was no major for social media on campus, those gathered were stumped. What then should she major in? The audience suggested web-content development, advertising, or writing for digital media, but none of those majors were of interest to Carla.

In the hidden job market, the world of work is a complex environment, with many more pathways into professions than colleges acknowledge with their rigid departmental structures and academic majors. For Carla, what didn't exist as a "designated major" for social media in fact did exist, if only she could learn how to fill in the blanks.

The Research Investigative Inquiry

Carla had to learn how to research the possibilities—and do so outside the structures of the academic environment, through a research investigative inquiry. The aim of the research investigative inquiry, or RII, is to explore, find people with similar interests, and pick their brains. Through the RII, students get critical information they need to design their undergraduate plans, and they begin creating a network of potential mentors who can offer experiential-learning opportunities. The conversations a student has with an insider are not generic, focused on job trends, office life, or the biography or career path of the person interviewed. Instead, the RII focuses on the deep personal perspective of someone who works in a particular position in the hidden job market, who can convey an insider's view of an industry and the unspoken skill sets necessary to deal with the complicated situations that frequently arise. In a sense, the interviewee begins to take on the role of a mentor, career coach, or guide for the student.

This is not the typical informational interview often recommended on career-center websites. For example, the slate of twenty-three sample questions offered on the career site at the University of California at Berkeley represents much of what's out there: the questions ask about industry trends, generic career paths into the field, and bland work-lifestyle questions, with precious few focused on the skills needed for the job. Here is a sample: *What is a typical day (or week) like for you? What do you like most about your work? How does your job affect your general lifestyle? What related fields would you recommend I also look into? Can you recommend trade journals, magazines or professional associations which would be helpful for my professional development?*[17]

A student asking these questions in an informational interview might come across as someone who has not done the basic homework on the profession. Berkeley's long list of suggested questions includes only three pertinent to skills and training: *How relevant is your undergraduate major to your work? What kind of education, training, or background does your job require? What skills, abilities, and personal attributes are essential to success in your job/this field?* (Students have to decide how many of the twenty-three questions they can pack into a thirty-minute interview.)

Worse yet, most of these questions may not yield the granular information students will need to design an integrated and marketable undergraduate experience for a particular position, and the answers won't likely lead to an experiential-learning opportunity. In fact, Berkeley's site expressly discourages students from asking about experiential or employment opportunities. The "objective is to get information and advice, not a job," the site says. "It is not a job interview, and the objective is not to find job openings."[18]

For students who desperately need real-world experiences before graduation—not only for their resumes but also to confirm their interests—this prohibition risks wasting a potentially valuable opportunity. It is fine to remind students not to fish for a job, but these interviews should be an entry point for discussing the possibility of creating experiential learning.

The questions students ask through the research interview focus on the complex, multidisciplinary "wicked problems" that people in any field face on any given day. Before students can even engage productively with someone in the hidden job market, they need to get a sense of those issues and conundrums. RII questions are more investigative, and they are deeper, designed to help a student understand the reality of the paths into a profession and the specific skills that practitioners truly value in the field, not what colleges believe students need. And, more often than not, the RII brings up unexpected and important information that students never would have considered. What students learn from the people they interview often contradicts what they hear on campus.

Carla, for example, was prepped with opening questions like these:

- Social media is fraught with pitfalls. With a few strokes, someone can create a microaggression storm. How do you avoid those risks?
- Social media can be unforgiving, and responses to a post can become toxic. How do you manage that? How do you know when you need to pull the plug on a post?
- When you are trying to expand your social media to a more diverse audience, how does that affect the language, appearance, or topics on a social-media platform?
- What keeps you up at night?

These opening questions are designed to engage the interviewee and draw out unexpected, unspoken information about the variety of skills at play in social media. These questions are intended to be provocative, leading to more questions and a more engaged conversation. By exploring the granularity of someone's experiences in their hidden job market, students learn insider information not found in a college catalog or course, and they add that information to the material they will use to devise their undergraduate plan.

The last few questions in the research investigative inquiry are intended to open the possibility for an experiential-learning opportunity with the interviewee.

- If someone wanted to come into this field and work with you, what do you want to see in that person's background?
- How important is hands-on experience?
- How can I get that experience with you?

Students interview several different people through the RII, which increases their chances of finding someone who is willing to engage and work with them. Many students are surprised to see how many people will talk with them and offer advice. This process proves to be invaluable to first-generation and historically underserved students, helping them build out their social and cultural capital. (We go into more detail about the research investigative inquiry in chapter 3.)

Students are also surprised to find that insiders in the hidden job market frequently recognize the intrinsic talents that students bring, talents that the students themselves may not see. In Carla's case, everyone she interviewed emphasized the difference between using social media professionally and using it with friends, so Carla would have to develop an appropriate skill set to understand the difference. Everyone also noticed she was bilingual, and they told her that managing social media in two languages would open up a range of employment opportunities, but she would have to develop those language skills as well.

After a series of interviews, Carla returned to the Center for the Junior Year to share what she had learned, and she revealed a better understanding of how to backward-map her undergraduate experience. Importantly, she also knew what her major would be. Can you guess what that is?

The Dilemma of Advising and Career Services

One might think that a capable student like Carla would have gotten some direction previously through traditional academic advising. Academic advising, after all, is intended to help students navigate the college maze, complete the requirements for graduation in a timely manner, and be ready to enter the job market or pursue graduate study. Researchers of higher education consistently note that advising, when done well, can change the trajectory for the average student, improving recruitment, retention, and postgraduate outcomes, which lead to happy, generous alumni. Advising is costly up front; CCRC points out that hiring new advisors is the most significant expense in implementing guided pathways. But personnel costs in advising should be looked at as an investment that will pay for itself.[19]

The data and public narrative on disappointing outcomes at many institutions suggest, however, that advising is not working as desired. Protracted time to degree completion, low graduation rates, troubling evidence of postgraduate underemployment, and a lack of preparation for the work world—all of these indicators point out that advising is not consistently effective at setting students up for success. Why is that?

We can glean some of the reasons from Carla's experience. Carla's choice of major was made on unwarranted assumptions that her high-school counselor, the advisors at her community college, and the transfer-admission advisors took for granted—until, that is, she started to stumble. This is a problem endemic in higher education. Much of what passes for "advising," as practiced at many institutions, is merely tracking students through the system. Many advising syllabi, which set an agenda for advising sessions, prioritize transactional interactions: introducing the requirements for completing a degree, performing degree audits, helping students understand the rules and regulations around adding and dropping courses, taking students through the procedures of registration, and meeting with students when flags pop up.

These syllabi do not identify the learning encounters that would help students clarify their hidden intellectualism or vocational purpose, teach them how to identify their hidden job market, or show them how to create experiential-learning opportunities. Much advising places the responsibility for clarifying personal, professional, and educational goals on the student, *before* they meet with an advisor; if they need help with that process, advising syllabi often recommend that students meet with career services. This means that students have to bounce between disconnected offices on a campus, and they are expected to do this while negotiating their course schedules, work schedules, and other activities occupying their time.[20]

Nothing in the average advisor's preparation indicates an expertise in helping students clarify their hidden intellectualism or vocational purpose, spot connections to the hidden job market, or understand how to fill in blanks to create an integrated undergraduate experience relevant to the world of work. Professional advisors, those hired by institutions to advise students full-time, come from all sorts of backgrounds: recent undergraduates who want to start a career in student affairs, graduate students from various programs, doctoral-degree holders who could not find a faculty job, and more. Just because somebody graduates from college does not mean they have a good understanding of how college works. In fact, many job postings for entry-level advisors require little employment experience, and colleges are often hiring entry-level advisors because turnover in the field is so high. "You know what it takes to be an advisor on my campus?" one community college president told Scott in a moment of candor. "An undergraduate degree and a heartbeat."

Professional advisors sometimes get their training from graduate programs in higher education and student affairs. Typically, though, these programs are broad in scope, preparing students for the spread of student-affairs roles across campus. They do not cover the depth and breadth of the college curriculum and how knowledge in one discipline connects to the learning in another, nor do those programs detail how curricula connect to the vast opportunities in the world of work. Not having this outlook limits the sorts of relationships advisors can have with students. For most advisors, on-the-job training about the college curriculum focuses on learning the general-education requirements, the requirements for majors and minors, and how to work with the degree-audit system.

When advisors start their position, from the get-go, they labor under a variety of pressures. The average pay is modest; various job sites list salaries around $45,000 to $55,000, but some positions start as low as $35,000.[21] Advisors consistently complain that they are overworked, with unmanageable caseloads, and that administrators often disregard their suggestions for improving conditions for students.[22]

Moreover, advisors are on the front line of a conflict of interest at the core of the higher education system. Many advisors are pressured, tacitly or explicitly, to keep a student "on track" at the institution, even if that student's best interest might be to change majors, change schools, or pursue another life course altogether. For those advisors who are housed in academic departments, that pressure could mean keeping students in the department and maintaining full-time enrollment numbers; for centralized advisors, that often means keeping students within a specific college. Many begin to feel that their role in student success—*real* student success, beyond merely getting bodies to graduation—is not the focus of their job.

In consequence, the important conversations that students need to have in advising do not seem to be taking place. For instance, it's not unusual to have students who express an interest in law be referred to a prelaw advisor housed in a political-science department, even though there is no major or courses required to get into law school. The prelaw advisor is frequently found in political science because that department offers courses in constitutional law, which, incidentally, have little to do with how constitutional law is taught in law school. Still, the bureaucracy of the institution holds sway: students with an interest in law are almost reflexively directed to declare political science as their major.

If colleges were thinking seriously about preparing students for law school, instead of their established bureaucracy, why wouldn't the prelaw advisor be in the philosophy department? There, students would learn logic (critical to doing well on the standardized test required for law school admission), ethics, and theories of justice. Alternatively, students interested in law could get much out of designing their studies around a major in theater, where they could master the performance skills essential for a courtroom litigator, while they fill in the blank spaces of their degree with courses in philosophy, political science, and rhetoric. In fact, if colleges put students' interests first, they would help undergraduates plan their prelaw studies around what genuinely calls them to the field (be that environmental protection, children's rights, or technology patents). The advisor, independent from any college or major, would help students plan a program of study, including experiential learning, around their vocational purpose and their academic strengths.

So, if professional advising is compromised, what about faculty advising? Many colleges rely on faculty members to offer advising, on the assumption that they have a better sense of the whole college curriculum and how a particular major might translate to the world of work. But this assumption is unwarranted. Faculty are hired to contribute expertise to their department, to publish in journals and present at conferences, to raise money for their discipline, and to contribute to shared governance by sitting on various committees. These tasks alone are burdensome; and at many institutions, most of the rewards for tenure and promotion are tied to performing these activities and not typically tied to teaching and advising. Unless faculty members are at a college that rewards teaching and advising for tenure and promotion, it's against their best interests to invest more-than-minimal time in working with students. Given the requirements for tenure and the running tenure clock, many new faculty members are told to "waste" as little time as possible with students.[23] Typically, those who have tenure look for ways to reduce their teaching load so they can focus on research and publication.[24]

Faculty advising, whether administrators like it or not, is at odds with itself. Professors have to choose between spending time working with undergraduates versus devoting time to their own professional development and advancement. Mentorship with faculty works best with those students who show a genuine interest in a professor's discipline, because those students can assist the professor in his or her research.

Where does that leave the majority of students who are pursuing a terminal bachelor's degree or looking at their undergraduate degree as an entree into a professional school? For them, the value of faculty advising becomes even more questionable. First, it's not clear that faculty members understand how students in their discipline could use their studies to launch into various possible jobs; many faculty members never had to do this themselves and, in fact, wouldn't know what to do with their own academic credentials should they ever have to leave the academy. Second, we cannot assume a professor in one department has a good working knowledge of the whole curriculum—and in a way that would help students fill in the blanks on their degree audit. Lastly, many faculty members are wary of looking at the bachelor's degree as career education, categorizing disciplines like engineering and business as "vocational training" and the liberal arts as "nonvocational education." In the end, the quality of faculty advising depends on the goodwill and engagement of a particular professor.

Career-services offices are often seen as the backstop for gaps in advising. But in most cases, a career office gets students toward the end of their advising encounters, if the office sees them at all. Only 22 percent of students reported using career services "often or very often" before graduating, according to a 2018 Strada-Gallup survey.[25] It's not unusual to hear career advisors complain that students come into their offices with empty college degrees.

People in career services are strapped, too, by the college structure. They are held accountable for helping students land good first jobs, ones that satisfy student and parent concerns about return on investment. Although versed in job trends in major industries, they usually do not get trained on how to translate those job trends into course selections for students, especially those in humanities, social sciences, and the fine arts. In fact, in many cases, career-services staff are discouraged from crossing over to the academic side of the institution. When it comes to reaching out to alumni to offer their mentorship to students, staff often have to battle with the fundraising office to get a list of names.

Often, career offices don't think about the hidden job market, as we define it in this book, perhaps because they don't have the resources to explore it or because too few small- to mid-size employers have personnel who reach out to colleges to form a recruiting relationship. Career offices generally prioritize relationships with major companies and locally or nationally known employers, in industries like engineering, technology, allied health, and finance. They also tend to lean into a basic equation: a major, by dint of its name, links to a job track in a prominent industry, mainly because that operation is the easiest to scale. A career trajectory in a major like international business appears to be relatively clear. But there's an irony here. A foreign-language major, for instance, could easily form a path into international business, yet many of the jobs for language majors lie in the hidden job market, positions concealed deep inside large corporations and in small- to medium-sized employers overlooked by colleges.

The website called What Can I Do with This Major?—a service produced by the career center at the University of Tennessee and sold to career offices across the country—seems to encapsulate the mixed messaging. Apparent even in its title, the site assumes that students pick a major first and then figure out what to do with that major later on. The site could be valuable to advisors and career counselors who need a more expansive sense of what students can do with degrees in liberal arts, but it mainly offers generic suggestions for next steps in pursuing those careers. When you explore the site, you notice how many of its suggested occupations are found in the hidden job market. Students would still need someone to help them clarify their vocational purpose, coach them in filling the blanks, and show them how to cut their own path into an entry-level position.[26]

The reality for students on campus is that they often bounce between the advising office and the career center. One entity has an inward-looking perspective on completing degree requirements, and the other focuses outwardly on major employers and general job trends beyond the institution. In the middle are the students, who are mostly looking for spaces in the hidden job market, which they don't see or understand and for which they need preparation. Doing that depends on how students learn to fill in the blanks.

As it stands, most career counselors find themselves faced with students needing to construct a career-readiness narrative from a cafeteria-style degree. Much of the time, these conversations don't happen until the last months before graduation, or even afterward, when it's too late.

Carla Solves Her College Conundrum

Carla returned from her research investigative inquiry knowing the skills she needed to enter the work world of social media. The problem was that she didn't know how to start acquiring those skills in the college environment—because, like most students, if she didn't see what she wanted to do in the name of an academic department, then she believed it didn't exist on campus. What she was not looking at was how the blank spaces could provide her with a tool to design her undergraduate experience.

Building an integrated, meaningful, and marketable undergraduate degree does not start with the title of a major or minor. Carla had to be taught to look first at the learning opportunities in the course catalog and in the academic interests of faculty members.

Realizing this fact was a lightbulb moment for Carla. On her campus at the time, the marketing major did not include any courses on creating or managing social media. When she typed "social media" into the course catalog search engine, she found a cluster of four courses in communications studies, on a completely different side of campus from marketing.

However, her research and her reading of course descriptions suggested that there were still valuable things to pull from the marketing program. She could use courses in content marketing, consumer behavior, and marketing across cultures—but they didn't necessarily add up to a minor. She also discovered that she did not need the math courses required for the business core. She only needed a statistics course that would satisfy a general-education requirement and provide the literacy she needed to understand the number crunchers' analysis of audience engagement.

Finally, she found two courses in public relations that would introduce her to the strategies organizations use to communicate with the public, which tied together social media and marketing. All she would need to complete her "career readiness" was a well-rounded experiential-learning opportunity.

A smattering of courses in social media, marketing, and public relations does not constitute a major, however. So, what should she major in? The audience at the Thrive Conference could not come up with the answer.

Carla did. It was obvious: Spanish, a humanities program but one that made good business sense. Combining Spanish with the skills taught in the courses she discovered in the catalog, she could pursue her cultural heritage, master her language, have a better sense of her personal identity, and learn to think across cultural boundaries—and she could create social media in two marketable languages, which could help her land a job. Her first gig was a work-study opportunity in her college's admissions office. By her last year, she had a solid portfolio and interviews lined up. She graduated in less than five years, faster than the national average.

Colleges are pressured today to put a premium on getting students into and through undergraduate education, partly to have satisfactory data on graduation rates and other elements that colleges are ranked on. Students like Carla get lost in this emphasis. Ironically, pushing students through the system undercuts higher education's credibility and raises a question: Are colleges genuinely serving students, or are they driven by other accountability concerns? Colleges could have admirable graduation rates and genuinely work for student success if they would redefine the problems and take their existing resources and use them differently.

Carla's story represents the tension that so many students feel. They find themselves caught between the siloed programs colleges create— with their inward gaze at majors, minors, and guided pathways—and the reality of the world of work, which calls for a multidisciplinary skill set. It's no wonder that the administrators at the Thrive Conference, in trying to solve Carla's dilemma, could not see outside the academic frameworks they inhabited.

Completion of college alone is not the goal. The goal is to launch students into a promising work opportunity, and they prepare for that by designing their undergraduate education through the information they gather in the real world through their research investigative inquiry. Carla's story represents what could happen on campus, if we change the conversations that students have. Her declaring Spanish as her major might seem obvious to readers with the cultural capital to imagine jobs for Spanish majors that go beyond teaching Spanish or working in translation.

But a maxim holds true for many low-income and first-generation students: you don't know what you don't know. Carla never would have seen Spanish as a viable major for working in social media. As a matter of fact, she could have been dissuaded from choosing Spanish by her advisor, who might have steered her instead toward a major associated with a higher average salary. Without a deliberate and coached engagement with people in the world of her hidden job market—and the conversations that let her see college learning opportunities differently—Carla would not have been able to pull together her intrinsic strengths into a Field of Study that ultimately launched her on a viable career path.

3

The Wicked Problem

SASHAY BUTLER GREW UP in Cross, South Carolina, little more than a handful of dirt roads on the western shores of Lake Moultrie, about an hour north of Charleston. Cross sits on the border of a rural section of the state known as the Corridor of Shame, with widespread poverty, blighted schools, and a dearth of employers, services, and infrastructure for the locals.[1]

"When I was in elementary school, we used to have a Piggly Wiggly," says Shay, as she is known to friends and family. "It brought in some good revenue and jobs for people, but ultimately the community was too small to sustain it." People in Cross, she says, now mainly get groceries from one of two dollar stores in the area or from the gas station.

Shay's mother was labeled the "smart one" in the family and went to Claflin University on a music scholarship for a year but left after she got pregnant with Shay at age nineteen. Shay says she was "adultified" early, helping to care for her siblings and her mother, who suffered from depression and mental illness. Shay pushed herself into academics and extracurriculars to distract her from the chaos at home—after all, she was now the family's "college baby," as expectations for mom got passed down to daughter.

Shay took up percussion in the high-school marching band, earned a spot on the basketball team, and signed up for dual-enrollment courses at the local community college. Along the way, she found a passion: poetry. One of her cousins was a rapper, who made poetry feel "cool," and a high-school English teacher invited Shay to join the poetry club and talked to her about metaphors and other literary devices to spice up her verse. Her journal became an emotional outlet. "Poetry was this space where I could tell my story, even if I couldn't say it out loud," says Shay, who realized early that "consequences would ensue" if she told people in Cross about the trials of her home life. "The page is not going to tell anybody."

In her junior year, she joined College Summit, an organization that offers advising, career coaching, and college-immersion experiences to rising seniors from low-income, predominantly Black communities and under-resourced high schools. Shay was offered several music scholarships from historically Black colleges, but she wasn't interested in music. Her skills on the basketball court weren't good enough to earn an athletic scholarship, but a recruiter at Columbia College in South Carolina liked Shay's attitude and work ethic and offered her a scholarship as a manager of the basketball team. There, Shay felt she had an opportunity to pursue something meaningful. Coming from a community like Cross, "you felt like you escaped," Shay explains. "And you want to do something to help other students escape."

Shay shared that drive with her high-school counselors and her advisors at College Summit, and they suggested that she major in political science and go to law school, on the simple reasoning that lawyers make a good living and can impact communities through policy.

But soon after Shay arrived at Columbia College, she realized political science and law school were not for her. The issues discussed in her political science classes were distant from the individual stories of people in Cross and communities like it. Sure, she had the smarts to gain admission to law school, but "just because you can do something doesn't mean it's the thing you're supposed to do," she says. "I'm not passionate about being in a courtroom. I am passionate about being an advocate for young people, for youth development. I'm passionate about poetry. I'm passionate about helping each student reach their ideal version of success."

But what could success look like for Shay? Her avocation in poetry and spoken-word performance became more important to her as she started seeing what she wanted to do, but she struggled to find her space in college. She talked to faculty members in social work, but they didn't see a place for spoken word in their program. She considered psychology but had a similar conversation with faculty there. She talked to people in the English department and discovered the college offered only one course in creative writing in poetry, taught occasionally by adjunct faculty. Advisors told her that she couldn't double-major in English and either social work or psychology if she wanted to graduate on time. Career services offered a pat answer: she could minor in English, but if she wanted to earn a decent living, she would need a master's degree in social work or psychology.

Shay faced that complicated, wicked problem that so many other undergraduates struggle with: How could she pursue something meaningful in college, while also meeting the expectations of her family to live up to her potential and find a viable career? As a last resort, she turned up at Columbia College's Center for Engaged Learning, which used a Field of Study approach.

A World of Wicked Problems

We have already mentioned wicked problems a few times in this book, and the concept of the wicked problem forms a crucial underpinning to the argument we're making about designing an undergraduate experience. The design theorists Horst Rittel and Melvin Webber introduced the term "wicked problem" in 1973 to draw attention to the complexities and challenges in planning and in social policy. Some problems, they said, are "tame"—that is, they have a well-defined and stable problem statement, a solution that can be objectively evaluated as true or false, and a definite stopping point when that solution is reached.

Wicked problems, by contrast, do not have that same level of clarity. They are grounded in the messy and fuzzy complications inherent in real-world problems, like climate change, border security, or forming social policy to address poverty or health-care disparities. Their solutions can defy conventional wisdom, must draw from a range of expertise and disciplines, and almost always have intersecting social, cultural, and pragmatic implications. In a world with multiple cultural perspectives, even defining a wicked problem is crucial, as they don't always lend themselves to a single definition—or even a single solution. Wicked problems can have multiple resolutions, without requiring that any particular solution stand as true or false.[2]

Wicked problems represent the reality outside the walls of academe. We live in a complex, interdisciplinary world, where problems have layers that cut across areas of expertise and zones of culture. For an example we need look no further than water. This essential component of life on earth touches everything. We need water to mine precious minerals, manufacture computer chips, irrigate golf courses and farmlands, generate electricity, and drink simply to stay alive. With so many competing interests, the way we define the problem holds a key to how we address it. Approach water from the perspective of western water-rights laws and the business interests of major breweries in Colorado, and you raise multiple complications. What are the implications of redirecting water from the western slope to the eastern slope of the Continental Divide, and how does that impact farming, fire prevention, development, and electricity generation? Approach water from the perspective of green architecture, wastewater treatment, or drinking systems, and you raise entirely other sets of complications.

In a 2009 *New York Times* opinion piece, Mark C. Taylor, a professor of religion at Columbia University, proposed reorganizing the American college or university under broad "zones of inquiry" like Media, Mind, and Water. Higher education has lost touch, he argued, with its focus on highly specialized academic topics, so distant from the real problems that colleges and universities should be training students to solve. Abolish the departments, he recommended, and create "a curriculum structured like a web," with cross-disciplinary and cross-cultural programs. "A Water program would bring together people in the humanities, arts, social and natural sciences with representatives from professional schools like medicine, law, business, engineering, social work, theology and architecture," Taylor argued. "Through the intersection of multiple perspectives and approaches, new theoretical insights will develop and unexpected practical solutions will emerge."[3]

The idea landed with a thud at the time. When Taylor brought his thoughts to his colleagues, "people laughed in my face," he told the *Chronicle of Higher Education* in 2020. "I was in a big meeting at Columbia where they actually mocked it."[4] He noted, with bitter irony, that Columbia changed course that year: the university announced that 2020 would be the institution's interdisciplinary "Year of Water"—but it was as an initiative that existed mostly outside the curriculum, in the form of lectures and events.[5]

The culture of higher education resists change, and it has long had a conflicted relationship between its rigid departmental structures and the clear need to grapple with real problems across disciplines. In the late 1960s and early 1970s, at a time of experimentation in academe and society, institutions like the College of the Atlantic, Hampshire College, and Evergreen College challenged students to design majors around interdisciplinary problems and urgent issues. For some institutions, it was a practical decision: the smallest start-up colleges did not have the infrastructure to support substantial stand-alone departments in specific disciplines, along with the majors to go with them. At the College of the Atlantic, for example, all students major in "human ecology," which can mean whatever a student wants to bring to it.[6]

In this era of experimentation fifty years ago, even established colleges and universities were developing models that would allow students to design their own education around the notion of an interdisciplinary problem—what Taylor might have called a "zone of inquiry." At the University of Illinois at Urbana-Champaign, for instance, students could take advantage of Individual Plans of Study, which allowed them to design interdisciplinary programs that cut across majors in the existing collegiate and departmental structure.

Colleges saw promising side effects to students pursuing these programs. Through the work and interests of their students, faculty from disconnected disciplines, even distant parts of campus, would come together and begin talking. These conversations would sometimes lead to new programs in, say, cinematography, Middle Eastern studies, and neuroscience. Here and there, universities began to see the need to institutionalize collaboration and interdisciplinarity to support research across departmental boundaries. The University of Wisconsin at Madison, for example, introduced its "cluster hiring initiative" in 1998, recruiting cross-disciplinary faculty who can teach, research, and communicate in about seventy wicked problem areas, including biomedical engineering, disabilities studies, Wisconsin bioenergy, emerging polar regions, freshwater sustainability, and a cluster known simply as "Vitamin D."[7]

Colleges have tried to create spaces to tackle wicked problems not only at the departmental level but also at the course level. The capstone course stands as a key example. This is where an academic department (or even the college itself) formulates a problem with the trappings of a real-world challenge, then asks students to identify and analyze different facets of that problem and to use the training from their major to find solutions in a final project. Many educators talk about these courses as an opportunity for students to reflect on their time in college and retroactively identify the useful skills and knowledge they gained through their undergraduate studies.

For some in higher education, this counts as an exercise in "integrative learning," another catchphrase meant to highlight the need for students to tackle complex, real-world problems to bring context to their education. Organizations like the American Association of Colleges and Universities believe that courses like these create a learning experience where students can grapple with diverse and even contradictory points of view, using insights from different disciplines across the curriculum to develop a more complex understanding of the world. As students work through these issues, they have to reflect on how their own race, class, gender, sexual orientation, political persuasion, religious belief, and more influence their perspectives and how they work with others to develop solutions. To some extent, integrative learning is meant to counter persistent criticisms from employers—that students don't seem to know how to synthesize and apply their learning to real-world settings, use their learning to interpret knowledge and data, demonstrate complex problem-solving skills, and work effectively in teams.[8]

But a capstone course—with its wicked problems devised by an academic department or college, offered at or near the end of a student's undergraduate journey—has several obvious limitations. It's fair to say that these courses, on the whole, may not be achieving the grand goal of helping students understand how their learning integrates across their undergraduate experience.

For starters, capstone courses are found only in select departments and majors on any campus and may not be found on many campuses at all. Many capstone courses are taught by teams, which means they are expensive for the institution to offer, yet they are also typically limited in enrollment, to help ensure that the institution offers a robust pedagogical experience. Capstone courses are also subject to the whim of a department or leading administrator, who might decide that the attention of the capstone curriculum needs to switch to the next educational fad.

What's more, in capstone courses and similar offerings, it's often the faculty members, *not* the students, who are defining the problems and their parameters. These courses might provide a memorable learning experience for a student in a particular major but may not help that student make connections between their *own* hidden intellectualism or vocational purpose and the courses they took in the previous four or more years. And all of this happens far too late, at the culmination of an undergraduate degree, not when laying the groundwork at the beginning.

The typical college or university—with its courses and concentrations, specialties and expertise, offered across an array of academic and professional fields—is *already* an interdisciplinary environment. Students, and the people who advise them, just have to be taught to see it that way. Rather than pick a major and try to find context through artificial problems devised by the institution as a capstone experience, students should grapple with their own wicked problems and personal passions, by learning how to design personally meaningful undergraduate experiences.

Higher education typically sees interdisciplinary majors as zones for the rare student with offbeat interests or highly specific educational goals. But the techniques of designing an interdisciplinary degree are not limited to students enrolled in special programs, like an Individual Plan of Study. Any student, regardless of major, can pursue a vocational purpose or a strand of hidden intellectualism—a passion, a problem, a "zone of inquiry" as Taylor would have it—within the traditional structures.

This potential rests on teaching students how to see an undergraduate degree as a Field of Study, where the blank spaces of the degree knit together with the major and extracurricular activities to form a cohesive whole. It depends on showing students the rich backgrounds and interests of their professors, who are themselves interdisciplinary field-of-study specialists, and on helping students build a curriculum around an interest using those faculty as a model. By taking on their wicked problem through a Field of Study approach, students understand from the start the relevance of the pieces and skills of their undergraduate education. They *build the meaning into* their curriculum, rather than trying to decipher the meaning on the back end.

The Field of Study Process

For students, planning a meaningful undergraduate education is their most important and pressing wicked problem—a real-world puzzle about the relationship between their education and career aspirations. Looking at a Field of Study as a wicked problem provides a better framework for designing an undergraduate education, by taking a student out of the simple equation that the right major will lead to a good job. Field of Study—not the major, not average salaries—should be the guiding principle that shapes our conversations with students.

What follows are the steps of the Field of Study method, but it's important to remember that these steps are fluid and should be adjusted based on the circumstances of individual students and their unique situations. The steps don't necessarily lead only in one direction. Some steps, like the research investigative inquiry, may have to be repeated if a student discovers unexpected things or changes direction.

For each of these steps, we describe the rationale behind it and explain how it might differ from other methods out there. That way, a college staff or faculty member could incorporate aspects of the Field of Study method into already-established mentorship and career-counseling programs.

This process is a curriculum. It has assignments and expectations for the students on a Field of Study journey. The purpose is to teach students the steps of Field of Study so that they can repeat the process themselves throughout their undergraduate careers. Many could even share with other students how they navigated through college, encouraging friends to take similar steps, playing the role of an informal peer mentor.

Ideally, the Field of Study method transforms an office into a learning organization: Students bring back information and tips from their research interviews, which are shared among staff and peer mentors who work in the office, who then use that information when working with new students coming in. Those new students go through the Field of Study process and start the cycle anew.

Step 1. Clarifying hidden intellectualism and vocational purpose and learning about the hidden job market

Discernment of a career path is the starting point—and the sticking point—for many students as they start to lay out their plans for a college degree. Scores of books have been written on career discernment, and some of those books have influenced how advising and career services approach the most stressful question weighing on a freshman: "What do you want to do after you graduate?"

In general, the conventional approach includes a handful of steps oriented around companies or job slots associated with college majors. For example, students are asked to list some companies they might want to work for, even though most students can name only a handful of major corporations, with no sense of the granular world of work within them or how to navigate into them.

Students are sometimes asked to look at a list of majors and to pick five or ten that seem most interesting—an institutional approach that, once again, is inward-looking and leans on the false major-equals-job calculation.

Some career educators are now directing students to ask ChatGPT, or other applications of artificial intelligence, how to combine coursework in a major with a personal interest, but the chatbot tends to kick out a generic list of occupations, still closely tied to major-equals-job, with no information about how a student can locate a particular interest in the hidden job market. Worse, relying on AI bypasses the interpersonal interactions students need for building out their social and cultural capital, and it provides them with no hints on how to find the people in their hidden job market that they need to talk to.[9]

A growing number of colleges and organizations have turned to career-assessment tests. Myers-Briggs, Strong-Campbell, and Focus-2Career are well-known ones, and recently the College Board and the State of Texas have developed tests of their own.[10] These tests largely resemble one another. The Texas Career Check puts users through a battery of questions on occupational preferences, like "Manage a retail store" or "Study the movement of planets." From the weighted characteristics of a user's interest profile (realistic, investigative, artistic, social, enterprising, and conventional), the assessment kicks out a disparate and disconnected list of job titles and associated salaries. When Scott recently tested it, Texas's interest profiler recommended floral designer, choreographer, foreign-language interpreter, and professor of architecture, among others, as possible career routes. (Journalism, his career for almost thirty years, landed near the bottom.)

Under a Field of Study frame, the approach to discernment comes at that most stressful of questions for a freshman from a different perspective. Field of Study is not interested in job titles or majors as orientation tools. Rather, it focuses on a student's wicked problem and how the student can work on that wicked problem in the granularity of the hidden job market.

Some students arrive on campus projecting certainty, confident in declaring a major in business, environmental science, or premed or prelaw—often with unspoken assumptions about what they think those majors mean. The Field of Study approach, by contrast, makes no such assumption: "We have no idea what you're talking about. Can you explain what you mean by business?" Or environmental science? Or premed or prelaw?

We want students to pause. Most get stuck on this question—and more important, they have never been asked anything like it. We want to disrupt what, for example, they think a business major leads to. Microbreweries are part of the business world, as are tennis, comic books, and tourist railroads. For the most part, *everything* is a business, yet students can have a difficult time seeing that they could make a living working for Goose Island Brewery, the United States Tennis Association, Comic-Con International, or a tourist steam railroad in a rural community. They could consider a role that isn't in a traditional business setting at all by applying business techniques to a life in the world of art or by working for the government or a nonprofit. We want to take off the blinders of the major and get students thinking about the relationship between their hidden intellectualism, their undergraduate plans, and the hidden jobs out there.

For those students who are "undecided," Field of Study asks a different question: "If you could do whatever it is that you genuinely care about, no matter how crazy it might sound, and we could guarantee you a comfortable living, what would you pursue?" The intent behind this question is to get them to explain themselves honestly, passionately. Freed from the mooring of the major, conventional job roles, and income worries, in this thought experiment, students begin to examine what drives them and what defines their vocational purpose and hidden intellectualism. The way that students answer the question often comes out unconventionally, driven by personal experiences. Here are some examples of responses from real students:

- "I eat, drink, and dream about anime."
- "I want to go into financial planning, but I want to work with low-income populations."
- "I love baking, but I'm also interested in how people eat healthy."
- "I emigrated from Egypt when I was five, and I want to go back there to open a breast-cancer clinic."
- "I can't get enough of looking at antiquarian books."
- "I'm from Houston, and I want to save watersheds from the impacts of housing developments."
- "I want to study consciousness and the effects of psychedelics."
- "I want to develop mobile diagnostic clinics for visually disabled Arab and Bedouin populations in the south of Israel."

Or, to quote Cameron Hardesty from chapter 1, "I love flowers. Always have."

These statements do not represent majors or job slots; they represent a student's hidden intellectualism or vocational purpose—it's that world they want to enter, what they would do to make the most of their gifts and talents. It can be that thing they feel they were "meant to do." But all of these statements represent real possibilities in the hidden job market. How a student might approach these possibilities within the college curriculum still depends on how they define their space in that job market. Cameron Hardesty's skill set could have led her in any number of directions, but the combination of her hidden intellectualism and vocational purpose called her to marketing, entrepreneurship, and e-retail in the world of flowers.

The relationships among hidden intellectualism, vocational purpose, and the hidden job market form a broad world of work, with roles in companies and organizations that can match just about anything a student can imagine, with multiple ways to approach those roles. The avenues come from how students match their aspirations and best academic strengths with what they discover in the world outside the classroom. This process begins with the research investigative inquiry.

Step 2. Conducting a Research Investigative Inquiry

The research investigative inquiry is the engine of the Field of Study process. Higher-education institutions cannot know, outline, or map all the possible roles in the hidden job market, so students need to learn how to discover them. Only by going into the professional world to talk to people can students understand how colleges and universities provide myriad possibilities to prepare them for real-world roles. As a component of the Field of Study curriculum, the research investigative inquiry is a learning agenda—it depends on formulating good questions to ask and utilizing the answers. The RII needs to begin early in a student's college career, during the first or second year, before they are locked into a major.

There are four components to the research investigative inquiry.

First, students need to research who is doing what they want to do or something similar. This stage of research starts to make the hidden job market visible for students, and it can begin with a simple Google search. Students can also work with staff members who have expertise in broad research of the world (reference librarians are a great resource) or in the specifics of a student's vocational interests. Taking an example from above, the student interested in baking and health would find expertise in bakers at a local vegan restaurant, nutritionists at corporations specializing in organic foods, those working in hospital food-service operations, or a professor in a culinary-medicine program at a medical school. Students should look for people working in their specific field of interest—experts who might be buried within an organization. Students should avoid general corporate gatekeepers, like human-resources managers, who might erect barriers to the students and likely won't have the granular information about skills and personnel that students need.

Second, students need to set up personal interviews. Students should identify four to five people to interview. Setting up those conversations is relatively straightforward: make a phone call. (Calling can be more successful than an email. Much of the time, a student will reach an assistant who manages the expert's appointments.) The strategy from there is simple: Students should say that they are calling from their college and doing research, looking for information about a particular field, topic, or role related to their hidden intellectualism and vocational purpose. For example: "I'm researching the antiquarian book market and how libraries and private collectors acquire such books for public special collections. I am wondering if I can get thirty minutes of your time." Students will be surprised how often they are granted an appointment.

Third, students should research the field and bring substantial questions (and genuine curiosity) to the interview. Students should bring a notebook and set several goals for gathering information. They'll want to get a deep understanding of the everyday issues and challenges that these experts face, the unspoken or little-known skill sets that are crucial to the work, and the sound professional advice that an expert has to share about the role. Students should begin to understand whether the reality of the work matches their perceptions of it and how they might further define or sharpen their personal goals by working in the field.

Students bring substantial questions that raise wicked problems related to the day-to-day challenges these people deal with, and additional topical questions may arise during the opening part of the interview. A student interested in low-income investors might ask questions like "What are the problems you run into when you're trying to develop financial plans with low-income individuals? What are the strategies you use to help low-income families budget their income so they can develop a financial plan?" The student is drawing this professional contact into a conversation about their mutual interests and is building cultural capital in the process.

The four closing questions follow a pattern. The first two—"What keeps you up at night?" and "If you were to advise somebody who wanted to get into the same area you are in, what would you want to see in their background?"—often elicit unanticipated responses. Here, students start to see the multidisciplinarity and insider knowledge of their preferred field, and they get crucial information to fill in the blanks in their degree. In researching work in financial planning, for example, a student might begin to see the importance of adding perspectives from sociology, Chicano studies, or public policy.

The last two questions—"How important is hands-on experience?" and "How could I get that experience with you?"—lay the groundwork for an experiential or work opportunity and help a student start to build a mentoring network in a particular field. Students are surprised how often these field experts are willing to work with them or refer them to another opportunity.

Fourth, students need to identify faculty across the curriculum and staff across the campus who have similar interests as those experts they are finding in the hidden job market. This critical step helps students understand that faculty are not generic; rather, they are field-of-study specialists who defy conventional thinking about connections between career and major. Faculty with interests in watersheds and housing in cities like Houston don't necessarily come from environmental science. They might be found in departments of political science, urban planning, finance, or economics. Students can engage these faculty members to help them get a better sense of the breadth of the issues, clarify their own interests and potential roles in the field, and further connect to other experts and experiential-learning opportunities.

Students usually need help figuring out the disciplinary interests and hidden intellectualism of their own professors, and they need to learn how to go digging for it. Sometimes the specific interests and areas of study are found in the profiles of faculty members on departmental websites, particularly on departmental sites devoted to graduate programs. Media-relations offices at some colleges compile lists of faculty expertise for journalism organizations seeking comment on a current hot topic or news event.

Even on campuses where the departmental websites are sparse, outdated, or poorly designed, students are not hamstrung. They can peruse the current semester course offerings, looking for relevant senior-level courses, senior seminars, and graduate seminars, and then sit in on a class or two. Focusing on upper-division courses is key. Students are usually advised to take an introductory course in a discipline to get a sense of it, but introductory courses generally do not give students a sense of the richness of the discipline and the potential connections to students' hidden intellectualism. Psychology 101 would not introduce a student to a field interest in mindfulness and health, but a senior seminar would. Sitting in on an advanced class or two works like a movie trailer, offering the student a sense of the faculty member's personality and interests and how those line up with the student's own interests.

Students come away from these experiences with a new view of their professors: They are not just harried academics who teach bland introductory courses. They are field specialists in environmental studies, psychology, or Arabic studies with deep specific interests that intersect with a student's own, and they are everyday people who have compelling hobbies and personal stories outside their academic role. When students and faculty members connect on these different levels, students will hear faculty talking emphatically about their areas of interest and expertise. These connections are particularly important for first-year and underrepresented students, who can use these experiences to build out their social and cultural capital, college literacy, and mentoring networks.

Why stop with faculty? A college is a complex organization with a range of staff members with their own areas of expertise, which students are rarely introduced to. A reference librarian, for example, might have an obsession with manga and anime that resonates with a student's hidden intellectualism. Specialists in a university's human-resources department might focus on retirement plans, in a way that could offer experience and guidance to a finance student.

Step 3. Identifying learning opportunities on and off campus

The research investigative inquiry is an assignment, so students have a deadline when they'll meet with a staff mentor or peer mentor to report what they have learned. That assignment makes the Field of Study process a pedagogical activity. After any research activity, a researcher has to sort through the information gathered, and Field of Study is no different. Student and mentor lay out the skill set, trends, and other information the student discovered, and they begin to translate those into different types of learning activities on and off campus: courses, service-learning or community based-learning, volunteer experiences, student organizations, and internship opportunities with the contacts they found during the research investigative inquiry. This provides the raw material that students use to fill in the blanks and design their undergraduate education.

Step 4. Designing an educational plan

Working with their mentors, students begin to look at the different ways they can fill in the blanks on their degree audit—and the various ways that learning opportunities across general education, a major, and electives/minors inform each other. Students can strategize how and when to fit in experiential-learning opportunities. This works just like design theory: students can prototype different undergraduate plans to compare various options and decide which options best fit their professional interests, their academic strengths, and their vocational purpose. A student who assembles a prototype can explain why they are choosing a major and how the other pieces of the degree fit together to support their whole educational plan. In this sense, as we pointed out in chapter 1, students create their curriculum and become agile learners because they have learned how to integrate their education. This is the intrinsic strength of a Field of Study.

Shay Works Out Her Wicked Problem

As we noted above, the sequence of steps in the Field of Study process is not always linear. There are always overlapping stages and redoing, as students discover new bits of information in their research that may require them to revise their plan. This is part and parcel of any design process. People probably best learn about the Field of Study method by seeing it in action or experiencing it themselves. Shay's story is an illustration of how it works. Along the way, we point to its various stages, even if they appear out of place in the sequence.

Shay had a clear sense of her hidden intellectualism and vocational purpose: poetry and a desire to help people from backgrounds like hers. She had the courage to commit to those interests, bypassing a "safe bet" like law school. What she didn't have was a sense of how she could find a path in college.

After she arrived at the Center for Engaged Learning and explained her conundrum, she had to be challenged: Who out there in the world is using poetry to lift up communities of color? A few keywords typed into Google brought up the trailer for Louder Than a Bomb, a documentary about the world's largest youth poetry slam (now called the Rooted and Radical Youth Poetry Festival), which draws five hundred young poets from high schools and community groups across the Chicago metropolitan area. Founded in 2001 by Young Chicago Authors, Louder Than a Bomb inspired more than a dozen other slam-poetry competitions in other cities.[11]

Watching the trailer, which features students reciting onstage their struggles with poverty, drugs, or disability, Shay teared up. "I had never seen anything like that before," she tells us today. "The things the youth were talking about were things I'd experienced. Traumas. Violence. The questions I had that I would ask only on the page or share on the page. There was nothing like that happening in South Carolina."

This stage of clarifying a student's hidden intellectualism and vocational purpose isn't simply about setting up a career path or finding an opportunity in the hidden job market or finding contacts for a research investigative inquiry—or about anything else related to the practical, career-oriented portions of Field of Study. Clarifying students' hidden intellectualism and vocational purpose is primarily about legitimating their voices. It demonstrates to students that their interests are often grounded in pragmatic career pathways and that their aspirations may not be just pipe dreams. This is the beginning of building out a student's social and cultural capital.

"I didn't know other people felt about poetry the same way I felt about it," says Shay. "I didn't know there are people actually making careers and a living teaching poetry to youth. And it's not just about the poetry, right? It's about the life lessons and the kind of therapeutic, creative expression that comes along with it."

Her world in the hidden job market legitimated, Shay now had to research the people, parts of campus, and places in the community that could support that vision. Her first call was obvious: she reached out to Young Chicago Authors and talked to a staff member. That call opened up the granularity of a hidden job market she didn't anticipate. She learned that YCA was involved in so much more than the annual Louder Than a Bomb poetry slam. The organization built corporate and community partnerships; developed partnerships with high schools and ran programs in those schools; created workshops and pedagogy for high-school teachers and youth; held open-mic events and youth-outreach programs; managed a robust fundraising operation, and more. But more important, Shay learned that there were numerous other organizations across the country using poetry in youth programming and education.

She also went looking for people on campus who could support her interests in spoken-word poetry. She found Professor Joyce Fields, who was the department chair of the Child and Family Studies program at Columbia College. Shay explained her interests, and Fields talked to her about how her interdisciplinary program—which drew from sociology, psychology and social work—would provide Shay the flexibility she needed. "I could still take some of those political science classes that I was interested in" to understand the political systems that affect low-income families, she says. "And I was able to incorporate the communication studies classes, thinking about interpersonal communication and intercultural communication," so relevant to the spoken-word interest and the youth she wanted to serve.

Shay was learning how she could fill in the blanks and integrate the different parts of her undergraduate experience.

She couldn't fully explore poetry on campus, however, with only an occasional course offered by the English department. So, with another Google search—"spoken word in Columbia, SC"—she found a spoken-word night at Art Bar, a local watering hole that supported various artistic performances. There, she would hone her spoken-word skills onstage and also learn about other venues and spoken-word artists in Columbia. She was beginning to understand the importance of off-campus opportunities, as well as the networking that comes with it.

Shay was hired in the Center for Engaged Learning. The center hired students, those who had gone through the Field of Study process, as peer success coaches; they could then share their experiences with other students. Peer success coaches were required to take a MAPP career assessment, among the many tests designed to narrow down a student's innate talents and point to potential career interests, so they could learn how to interpret the results when working with other students.[12] When Shay took the MAPP (Motivational Appraisal of Personal Potential), she was disappointed: It said she was good at organizing and motivating people in working toward goals and suggested that she become a business manager, which, she believed, had nothing to do with the vocational purpose and hidden intellectualism she had just uncovered in her academic journey. She buried her head in her hands, staring at the test results, feeling like she was being pushed back into a career-oriented box she didn't want. Or so she thought.

Within a week, Shay had joined a service-learning project to develop programs in the arts at Alcorn Middle School, where the poverty rate was so high that students could get three meals a day during the week. There, Shay would work on a spoken-word festival, which led to another epiphany: What does it take to run a poetry slam? Organization, motivational skills, pulling pieces together, and getting people to buy into a shared goal. "All of the sudden, it's like the lightbulb went off—there is no box," says Shay. "I needed these skills so I can get up on stage and throw the mic down."

In a sense, *everything is business*. At that moment, Shay learned that skill sets are transferable when they are refracted through a vocational purpose to reach a life goal. But in order to recognize those skill sets, and to realize how they connect to one's life goals, students often have to experience applying them in a real-world setting, not just in abstract assignments in the classroom or in a conversation with a career-development advisor.

Shay's "business product" was a hit. At the end of the fall semester, the middle-school kids put on a spoken-word play about their lives, their fears, their hopes. Students who wouldn't talk in front of a crowd during rehearsals, or even in front of peers in class, now strutted onstage and performed what they wrote with newfound confidence. Parents, teachers, school administrators, and other audience members were stunned, with many brought to tears by the performance. The Columbia Art Museum, a partner in the service-learning project, invited the students to perform at an opening event in the spring for an exhibition on contemporary Black artists.

At this point, Shay had proved something to herself: you don't just follow a passion; you have to craft a path that opens up the possibility of finding that passion. Shay's transcript would say that she majored in child and family studies, but this in no way summed up the Field of Study she was putting together or what the entirety of her undergraduate experience meant to her. She could, though, explain every piece. Each step that Shay took was part of a process, guided by her vocational purpose and driven by the information she gathered in her research investigative inquiry; she filled in the blanks so that any one piece of her undergraduate education informed the others. She created an integrated undergraduate experience.

College Is a Kaleidoscope

Too many students approach college as a kind of track: pick a lane (a useful major), follow a so-called degree map, check off the boxes, and you're on the way to a professional life. This is passive—a belief that college gives you something. But colleges, regardless of what they say about the services they provide students, are mainly neutral players in a student's life.

College is actually a kaleidoscope. It offers an array of disconnected pieces in the form of departments and courses, student clubs and extracurricular programs, community based-learning, study abroad, faculty and staff, and most of all, blank spaces to be filled in. Turn that kaleidoscope, and the pieces shift to form one pattern—a major in English combined with finance and history can open up the world of antiquarian book auctions. Turn it again, and a different pattern forms—a course of study in computer graphics, video storyboarding, and Asian literature and philosophy could open up the world of anime.

In a Field of Study process, the *students* turn that kaleidoscope, seeing the pieces of their education falling into patterns, refracted through their hidden intellectualism and vocational purpose. William G. Perry Jr., an educational psychologist at Harvard whose studies of undergraduates helped found student-development theory, pointed to the design elements of the learning process. He said that as students begin to accommodate new ideas in building a worldview—as they become mature learners—they engage in a synthetic and aesthetic process of blending their perspectives with the new experiences, information, and viewpoints they encounter in college.[13] Students engage in a synthetic and aesthetic process when they integrate a college's learning opportunities with their deep interests and vocational goals. And this takes place across an entire undergraduate experience, not just in a single capstone course near the end.

Learning is always an interpretive experience: we interpret new facts, day-to-day experiences, the television shows we watch, the food we eat, and so on, through the lenses of our personal experiences and backgrounds, which make up our cultural capital. Learning is also governed by positive emotions, where joy, creativity, and curiosity not only fuel engagement with a topic but also help brains encode and store information. When students engage in designing an undergraduate education, they become emotionally invested in it. In this sense, it's the student who builds the curriculum, not the college. The student defines the learning experiences and creates the meaning behind the array of major courses and electives.

Shay, in seeing clearly where she wanted to go, understood how learning in disciplines as varied as political science, communications, and child and family studies fit together as she interpreted her learning through her desire to use poetry to help young people. In her own way, she became a T-shaped professional.

Ms. Butler Goes to Washington

After the poetry show at Alcorn Middle School, Shay continued plugging away at her degree, while she helped other students make sense of their own undergraduate degrees as a peer mentor at the college. Through her child-and-family-studies program, she was engaging in various internships with different agencies, giving her multiple perspectives on the dynamics of working with high-risk youth and their families.

Upon entering her senior year, she needed a kind of capstone experience to unite much of what she had learned at Columbia College, an institution that didn't offer capstone courses at the time. Once again, she went hunting on campus for opportunities, found that the college offered an underutilized semester experience in Washington, DC, applied for a slot, and was accepted. The program's curriculum was cursory, consisting of a weekly meeting with an alumnus of the college, and students were given an assignment to explore some aspect of Washington and to share their experiences with the group. Students had to get an internship for the semester, but they were on their own to figure out how to land one.

Shay came to the Center for Engaged Learning in a panic. She'd looked into some of the organizations where past students had interned, listed on the college's website for the program in Washington, but those occupations and organizations were of no interest to her. At that moment, Shay had to be reminded of the Field of Study process: research, reach out to people in your field network, and create opportunities. She once again called Young Chicago Authors, which connected Shay to a sister organization in Washington called Split This Rock, a nonprofit that uses poetry for community building and social justice.[14]

Split This Rock had no internship opportunities listed on its site. Shay had missed the deadline to apply. But a key part of Field of Study is using connections with like-minded people and harnessing mutual passions, expertise, and life experiences to create opportunities out in the world. Shay wrote an email to the managing director of Split This Rock, told her about the poetry-play at Alcorn Middle School, and proposed doing an internship exploring similar work in Washington. The director scheduled an interview with Shay and offered her an unpaid internship for the semester. Unpaid internships are often difficult for low-income students, but Shay's transportation, boarding costs, and living stipend in DC were already covered through her tuition and fees at Columbia College, so Shay saw the offer as an opportunity to open more doors in her field.

"I literally just Googled and called an office," Shay says. "It was so bizarre at the time, and when I tell people about all the other times I've practiced this approach in gathering information or seeking new opportunities, they're shocked. When I was accepted for the opportunity, I was so geeked. I just made this thing happen, and I was about to do something I literally pieced together." Shay spent thirty to forty hours a week at Split This Rock, putting on youth workshops at Martin Luther King Jr. Library, designing and creating fliers for poetry events, canvassing schools to implement the Louder Than a Bomb model, and going to Howard University for poetry readings.

Suddenly, Shay—a kid from tiny Cross, South Carolina—found herself hanging out at the house of Andy Shallal, the founder of bookstore-cum-restaurant Busboys and Poets, in the middle of the Washington scene of spoken-word artists and African American celebrities. "I am meeting Dr. Cornel West, Angela Davis, Hill Harper, DJ Questlove, Elizabeth Acevedo, Danez Smith," she says. Sometimes she would hang out at a party or ride in a taxi with a celebrity she didn't recognize, later see their picture on the internet and realize she'd had a brush with fame. That year, the DC Youth Slam team, the reigning champions of slam poetry, had just won another national competition, and Shay was working with them. "We got real in the weeds and nerdy with the poetry stuff," she says. "They'd get an invitation 'to go spit' at the White House, in front of Barack and Michelle."

Shay's knack for business skills came into focus that semester. Working with young poets, she gave them advice on their verse, their delivery, their tone. "It's an entrepreneurial space, right?" Shay explains. "Not only do you have this outlet for high schoolers to express themselves through social justice, spoken-word poetry, but you're teaching them graphic design, how to edit, and how to market their chapbooks. We're printing them out, assembling them, and selling them. It's just dope."

After graduating from Columbia College, Shay counseled youth in the social-services system and joined AmeriCorps, where she worked on programs in under-resourced schools in Charleston. But she had her eyes set on moving to the Windy City to work with Young Chicago Authors. She applied and was accepted to two graduate programs, at Loyola University Chicago and the University of Illinois at Chicago; ultimately she chose UIC for its master's program in youth development. While in graduate school, she counseled abused and neglected children at Chicago's Mercy Home for Boys and Girls and also worked with boys in the Chicago juvenile justice system, incorporating "hip-hop critical pedagogy" into her work. And of course, she continued to volunteer at Young Chicago Authors.

Shay has come back, again and again, to the research and design methods she learned in her Field of Study process as an undergraduate, particularly the networking and information-gathering components. For Shay, the most nerve-racking aspect was always the research investigative inquiry, which involves picking up the phone and asking a stranger for some thoughts and advice. But she remembered that, in high school, she got practice reaching out to neighbors and strangers to sell donuts or to raise donations for purchasing gym shoes for basketball or a band uniform. If she asked for advice, she reasoned, the worst people could say is no. But most didn't.

"People are willing to help," she says. "That's something that surprised me, just coming from where I came from and just not wanting to feel like a burden." When Shay was deliberating over graduate programs, she reached out to professors at both Loyola and UIC by email to ask questions about the curriculum, the current research of the faculty, and how her interests might blend with theirs. Faculty at Loyola blew her off, but at UIC, she made a connection with several professors, including David Stovall, a professor of educational policy and African American studies who had researched spoken word, youth development, social work, and education. This interdisciplinary approach persuaded Shay to pick UIC for graduate school. She exchanged more emails with Stovall from South Carolina, and later, before starting graduate school, she ran into him at a coffee shop in Chicago's West Loop. He sat down with her for a casual conversation, picked up on her deep interest in poetry and youth, and asked her to join him at various events on the South Side. "Moments like that surprise me—like, wow, I didn't even know this man before I came to Chicago," Shay says, "and he's inviting me to events to fully invest and immerse myself in these experiences."

Field of Study helps students build out their social and cultural capital by pushing them to develop the confidence to identify and contact experts in a field, which puts them in situations where they practice the skills of networking. From their discoveries, students learn to become self-directed and self-empowered.

In this sense, the Field of Study process can be transformative. Where other methods try to speak to students about promising job slots and careers, the Field of Study method asks students to define the promise and potential within themselves. Shay came out of a deeply impoverished community and had the courage to pass up "sure bet" pathways, like law or business, to pursue her hidden intellectualism and vocational purpose in an unlikely field, poetry and youth development. Fueled by her interests in verse and Black culture, she found an avenue to a comfortable life, living out her own vision of what success looks like.

"I created my own pathway—and that's something I talk about in my interactions with every youth," says Shay. In other words, the Field of Study process is transferable: students learn the method and use it throughout life, and they can teach it to others. Field of Study, in the context of curriculum, transforms the mentorship role to something more akin to a thesis advisor—with the thesis research being how a student can integrate their undergraduate experiences with their deep interests and vocational goals, how the student can solve their wicked problem.

Today, Shay is an assistant director in student enrichment at Northwestern University, where she works with first-generation, low-income, and undocumented students. Here, and in past roles, she talks to students about how she found her way, and she uses the Field of Study process to help students find their own.

"I'm working with a lot of youth that came from spaces that I came from, dealing with significant trauma. How do we begin to unpack that stuff—but also get to *you*, right? What is it that *you* want to do despite what has been ascribed to you?"

4

The Hidden Job Market

AMANDA BELEU ALWAYS WANTED to work in a museum, where a kid like her could gaze at objects that opened up a range of experiences and possibilities in the world—tickets of imagination that allowed her to escape her rural South Carolina community. "I saw museums as a vehicle for education and enlightenment," she tells us today, "and I wanted to be a part of it." For her senior project in high school, she curated the items and artifacts in a small law-enforcement museum in Greenville, her first taste of that world of work.

But among her friends and family, nobody thought that working for a museum was a real job—especially her father, a second-generation policeman who pushed Amanda to become a traveling nurse or to get into some other high-paying career. "Everybody thought I was throwing my smarts away. That was something a friend of mine told me once," she recalls. "So when I was looking at colleges, I was not looking to stay in South Carolina because I was fed up with nobody listening to me." Only Amanda's mother, who lived below the poverty line, supported her dream to work in a museum.

One midsummer day after high-school graduation, Amanda's best friend and her mother dragged her to a recruiting event for high-achieving students at Columbia College. She attended a talk by Ned and by Fiona Lofton, then the college's director for career development, as they described the Field of Study approach: it wasn't the major that mattered, but how students composed the pieces of their undergraduate education. During the session, the students introduced themselves and talked about their interests and goals; then Ned and Fiona pointed out some of the learning opportunities in the curriculum and community through which students could build out their aspirations.

During her turn, Amanda said she wanted to work in museums and asked if she would have to wait until her junior year to apply for an internship, as she'd heard that was the case at many colleges. "No, it depends on the experiences you have," Ned and Fiona told her. "Give us a semester to figure it out with you." Encouraged that someone was finally listening to her, Amanda filled out an application for Columbia College that afternoon.

Little over a month later, Amanda walked into the Center for Engaged Learning, looking to test what she had heard at the recruiting event. Her first-semester courses were fairly standard: a smattering of general-education courses, including composition, history, and a first-year seminar. She shared that she had already worked in the police museum in high school. Ned and Fiona pushed Amanda to call the South Carolina State Museum to set up a research investigative inquiry. They quickly coached her on how to make an appointment, picked up the receiver, dialed the number, and passed the phone to Amanda on the spot. Although she was terrified, Amanda took the phone and seized the moment. She reached the director of visitor services, who also happened to be the intern coordinator, and set up a time to talk.

In the interview, Amanda demonstrated her love for and knowledge of museums and showed she could speak the professional lingo. The visitor-services director "was surprised that I had terms for things," Amanda says. The director asked Amanda where she would want to work in museums, hinting at a hidden job world that most patrons never see. Amanda indicated that she leaned toward the curation of collections, but she wouldn't be picky. "I'm just interested in getting my hands dirty—whatever you need me to do, I'll do it," Amanda said.

The State Museum did not have a collections internship at the time, but Amanda had nevertheless talked her way into an unpaid position there. The visitor-services director placed her in the role of "caboose" on group tours of the museum, to handle technical difficulties or other problems on the tours. In observing how audiences reacted to the exhibits, Amanda started to see an unanticipated role for herself in attracting museum visitors and telling the stories behind items on display.

"One of my favorite things," says Amanda, "is when visitors get sucked in—like, there's always that one kid who presses a nose against the glass, really interested. And you just ask them why, and then they just open up. It's an amazing experience. I wasn't stuck in the back, working with the staff." This allowed her to "lean into that storytelling and audience-building aspect" of the world of museums.

Amanda drew two lessons from her experience at the State Museum: First, it validated for her that the museum world is a real job market, and although no one was getting wealthy working for the museum, many of the people she met led comfortable and fulfilled lives. Second, it introduced her to new and different ideas of what was possible for her in museum work, showing her the variety of roles available.

She had taken her first steps into her hidden job market.

What Is the Hidden Job Market?

Media outlets in the world of business and finance sometimes discuss the "hidden job market." The term usually refers to positions and careers that are not advertised on major job boards like Indeed or Handshake but rather are landed through personal relationships and employee referrals. Such jobs, articles frequently say, could compose 80 percent of the actual job openings out there.[1]

In this book, we want to expand the definition of the hidden job market to provide a broader perspective on the relationship between college learning and the world of work. For many students, and even advisors and career-development counselors who work with them, hidden jobs are not just those positions that aren't advertised. By our definition, hidden jobs constitute the occupations found "behind the curtain" in the world of work—that is, the wide range of critical positions that make any organization function but that people rarely think of. Hidden jobs can also be those positions found in organizations that are too small or outside the mainstream to capture the attention of students, who conceive of jobs through brand-name companies they recognize (Amazon, Deloitte, Goldman Sachs) or occupation areas that get a lot of attention (like law, business, allied health care, and tech). These limited perspectives are reinforced by advising and career services, both of which tend not to look beyond industry and corporate types.

Let's take a brief look at the hidden employment possibilities in the world of museums, for example. When most people think of working in a museum, they think only of curators and collections specialists. But museums run on a complex array of professional skills, much of which the public never sees when a new exhibit opens.

The Walters Art Museum, a mid-sized institution of 36,000 items in Baltimore, employs a head museum director, along with a director of curation and collections, with support staff who have specialties in specific areas, like Islamic art, material culture, and rare books. It also employs a director of conservation, who oversees specialists in the preservation of various media (wooden or metal objects, paintings, books, and paper documents). The museum has a large roster of security officers who stand guard around the items and numerous (often volunteer) docents who guide visitors through the galleries. All of those positions are part of what we might consider the *visible workforce* at the Walters, which a layperson would expect to see in any museum.[2]

But the hidden workforce at the Walters is bigger. Deep inside the organization, a head of exhibition design and installation planning, along with a staff of designers, lay out the exhibits. To produce those gallery designs, the Walters employs a head of installation and production, a lead art handler, a lighting technician, even a cabinetmaker, among other staff.

But go deeper. An average student interested in museums might not know that the Walters also employs directors and managers of visitor experience and "audience insights," who look for ways to improve how patrons interact with galleries, exhibits, and retail attractions. A retail-operations manager, assistant manager, and floor supervisor—along with positions in shipping, sales, and food service—handle the museum's cafe, gift shop, and products. To connect with the community and draw people in, the Walters's staff includes a number of people who run various parts of educational and outreach programs, for adults, teachers, college students, teens, and schoolchildren. The museum has a team of people who produce content, among them writers, copyeditors, photographers, videographers, and video editors. The museum's head of graphic design and its specialists in marketing use much of that content in their duties. In fundraising, one director handles individual and major gifts, while another director handles institutional gifts and government grants, and both oversee managers of special events and donor relations, along with support positions in that office. On-staff specialists advise the museum on intellectual property issues and other legal matters. The Walters's building complex, which includes structures from the 1800s through the 1970s, is managed by a team of engineers and technicians who oversee operations, maintenance, safety and security, and information technology. Of course, crucial to any complex organization, the Walters employs a chief financial officer, a comptroller, a human-resources director, and support staff.

Those are just the jobs *within the walls* of the Walters Art Museum. Institutions like this interact with many small- to medium-sized firms specializing in the museum sector, offering services related to architecture and interior design, audio and visual services, donor relations, foreign-language translation, accessibility services, marketing, preservation, publishing, art transport and security, custom fabrication (for exhibitions and displays), and technology, whether that's an app to guide visitors through a gallery space or an entire virtual-reality room to recreate a historical setting or experience.

The world of museums is huge, if you could see all of it. A student like Amanda who wants to enter the world of museums can do so from a range of angles, skill sets, and agendas. And what's true of museums is true of nearly any business or organization out there. Almost every organization, regardless of size, has a hidden world of work within it.

Even the world of work closest to students—the average college or university—is itself a complex organization with a range of "hidden jobs" embedded within. Most students look at a college or university and see the president, their professors and instructors, and the people attending to them in student-affairs roles. Students (and often their advisors and mentors) don't see their institution's offices and activities in governmental affairs, fundraising and development, master planning, facilities, procurement, marketing and communications, human resources, regulatory compliance, risk management, or the backstage logistics of running an athletic program. A student interested in supply chains could glean knowledge from a university's procurement officer or facilities director, for example, while a student pursuing data analytics could find valuable work opportunities with the office of institutional research. On most campuses, though, these spaces and areas of expertise remain undiscovered resources for students.

Seeing the hidden job market is important for students, because in seeing the granularity of the world of work, they see the possibilities it contains. By examining the hidden job market, students open up greenfields of experiential opportunity. They find people who share their interests and skills, often at companies and organizations ignored or unnoticed by college career counselors and advisors, companies that don't have a stream of undergraduates knocking on their door, begging for internships and other experiential opportunities.

When students talk with people who work in different organizational settings, they begin to see that skill sets take on different hues, depending on the culture and mission of the organization. Even in a relatively straightforward discipline like accounting, the nature of the work changes depending on the focus. An accountant working for one of the Big Four firms in public accounting has a different orientation compared with an accountant working for an arts organization or for a state university. Business leaders need finance experts who can help them think around corners, and much of that thinking depends on the training and experience that accountants get outside the basic curriculum of accounting—in the blank spaces. Valuating the assets of an art museum requires a different professional orientation and set of skills than does performing an analysis of the assets of a big corporation or a public university.

In seeing the hidden job market, often through a research investigative inquiry, students begin to understand why they need to connect their hidden intellectualism and vocational purpose with learning opportunities in the blank spaces across the curriculum. They start to see how they can marry a love of art to the practice of accounting—and open a pathway to arts administration, or arts investment and appraisal, or another personally and professionally meaningful niche in the hidden world of work. Their discoveries help define their sense of "why," the angle on a profession that helps students understand the skills they will need and the particular route they want to take to enter the field. The importance of clarifying this "why" cannot be understated.

What Is the *Why*?

Hidden intellectualism, as we have mentioned, is a personal inner drive, fueled by a love of something or by a curiosity or a civic concern. It's anything a student is intellectually or emotionally committed to, which may not be represented in the title of an academic program. *Anything is valid.* The flip side of hidden intellectualism is vocational purpose—the understanding that this hidden intellectualism exists somehow as paid work out there, somewhere in the hidden job market. Amanda, for example, had a keen interest in museums, fueled by the way they had opened up her world when she was a child; this was her hidden intellectualism. She had the courage to defy her family and friends to pursue museum work, which became her vocational purpose.

As she took her first steps into the museum world, she discovered a range of professional possibilities within it. What struck her was the storytelling aspect, the space in the world of museums where she felt engaged and comfortable, where she felt her strongest sense of vocational purpose. This is the beginning of discovering her "why."

Why and passion, like hidden intellectualism and vocational purpose, are also two sides of a coin. The why emerges when students step into an experiential opportunity and begin to understand how their personal dispositions and talents help them define their corner in the hidden job market. This is as true for a recent graduate stepping into the world of work as it is for someone who wants to pursue graduate research in a university setting. The why simply clarifies what students are drawn to.

Passion is the emotive expression of the why. It enables drive, grit, engagement, creativity, and innovation—many of the elements that lead to educational success, career success, and happiness. As students might put it, they get jazzed or pumped about what they are doing, and that passion gives them momentum through college and into a career.

Coming off her experience at the State Museum, Amanda realized she would have to strengthen her background to get into graduate school, a necessary step to landing a comfortable position in the museum world. During the spring semester of her junior year, while working as a peer mentor in the Center for Engaged Learning, Amanda found out about Columbia College's semester program in Washington, DC, where she thought she might be able to find an internship at one of the biggest museums in the world, the Smithsonian Institution. She started another research inquiry process and found the Folklife Center.

"Folklife is a really interesting sector," Amanda says. It's not just objects and recordings of music. "We're talking about people's life stories. We're talking about somebody's experience. And I was really interested in how museums collected experiences." In her research, Amanda learned that there were no lower- to mid-level managers she could talk to for her research interview; she would have to figure out how to land an interview with the Folklife Center's director.

At the time, Amanda was smart and headstrong, but also shy and insecure, and she was terrified of phone conversations. The Smithsonian has a regimented process for hiring interns, and Amanda didn't think the institution would give her a second look, particularly if she just dropped her resume on a pile with dozens, possibly hundreds, of others. Once again, she had to be forced to sit down in an office in the Center for Engaged Learning to make the call.

To her surprise, the director himself picked up the phone. "He asked me the infamous 'why' question," she remembers: "Why do you want to work here?" Drawing on her hidden intellectualism and passion, Amanda nervously but articulately rambled for about ten minutes. "I was talking about how living archives are incredible—an interesting intersection between objects, people, and community," she says. Amanda could feel that her passion for museum work resonated with the Folklife Center's director.

Perhaps to test her, the director told Amanda that most people who applied for internships wanted to work on the Smithsonian Folklife Festival—among the most visible of the center's activities. But Amanda said she wanted to work with him in the archives.

"Okay, but the work I have for you is boring," the director said. "We have this large letter collection. We have all of this ephemera, these notes. And it all needs to be cataloged, with metadata."

"I just want to be there," Amanda replied. The director told her to submit an application through the system, and he would flag it and push it through. It was a moment when Amanda realized that she was creating a network where her passions met the passions of others in the work world.

In the fall semester, Amanda started working in the Ralph Rinzler Folklife Archives and Collections, and the work was anything but boring. Rinzler had been a folk musician in New York in the 1950s—

Bob Dylan opened for his band—and he later went on to work as a folklorist and curator for the Smithsonian. "This guy went out into the world and just recorded everything—Amazonian rain sounds, blues musicians off the street, Pete Seeger, everybody."[3]

One afternoon, while Amanda was processing a collection of papers, an archivist handed her a box and asked her to look through it. Most of the material was documents on onionskin paper and receipts. From the pile, Amanda pulled out a letter from Woody Guthrie to Moses Asch, the record executive who published Guthrie's songs.

"I'm holding this piece of paper in my hands, and I just had this moment where I thought, holy shit. I had worked so hard after nobody had listened to me for years, because I wanted to work in museums since I was a kid. And here I was, sitting in a chair, actually doing it."

The letter was trivial—Guthrie and Asch were arguing over money, not discussing politics or music—but for Amanda it was a revelatory moment. "This object holds so much power, and they're letting me hold it. I mean, I'm nobody from the middle of nowhere South Carolina," she says. "It was just so affirming, that things like this—things that feel impossible to students—can actually be reality."

Passion versus Income

When they arrive at college, students have spent their school life in a lockstep K-12 curriculum, derived by somebody in a distant district office, increasingly designed around state and federal assessments. Going to college dangles the promise of finally being able to explore their interests and curiosity, with the hope of opening up a professional world that provides both enjoyment and a decent living.

At the core of this journey is the "why" (and the passion that comes with it), which doesn't strike like a bolt of lightning. The why emerges when students clarify their hidden intellectualism and vocational purpose and find where they fit in the hidden job market. This process of clarification isn't just reserved for students with idiosyncratic interests or design-your-own academic programs. It is just as appropriate for students in majors with a short "crosswalk" to a job, like nursing, data analytics, or finance.

Take, for example, the college-to-career trajectory of Adara, an immigrant and first-generation student, who majored in electrical and computer engineering at the University of Illinois at Chicago, with a fascination for signal systems in telecommunication. When she started looking for internships, her career counselors at the university offered to line her up with one of the many internships available with cellular-phone companies, but those opportunities didn't excite her.

When Adara started to ponder the vast possibilities in telecommunication, a mentor using the Field of Study approach asked her a question that disrupted her view of the industry and the possibilities within it: How would someone make a cell-phone call from Mars? Adara, fascinated with that question, started a research investigative inquiry by looking into the backgrounds of faculty on campus and organizations in the Chicago area, and she discovered the Far Horizons Lab, a joint project between NASA and the Adler Planetarium. Adara set up a research interview with a graduate student in the lab from the Illinois Institute of Technology, who was working on wireless communications for high-altitude missions. This started her journey as an intern with the Illinois Space Consortium, where she worked until graduation.

Much like Amanda, Adara used a research investigative inquiry to expand her world of opportunity to resources beyond her university and discovered an unexpected niche, where she found a "why" and a passion. That experience led to others (such as an internship working on advanced signal processing with a cellular firm and NASA's L'SPACE Mission Concept Academy), and it helped her fill in the blank spaces of her technical electives, for which she took courses to strengthen her background in circuit analysis and design and in communication engineering. Today, she is working for a major aerospace corporation, focused on mission systems.

The act of picking a major doesn't clarify a career direction, nor does it offer any guarantee in terms of income. Of course, anyone who has spent time on the job market after college would understand this intuitively, knowing how opportunities emerge organically and lead to unanticipated roles and unexpected financial reward. Many unspoken factors can affect a student's success after graduation, and much can rest on how that student assembles an undergraduate education from a sense of why. Too many students, especially historically underserved and first-generation students, miss the conversations that would help them clarify their hidden intellectualism and sense of why, discover their hidden job market, and then design a route through college to get to their goal.

Instead, much of the conversation on campuses—and in advice columns, books, and policy circles—pushes students to concentrate on return on investment, as measured by the median incomes associated with various majors. This focus on ROI is rapidly becoming the new version of the *U.S. News and World Report* rankings: a metric that approximates certain factors that could lead to monetary success but perhaps more often misleads students into wrong choices and a false sense of security. In the process, *why* and passion get set aside.

In *Making College Pay*, Beth Akers, an economist for the American Enterprise Institute, urges students to consider the average salary outcomes of various majors. She describes the college experience in investment terms—choosing a major is like selecting a mutual fund. "The best way to pick a major, like the best way to pick a school, is to first understand your goals for enrollment as well as your tolerance for risk," she writes. "Your tolerance for risk has less to do with personal preferences and more to do with your specific financial situation." In other words, if you lack a financial safety net, beware the risk of a major with a low median salary.[4]

As a lesson for her readers—students and their parents—Akers recounts her own story of going on "the quintessential privileged-kid college search" and picking a major. She "wasn't much of a student in high school," but "one thing I did know was that I was an artsy kid." Stopping at Syracuse University on her tour of colleges, Akers told an admissions officer of her interest in majoring in art. The admissions officer informed Akers that fine-arts majors end up designing consumer products, like toasters or wrapping paper, which didn't interest Akers. Then the admissions officer issued a warning: "Do you love creating art so much that you'd be willing to be poor for the rest of your life in order to pursue it as a career?"[5]

Akers took to heart this sobering advice, so when she later matriculated at Ithaca College, she gave up on art, haphazardly enrolled in a range of general-education courses and electives, and landed in an economics course, which fascinated her. She set a goal of becoming a tenured economics professor, choosing a math major and her electives "on the sole criterion of how well they would prepare me for graduate school in economics." Her approach was mechanical: the right undergraduate major should lead to the right graduate school, which should lead to a tenured professorship in economics.[6]

"The idea of 'following my passion' was a nice one. And it was the only one I really recall being given as a framework for thinking about what to study in college," Akers writes, reflecting on her choice between fine arts and the "more secure" quantitative major she ended up pursuing. "But at the same time, it didn't sit well with the pink-clipboard part of me that knew this decision needed more practical consideration than my passion could provide."[7]

Let's pause her story there for a moment. That Akers was allowed to follow a passion is more than "nice." It's a tremendous privilege. Many students from lesser means are pressured by parents to pursue supposedly lucrative and prestigious careers in medicine, law, or engineering, regardless of whether it ignites a passion.

It's not clear that Akers had any commitment to or talent for the arts, so maybe it's no loss that she didn't pursue it. But the advice she got from the Syracuse admissions officer was misguided. The fact is, fine-arts students don't just wind up designing wrapping paper or starving to death. They find work and comfortable livelihoods in a range of professional settings in the hidden job market, especially if they deliberately connect their training in the arts to the training one can find in the blank spaces. If Akers had encountered the conversations that would have helped her unpack the arts and economics, she could have found ways to unite the two disciplines in a manner that satisfied her practical consideration for money and her desire to pursue her passion. In fact, if Akers had more consciously built her undergraduate experience, she probably would have had a better chance of becoming a fine-arts major making a comfortable living than of becoming a tenured professor of economics, given the intense competition for tenure-track positions in academe and the narrow goal Akers set for herself.

Despite going to Columbia University for graduate school, Akers never became a tenured professor, perhaps because the passion, the why, got lost somewhere along the way. In her book's preface, Akers makes a stunning admission: she was two years into her doctoral program before realizing that she didn't know why the study of economics mattered to society or culture.[8]

But Akers got lucky. "In some bizarre and strange twist of fate, the opportunity of a lifetime fell into my lap," she writes, when she landed a yearlong appointment in the White House, working on the President's Council of Economic Advisors to study student loans amid the financial crisis in 2007. "My understanding about public policy and real-world economics jumped from nil to 'firsthand experience' in an absurdly short period of time. And I suddenly had the motivation, and knowledge, to be able to return to my PhD program and complete a dissertation on student debt." In other words, she finally discovered her why and her passion.[9]

Her saving grace wasn't some bizarre "twist of fate," however. It was the happenstance that comes with the privilege of attending an elite institution and having the social and cultural capital that comes with it. Akers clarified her journey in a series of emails with us: One member of the economics faculty at Columbia University who had worked on the White House council in the past—a professor with whom she had never had a class or a conversation—forwarded a recruiting email from the council to the program's doctoral students. Akers applied and landed a spot on the council after one of her peers turned down the position. Akers told us she felt isolated at Columbia and might not have finished graduate school without the White House job. The scholars on the council—particularly Eddie Lazear, a Stanford economist—became her mentors and offered to help, "since no one at Columbia seemed to be paying much attention to me anyway." Lazear pushed Akers to finish graduate school and encouraged one of his friends to serve as her formal advisor at Columbia.[10]

In her book, Akers attempts to outline a method for choosing a major, finding a college, and laying out a path to a good ROI after graduation. But if Akers hadn't stumbled onto the Council of Economic Advisors—if her friend had decided to take that White House job, after all—she might have been just another all-but-dissertation doctoral student, trying to make sense of her college journey and looking for a next-best career slot, since it would never be a professor of economics or a think-tank policy wonk. It was social privilege that opened doors for Akers and provided access to a network of people who helped her see the possibilities in the world of economics, find the topic of her dissertation, and discover a pathway into the hidden job world of economics and think tanks.

Why the Research Investigative Inquiry Is Critical

Akers's pathway through college just doesn't work for low-income or even middle-class students. It hardly works for students at elite universities and colleges but for the advantages and networks that elite institutions bestow upon their undergraduates.

Networking is the currency of the job market. Social-media platforms and professional conferences are built on the networking economy, which has prompted a para-industry of books, blogs, private career consulting, and more—all devoted to helping people understand how to develop and use professional networks to open a door to the next job. For colleges, networking is one of the selling points for enrollment. Elite institutions, in particular, recruit students on the promise of the access they provide to social and professional networks: their alumni and corporate partners. However, as Anthony Jack discusses in *The Privileged Poor: How Elite Colleges Are Failing Disadvantaged Students*, networking on an elite campus sometimes doesn't work for low-income students who lack the financial resources and social and cultural capital to participate in those casual encounters, on and off campus, where connections are formed.[11]

In general, colleges don't teach students how to network. Colleges and nonprofit organizations working with low-income students might establish partnerships with alumni or local employers to speak to students during campus visits or to become career mentors. But those institutions and organizations, not the students, are the ones picking the mentors and lining up the connections, which are typically limited to major industries, large corporations, and jobs linked with the most popular majors and common career pathways.

These opportunities do not necessarily offer students the expertise they need. For example, job fairs attract recruiters, who are gatekeepers for human resources, not subject-matter experts in a particular industry or company. Alumni mentors are limited in number and may not connect to every student's hidden intellectualism or vocational purpose, particularly among those students in humanities and social science. And institutions that most often serve first-generation and low-income students just do not have the drawing power, financial resources, and hyperconnected alumni to support mentorships at scale.

Building the right professional network is a key piece of acquiring social and cultural capital. One of the biggest knowledge gaps between rich and poor is the ability to build such a network. The research investigative inquiry helps students bridge that gap by teaching them how to strategically reach out to strangers to gather essential information and to open up opportunities in the granular spaces of the hidden job market.

For the most part, advising and career centers do not talk about the granularity of the hidden job market, even though it offers so many possibilities for a range of academic interests. For instance, what student (or college advisor or career counselor) would readily see the relationship between linguistics and marketing? But it's out there. For example, NameLab is a consulting firm that invented corporate names like Acura, Compaq, and simplehuman. Normally, we'd consider this a part of the marketing world, and it is, of course. But it's a specialized corner of that world, focusing on "constructional linguistics," or how small units of words can be combined into new words to promote a product.[12] NameLab would likely never pop up in a career center, and neither would the Walters Art Museum or the American Enterprise Institute. For students, the research investigative inquiry serves as a "blue ocean" strategy, opening up unnoticed spaces in the job market where there are fewer peers exploring the same spots and competing for experiential opportunities.

In this process, students begin to experience the importance of *tailored networking* to create a career path. Students aren't simply given mentors picked out by a campus program or a nonprofit organization. The students themselves identify their potential mentors and make those connections. By learning how to navigate and network within a hidden job market, low-income students build out the social capital they need to begin to close that networking knowledge gap. With each successful conversation along the way, they hone pitches for themselves, develop their professional demeanor, and build confidence that makes the next interview and the next cold call easier.

After graduation, students will reuse these networking skills again and again—for the next job, for a career change, or to recover after hitting a professional pothole.

Amanda Stumbles—and Recovers

Many of Amanda's colleagues at the Smithsonian had gone to George Washington University's graduate program in museum studies, a top-ranked program in its area. Knowing she needed a master's degree to advance in the museum field, Amanda applied to GW and was accepted, but the offer was uninspiring. Amanda had a conversation with the program director, who was nice enough. "I don't want to say she didn't care, but really, she didn't care," Amanda says. "I was just another applicant." The university offered Amanda no financial assistance.

Amanda had applied to a number of other museum-studies programs, and her personal statement—about the role of museums in communities, drawn from the experiences she had gathered as an undergraduate—caught the eye of the program director for museum-exhibition design at the University of the Arts in Philadelphia. That program director forwarded Amanda's application to a professor in charge of a concentration in museum communications, and he called her. Amanda sat in her car in her mother's driveway—the only place she could get cell reception in her rural area—and talked with him about the stories that museum objects convey and the impact those stories can have on communities. "Do you think other people need to hear that?" the professor prodded. "You need to come to this program." He offered her a partial scholarship, which was important, but more important to Amanda was the developing relationship with faculty that started in that driveway. Again, doors opened when passion met passion.

A few months after finishing her graduate program, while preparing to pursue various job options in the museum world in and around Philadelphia, Amanda caught pneumonia. She spent ten days in the hospital, nearly dying at one point. The doctors ordered Amanda not to work for three months to allow for a recovery. Amanda's parents drove six hundred miles north to pack up her things and bring her home.

"I was back on my mom's couch, which is not the place that a twentysomething wants to be," Amanda recalls. "I felt like I had messed up." Museum work had been her ticket out of South Carolina, intellectually and physically, and in her convalescence, Amanda felt like she was losing her momentum. After three months on the couch, Amanda's mother pushed her to get going again. "She was like, 'All right, time to quit sulking. What are you going to do?'"

Amanda turned back to the Field of Study's networking process, even dusting off the binder of training materials she had used as a peer mentor at Columbia College. She remembered that when she worked in the Center for Engaged Learning, she and her peers would talk about what a mystery networking is to most undergraduates. "Especially in higher ed, students have this idea that networking is this big, weird, unwieldy process, and we have no idea how to do it," Amanda says. But networking is the unseen "backstory" of the college-to-career trajectory. "It's not this magical, mystical process. It's doing a little bit of Google research, utilizing a little bit of LinkedIn, and then making a couple of phone calls and having a little bit of coffee."

To recover professionally from pneumonia, "I leaned into my networks," says Amanda. She reached out to friends on Facebook to tell people she was on the job hunt, and one of her former professors at Columbia College sent her a posting for a communications manager at the McKissick Museum at the University of South Carolina; she later contacted him, asking for help in landing the job. Amanda was not relying on blind chance but was falling back on a network she had created—the sort of network that many wealthy students inherit from their social capital. "It's that systematic construction of your network and your resource pile that really helps you take that step up," Amanda says. It's manufacturing luck, "because luck doesn't just happen."

After six years at the McKissick, where she handled everything as the communications manager of a small museum—Amanda topped out in her position and wanted to get back to the urban Mid-Atlantic region. Looking for positions in Washington, DC, she found the Milken Center for Advancing the American Dream and applied for a job as a content developer, a position that didn't quite match her experience. Amanda didn't get the job, but she interviewed well, and the director of human resources contacted her two months later, encouraging her to apply for a position as a digital-content writer. At the same time, someone in Amanda's network alerted her to a similar position as a content writer at the University of South Carolina law school.

Amanda went back to her network to get help retooling her resume— to put a new spin on her skill in "telling stories." Repackaged as a digital-content writer, she was offered both jobs, with the law-school job paying significantly more than the position at the Milken Center. But Amanda took the position at Milken because the center was planning a sixty-thousand-square-foot museum in the heart of Washington and the job would get her out of South Carolina.

After a year, the center went through a reorganization; people working on the museum project started leaving, and Amanda was taken off that project and put in public relations. Dissatisfied, she reached out to her network again—this time, finding a college friend who worked at Hager Sharp, a DC public-relations firm focusing on education, the arts, and public health. Amanda's friend helped her set up a meeting with a vice president overseeing the education and labor team. After a few conversations, the firm offered Amanda a job working with education clients. The job more than doubled her salary and offered invaluable communications experience.

The kicker: Amanda will be helping Hager Sharp develop proposals for possible museum clients, while working in a town full of them.

Her hidden intellectualism and passion weren't just pie-in-the-sky goals, as Akers might put it. They remain practical, differentiating factors that will help Amanda stand out in the hidden job market and help her think entrepreneurially about her work life.

Rethinking "Follow Your Passion"

LinkedIn and the business press are awash with authors telling young people *not* to follow a passion. The entrepreneur and *Shark Tank* judge Mark Cuban calls it the "worst career advice." Instead, Cuban suggests, you should "follow your effort," and you will find what you're good at—and passion will follow later.[13] Cal Newport, an associate professor of computer science at Georgetown University and author of a series of advice books for people in the workforce, says following a passion could be dangerous because passions change. Drawing on stories about Steve Jobs, the comedian Steve Martin, and a young bluegrass musician named Jordan Tice, Newport argues that people should adopt a "craftsman mindset": a dedication to sharpening skills and to being "so good they can't ignore you."[14] Julia Korn, in an article in *Forbes*, noted that following your passions is bad career advice, even as she argues in the same piece that you should dedicate yourself to what sparks your interests and to "commit to learning and re-learning what energizes and drains you."[15]

Isn't that akin to passion? You do not develop a commitment to sharpening skills—to cultivating a craftsman's mindset—in a vacuum. You sharpen skills in the context of your hidden intellectualism, your vocational purpose, and your "why," all of which are influenced by your origin story. Newport, confoundingly, never addresses what pulled Steve Martin into the world of comedy or Jordan Tice into the world of bluegrass—or how, from that gravitational pull, passion emerges. "I really don't care if Jordan Tice loves what he does," Newport writes. "I also don't care why he decided to become a musician or whether he sees guitar playing as his passion."[16]

On podcasts and in interviews, Scott Galloway, a New York University business professor and marketing guru, has made the most noise about the pitfalls of passion, drawing from his book *The Algebra of Happiness: Notes on the Pursuit of Success, Love, and Meaning*. Like much of the advice in the literature straddling business and self-help, his is a superficial and often contradictory message. Like Newport and others, Galloway sets up a straw-man argument by equating passion to the pipe dream of becoming a Hollywood star, a fashion model, or a professional athlete.[17]

"The person telling you to follow your passion made their billions in iron-ore smelting," Galloway said on *Habits and Hustle*, the podcast of the fitness personality and entrepreneur Jennifer Cohen. "Ideally, you find something you like that has a 90-plus percent employment rate—which acting, modeling, and sports do not have; they have a 2 percent employment rate—and then commit to becoming great at it." Tax law, for example, might not sound very attractive or fun, he says, and certainly no child aspires to become a tax attorney. "But the best tax lawyers enjoy their work, have intense camaraderie and respect, they get to fly private, they have a larger selection of mates than they deserve, and they get the admiration of others." All of those external rewards—most of all, the money that tax attorneys earn—will make someone passionate about a career, Galloway argues.[18] Cohen called Galloway's perspective "refreshing." "Because you only always hear people, especially on social-media nonsense [saying], 'Follow your passion,'" Cohen told him.

But if you look at their stories, both Galloway and Cohen were driven by their interests, and their passions emerged as they strove for something fulfilling in their work lives. Galloway's initial driving motivation was to be a "baller," that is, someone who makes a lot of money and enjoys all the things that come with living in the spotlight. Even though he succeeded at this, his *Algebra of Happiness* reveals that this motivation could be a recipe for deep emptiness. "It didn't take long to realize that the secret is to find something you're good at. The rewards and recognition that stem from being great at something will make you passionate about whatever that something is," he writes. Investment banking, which initially promised wealth and seemed to signal success, was ultimately boring and stressful for a young Galloway. "Figuring out early that my hunger to impress was leading down a road of misery gave me the confidence to get out. I quit the path of success devoid of fulfillment."[19]

In the breezy narrative of her book *Bigger, Bolder, Better: Live the Life You Want, Not the Life You Get,* Jennifer Cohen describes her own journey to becoming a trainer for celebrities and an entrepreneur—much of which resembles a Field of Study approach. Growing up in the era of Jane Fonda and Denise Austin, an adolescent and heartbroken Cohen joined a gym after she failed to earn a spot on the Chai Folk Ensemble, an Israeli dance troupe and a "rite of passage" for girls at her Jewish high school in Winnipeg. Lacing up her athletic shoes after school every day, Cohen got more than just self-confidence from working out. She started to develop a hidden intellectualism. "Fitness was not just a habit; it became a part of my identity," she writes.[20]

Cohen also nurtured a dream of working in entertainment. While still in high school, she ambushed Keanu Reeves outside a Winnipeg theater where he was performing Shakespeare and persuaded him to sit for a taped interview, which she sent off to talent agents. In college, she and a friend recorded interviews with celebrities at a Montreal comedy festival to make a demo tape to pitch a Canadian version of *The View.* The pitch went nowhere, but the agents at the festival liked her hustle and invited her to come to Hollywood to work in talent management, a move that set up her career in the world of entertainment. She drew on her love of fitness, her interest in entertainment, and that hustle to create jobs for herself: as a fitness trainer for touring musicians, the owner of a line of athletic shoes, and an author and podcaster talking about success strategies.

Cohen's advice rests on helping people discover their "bold." It involves approaching strangers connected to an aspiration and asking for connections, help, a job—a process that seems very similar to the research investigative inquiry. "I guarantee that if you make ten attempts at anything, one will be successful," Cohen says in a TEDx talk, describing her method. "Either, one, you'll get the thing you want, or two, you'll get something that you never even knew was available. The reason why most people don't get the job that they want is because they don't actually go for the job that they want. They see what's available on Monster.com or LinkedIn."[21] In other words, they don't look for their place in the hidden job market.

Passion is not the problem, but how we define it is. The vocabulary around passion is so muddled that it's difficult to make out the relationship among passion, practicality, and professions. They are not at odds; in fact, they go hand in hand. When people talk about "following a passion," that's a shortcut statement to describe a long process of clarifying one's hidden intellectualism or "why," and then validating that clarification in a particular hidden-job world. Passion is not a pipe-dream aspiration; it's not the innate talent that drops a job into a student's lap, nor is it an impulse or emotion one follows to find a place in the work world. It's the emotive expression that comes when students discover that their hidden intellectualism and vocational purpose are real, practical, and achievable in the hidden job market.

Discovering hidden intellectualism and vocational purpose comes first—and that's hard work. One's hidden intellectualism may not present itself as a job title or a college major, and one may not find it posted on a job board in the career center. The problem for students is trying to make sense of the relationship among hidden intellectualism, practicality, and passion—these elements are not outlined in a college catalog, and any student would be hard pressed to find them discussed in any college's list describing its majors. In the absence of good advice or mentoring, how are students supposed to figure this out?

For first-generation and low-income students like Amanda, the Field of Study process provides them a means to contemplate and clarify their hidden intellectualism and their motivations, the means to explore the world of their hidden job market, and practical strategies to enter that world—and like Cohen says, some found what they wanted, and some found the unexpected.

We need only to look at the parallels between Beth Akers and Amanda Beleu. They both went to institutions called Columbia: one an institution of privilege, the other a beleaguered women's college. Both found their "why" through experiential learning and engagement with the world of work. Both refined their career trajectories through those experiences, found mentors and guidance, and landed in perhaps unexpected roles that neither had anticipated. They found the "something that you never even knew was available," as Cohen put it.

The difference is that Amanda had to learn how to create every opportunity for herself. First-generation, low-income, and underrepresented students can find their way into the hidden job market and, in doing so, express their passion, but they have to be given the tools. Amanda had to be taught to see the hidden job market and its possibilities and how to reach out and ask for what she wanted and needed. That is how she constructed the social and cultural capital that other students are born into.

5

The Liberal Arts and Field of Study

THE SCENE: THE ALFÂNDEGA DO PORTO in Porto, Portugal, along the Douro River, a city known for its town center (a UNESCO World Heritage site), its stately bridges and cobblestone roads, and, of course, the region's famous port wines. In September 2022, Porto hosted the Vacation Rental World Summit, a conference that covered the huge, hidden world of the boutique "homestay" industry—which includes not just the owners of Aspen ski chalets and midtown Manhattan apartments but also the technology companies behind websites like Airbnb and Vrbo, the trade journals covering the getaway locations, and the data crunchers selling services to optimize the property owners' market potential.[1]

Sarah DuPre, coming from AirDNA, one of those data-crunching companies, was a keynote speaker who highlighted how data analytics of the market can reveal unexpected insights. One of the takeaways: "It was all about, essentially, how larger property managers are losing in the industry," Sarah says over Zoom about a month after her presentation, sitting on a veranda in Barcelona, where she lives. "Essentially, the larger you get, the worse off your ratings are." Apparently, the human touch in boutique rentals is everything.

Her presentation killed. "When I got off stage, people asked me if I was an economist or a statistician, which is a compliment because I am definitely not either of those things. I studied French and Spanish."

Maybe that's a surprise to some readers—after all, among liberal-arts disciplines getting cut at colleges across the country, foreign-language departments appear on every list. From 2016 to 2021, according to a census by the Modern Language Association, enrollment in foreign-language programs fell by more than 16 percent, the largest decline in language program enrollments since the MLA started tracking them in 1958.[2] But languages are among many departments on the chopping block, frequently joined by philosophy, religious studies, sociology, mathematics, and others in the liberal arts.

Employers, academics, parents, pundits, and policymakers all have various ideas of what a liberal-arts major means to individual development and prospects on the job market. Depending on the person, that value lands somewhere between priceless and useless. "For years, economists and more than a few worried parents have argued over whether a liberal arts degree is worth the price," writes Anemona Hartocollis, a higher-education reporter for the *New York Times*, before confidently adding, "The debate now seems to be over, and the answer is 'no.'" Her November 2023 article captured that debate's polarized, caricatured views of faculty versus politically motivated state officials: Roosevelt Montás, a senior lecturer in American studies at Columbia University, told Hartocollis that colleges should resist a careerist view—that "it's not true that all students want from a college is the job." Meanwhile, Shad White, the conservative state auditor of Mississippi, wondered if the liberal arts served the professoriate's ideologies, rather than "a set of skills on how to approach problems in the world."[3]

Caught in the middle are administrators, whose decisions are driven by enrollment numbers and budget. The *New York Times* focused on Miami University, which had proposed cutting eighteen "low-enrolled" liberal-arts programs, and quoted Elizabeth Reitz Mullenix, a provost, who lamented the "existential crisis" of humanities programs because of the career focus of parents and students: "There's so much pressure about return on investment." Even amid the wicked social, economic, and geopolitical problems making headlines in the *New York Times* every day, students at Miami evidently couldn't see the practical use for degrees in critical race and ethnic studies, or religion, or Latin American studies, or Russian, East European, and Eurasian studies. Or, for that matter, French.

Higher education increasingly responds to market forces, but the key population driving those market forces—students and their parents—generally do not understand the nature of liberal-arts disciplines or how to apply them in the world of work. And neither do many of the people guiding those students and parents in navigating college to get a good return on investment. The Strada Institute for the Future of Work and Emsi, a labor market analytics firm now called Lightcast, called the phenomenon the "translation chasm": "Liberal arts graduates are too often left to stumble upon the valuable mixture of layered skills," said the report *Robot-Ready: Human+ Skills for the Future of Work*. "It's one of the reasons why, today, a liberal arts degree is under attack and fewer learners are pursuing liberal arts degrees. They lack visibility and clarity about the journey and the outcomes."[4]

Advocates for these disciplines often make the case for the liberal arts through anecdotes about students who studied humanities, social sciences, or the arts and later landed plum jobs at tech giants or big consulting firms. George Anders's book *You Can Do Anything: The Power of a Liberal Arts Education* features students who went to institutions like Bard, Dartmouth, and the University of Chicago and then found their way to jobs at Etsy, Morningstar, and PayPal. But Anders doesn't provide the backstory on how these students figured out their college-to-career puzzle. In some of his examples, the linkages seem serendipitous and random. At the very least, it's clear that most of these people used their considerable social and cultural capital to secure their job outcomes. In offering advice to students who do not have a coherent job-market strategy, Anders leans on career services, advising, career-exploration courses, and the like—strategies that, in reality, have mixed results on most college campuses, especially for liberal-arts majors and low-income students.[5] At a time when the cost of college is high, when low- to middle-income families are looking for a clear crosswalk from major to job, a major in a liberal-arts discipline can seem like a roll of the dice.

Sarah DuPre did not come from an affluent or connected background, did not go to an elite institution, and did not simply get lucky. She illustrates how a student from a small, unknown college with a liberal-arts major, armed with a Field of Study process, can open up unexpected career routes as she learns how to research the possibilities, fill in the blank spaces, and trade on the *hard, pragmatic* skills discovered in liberal-arts disciplines. For students like Sarah, what might look like luck is actually, as Seneca would say, where preparation meets opportunity.

Sarah grew up in an evangelical Southern Baptist family in Columbia, South Carolina. "You've seen that film *Jesus Camp*? That was me," she says. "Speaking-in-tongues kind of family, super religious." Those traditional values extended to the jobs the family would approve for Sarah: a teacher, a nurse, or a mom. Sarah didn't want children and couldn't stand bodily fluids. "So, teacher it was," she says with a shrug. Sarah entered Columbia College, the women's college her mom and aunt had attended, as an elementary-education major taking French and Spanish courses as electives, with the goal of becoming a French teacher.

Sarah had long been obsessed with France. She attended one of the "odd" public primary schools in South Carolina that offers French, starting when she was seven years old. Later, a high-school teacher who grew up in France lent Sarah novels and storybooks from francophone authors. "I would just sit with her and hear her fascinating stories about where she's from and how different it is," Sarah recalls. "She was married to a guy in the military in the US, and she was always saying, 'Oh, I'm trying to get him to retire back in France.'"

After she enrolled at Columbia College, she wanted to study abroad at Columbia's partner universities: the University of Angers, in France, and the University of Salamanca, in Spain. The problem, she soon learned, was that the education major did not allow her to study abroad. That led her to the Center for Engaged Learning.

The office's advice was to change majors from education to French, which could still lead to viable careers after college in the hidden job market. Taking that advice with a mixture of skepticism and relief, Sarah marched down to the registrar's office on the last day of the spring semester of her freshman year to declare French as her major and Spanish as her minor. "Are you sure about this?" a staff member in the registrar's office asked her more than once. Sarah nodded—she was certain that getting to Europe was now her goal. Then she packed up her dorm room and returned home for the summer to face the "wrath of her parents," as she puts it.

The Mystery of the Liberal Arts

Advocates have long lauded the liberal arts as a key ingredient to producing "robot-proof" employees, engaged citizens, and culturally rich personal lives. Studying in these disciplines, the story goes, nourishes undergraduates on a broad palate of arts and sciences that harkens back to Plato's classical educational framework, consisting of the trivium (grammar, logic, and rhetoric) and quadrivium (arithmetic, astronomy, geometry, and music). The liberal arts, its advocates say, are even a hallmark of American higher education—a course of study aligned with democratic values and free inquiry that attracts students from countries with more rigid, vocationally oriented education systems.

The problem is, for many students, parents, college staff, and faculty members—and perhaps especially hiring managers—the liberal arts are something of a black box. Talk to employers about how they value liberal arts, and you get a range of responses, many of them vague. Hiring managers and business owners who majored in a liberal-arts discipline themselves might say that their college training merely reinforced or sharpened talents and tendencies they already had. They might reflect on how a liberal-arts education gave them a broader sense of the world or a depth of thought, and they project their own experience onto job candidates.

They might see a liberal-arts major merely as a signal for traits that aren't necessarily there—that an applicant who majored in philosophy, for example, is more likely to be intelligent, or curious, or perhaps even bold or self-confident, for having picked a major with seemingly hazy connections to the job market.

Kathleen Duffy, the founder of the Duffy Group, an executive search firm based in Phoenix, works with Arizona State University's College of Liberal Arts and Sciences, helping students translate majors into skills. Her motivation comes out of her own experience graduating from ASU in the early 1980s with a degree in communications. "Nobody would even look at me because they didn't know what to do with that," she says. "We weren't having the same kind of conversations with our students back then as we are now in thinking about what are the skills, the talents that you bring to an organization that you can translate into a job."[6]

Her approach involves putting a major in context. A friend of hers, someone "wildly successful in the tech business," approached her recently, "devastated" that their child was going to major in philosophy. "Hold on. I want you to think about all the things that a philosophy major is going to learn and how their brain is going to work," Duffy counseled the friend. "It doesn't mean that they're going to graduate and be on your payroll for the rest of their lives. You have got to help them to understand how to tell their story."

Employers often "can't quantify the value of a psychology degree or an English degree or a sociology degree or a philosophy degree," Duffy says. She once sat on a panel with representatives from UnitedHealthcare who said they had trouble finding majors in actuarial science. "What an actuary needs to be is an expert in math," she told them. "I said, 'Well, have you ever considered liberal-arts majors who are getting a degree in math?' I mean, it was like I was speaking to them in a foreign language."

She herself has hired a number of dance majors to work in her recruiting firm. "Those individuals are really hardworking," she says. "Very disciplined, extremely driven. I can take those skill sets and see how to fit them in an organization." In speaking with administrators about the careers that might fit students in religious studies, she suggested playing up the morals of such majors. "If I'm looking to hire somebody in a field that needs to be very trustworthy, [with] high integrity, and be able to maintain confidence, why wouldn't I look at somebody in a religious-studies program?" she told them.

But Duffy is merely reading signals. Dancers aren't necessarily industrious, and religious-studies majors aren't necessarily honest, or even devout. There is an assumption that simply by studying in a liberal-arts (or even fine-arts) major, students will get infused with the personality traits that we commonly ascribe to that major. In this case, instead of major equals job, it's major equals a habit of mind or disposition.

Dance majors might be hard workers, given the competitive environment of professional dance and the physical rigors of dance itself. But dance students also get exposure to transferrable skills that would be relevant in any business setting. For instance, project management skills are necessary to mount a dance production, and a recital is a production much like those found in business conferences and fundraising campaigns; these require skills that could involve everything from planning an event program to the technical aspects of presentation, like staging and lighting. In putting on a production, dancers develop and work in teams to achieve a shared goal, and those team members need to learn how to deliver and receive critiques to improve the performance. Not to mention that dancers develop a physical presence that could be valuable when presenting in a boardroom, not just a ballroom.

Because the major-equals-job formulation doesn't work so well for the liberal arts, college presidents and other advocates have argued that the strength of these disciplines is that they are not tied to job titles at all. Compared to more vocationally oriented programs, the liberal arts—by providing broad exposure to different people and cultures, along with problem-solving and critical-thinking skills—are specially positioned to train students for a lifetime of adaptability. With the liberal arts, you're not trained for just one job but for a multitude of career possibilities.

These arguments intensified after the 2008 Great Recession, when families started putting a harder focus on ROI. "It's no surprise . . . that a growing number of corporations, including some in highly technical fields, are headed by people with liberal arts degrees," wrote Sanford J. Ungar, then the president of Goucher College, in a 2010 *Chronicle of Higher Education* essay. "Plenty of philosophy and physics majors work on Wall Street, and the ability to analyze and compare literature across cultures is a skill linked to many other fields, including law and medicine. Knowledge of foreign languages is an advantage in all lines of work. What seemed like a radical idea in business education 10 years or so ago—that critical and creative thinking is as 'relevant' as finance or accounting—is now commonplace."[7]

The problem is that college presidents like Ungar, and many of the people counseling students at their institutions, never explain how "plenty" of majors in philosophy or physics find work in the hidden jobs on Wall Street. What happens more often: students serendipitously figure out on their own how their studies in a liberal-arts major proved to be useful in an "unrelated" high-profile or high-paying career, and those graduates are later celebrated by their alma mater's public-relations office on the college's website. After getting a bachelor's degree in physics at the California Institute of Technology in 1986, Thomas Luke happened to take courses in empirical finance while pursuing a doctorate in physics at the Massachusetts Institute of Technology. There, he saw that finance problems were similar to physics and engineering problems—the same principles "but with different semantics," he told Caltech in an article highlighting his career successes.[8] Deciding that he could make a bigger impact in finance than in physics, he completed his MBA and went on to work for Deutsche Bank, Goldman Sachs, Merrill Lynch, and MAC Alpha Capital Management, where he is now president and chief risk officer.

In an interview with us, Luke pointed to a range of applications for physics in other fields. "I mean, genomics is fundamentally physics, right?" he said. His son did an internship at the Hospital for Special Surgery in New York City, which blended physics and biomechanics. "They were measuring hockey players and their physical aptitude, using accelerometers to see how strong they were, quantifying their physical ability to figure out that, 'Oh, this guy's phenomenal, and he's going to be a great NHL player.'"[9]

Luke complained, though, that students aren't introduced to these possibilities because faculty in physics programs are often focused on the pathway into academe and don't want to tell students there are limited roles in the world of theoretical physics, the main focus of many physics programs.

As the president of a company involved in hiring, and as a Caltech and MIT alumnus involved in admissions interviews, Luke sees students today as narrowly focused on technical and applied skills and obsessed with the brand names of institutions. Instead of committing to a challenging academic program that lights up their interests, he says, many students will downgrade themselves into any major that allows them to stay at a name-brand institution. "Now you're in a job, and you have a degree that you're not even sure you wanted."

Luke found the discipline-to-career connection on his own, like so many other students do. But liberal-arts departments will not survive on self-made-success stories. They need a deliberate "how" that would help any student—especially low-income and underrepresented students—bridge the translation chasm.

Liberal-arts departments are starting to understand the need to find that "how," because as budgets tighten and college leadership changes, those departments are first on the list for reduction or elimination. In 2018, four years after Ungar left Goucher, the college phased out its majors in math, music, religion, Russian, studio art, theater, elementary and special education, and—despite its utility on Wall Street—physics. To replace them, the college offered eight new majors, many of which had more vocational titles to help bridge the chasm: integrated data analytics, engineering science, integrative and digital arts, education studies, French transnational studies, literary studies, visual and material culture, and professional and creative writing.[10]

Even Sarah initially struggled with the translation chasm, but in her sophomore year, she began to engage in a Field of Study process that would help her bridge that gap. Now that she had changed her major to French to get to Europe through study abroad, she faced the hard reality that the registrar was hinting at. Summer was coming up, and she needed experiential learning.

"What do you do with a French major, anyway?" she sarcastically asked one day in the Center for Engaged Learning. To find something to do with that major, the center's mentors prompted her to play off a problem she'd long been concerned about: the number of South Carolina middle and high schools cutting their foreign-language programs.

Starting her research investigative inquiry, she Googled keywords related to the problem and discovered the office for Cultural Services of the French Embassy in the consulate in New York City, which had a program advocating for the expansion of French courses in American schools. Late on a Friday afternoon, she put together a short email in French, explaining that she was from Columbia College and outlining her concerns about dwindling language programs and her goals to address the problem, and sent it to the deputy counselor with a request to talk.

The following Tuesday, she received a reply asking her to stop by the cultural-services office on the Upper East Side on Thursday to discuss her email. Sarah panicked. Clearly, the deputy counselor thought she was writing from Columbia University in Morningside Heights, not a little-known liberal-arts college in the South. She called and explained the misunderstanding to the deputy counselor's assistant. It didn't seem to matter to the people at the consulate, who were captivated more by Sarah's initiative and interest in the French language than by the college she attended. The consulate set up a remote meeting over Skype.

Sarah took a day to prepare questions that addressed the social and political implications of keeping language programs alive. When she finally talked with the deputy counselor, he was impressed with her grasp of French and her concern about what middle- and high-school students would lose without exposure to foreign languages and other cultures. When Sarah asked him about opportunities for experiential learning, he offered her a summer position at the consulate.

Aside from a trip to Lancaster, Pennsylvania, with her grandparents when she was a child, Sarah had never been outside South Carolina. New York City was a culture shock in the best of ways, as Sarah absorbed new perspectives and experiences, growing her cultural capital. "That was the first time in my life I was in a place where race didn't seem to matter," says Sarah, who is white. Many of her friends and colleagues in New York were nonwhite or in relationships that crossed racial or ethnic lines. "You didn't have these weird undertones of silent racism that I feel I've always had in the background of where I lived. That was the first shocking realization—like, oh, I have tons of friends who are mixed-race couples and nobody seems to talk about it. It must not matter. That was incredible."

As Sarah's cultural capital grew, she began to see people in important positions—those she once regarded as unapproachable—as normal human beings, and she realized she could join their ranks. She had that epiphany one day when she was working on a project at the consulate and heard shouting and laughing in the foyer. There, the education attaché to the French embassy and another embassy executive were playing badminton in the middle of the marble entryway, while other embassy officials cheered them on. "They're just people," Sarah realized at that moment. "Everyone's just people."

This gave her the confidence to work the room at a gala a few days later, where she met the director of a dual-degree graduate program in business and French at New York University and one of the officers in a student organization that promotes French language, culture, and business within the MBA program at Columbia University. These conversations opened up her view of the hidden job market for a French major. She had so many other options than just teaching French to schoolkids.

Liberal Education and Soft Skills

Much of the attention on the labor market focuses on white-hot industries like data analytics and on Silicon Valley start-ups, where many of the desired skills can expire as technology evolves. Liberal-arts advocates have tried to create a narrative that counters the global, increasingly automated, and constantly changing labor economy: the liberal arts, often called liberal education, provides evergreen "human" or "soft" skills that every sector of the economy claims to need. The American Association of Colleges and Universities has been a key proponent of this view, having surveyed employers for years about their workplace needs.

It Takes More Than a Major: Employer Priorities for College Learning and Student Success, based on a 2013 online survey of 318 employers by Hart Research Associates, outlined the "capacities" that employers were looking for: "to think critically, communicate clearly, and solve complex problems"; "ethical judgment and integrity"; "intercultural skills; and the capacity for continued new learning." The report identified "five key learning outcomes": "critical thinking, complex problem-solving, written and oral communication, and applying knowledge in real-world settings." Surveyed employers wanted students to have a college education that included research, collaborative problem solving, senior projects, and community engagement.[11]

This AAC&U report and ones that followed assume that a liberal education delivers these skills and that employers want students who have had a liberal education. The 2013 survey offered employers a definition of liberal education: "This approach to a college education provides both broad knowledge in a variety of areas of study and knowledge in a specific major or field of interest. It also helps students develop a sense of social responsibility, as well as intellectual and practical skills that span all areas of study, such as communication, analytical, and problem-solving skills, and a demonstrated ability to apply knowledge and skills in real-world settings."

The survey then asked employers a leading question: Would this form of education be important for colleges to provide students (as future employees), and would these employers, as parents, recommend such an education to their own children? The report touted that "fully 94% of employers say it is important for today's colleges to provide this type of education," although the survey apparently offered employers only three options: very important (51 percent), fairly important (43 percent), and only somewhat important (6 percent).

It was a deft maneuver by AAC&U. What employer would admit to wanting workers (or children) who cannot communicate or solve complex problems or apply learning to the real world? In an increasingly complex cultural and professional environment, what company wouldn't want an employee who has expertise and can also think across domains of knowledge—the coveted skills of the T-shaped professional? And in a labor market upended by consolidation and automation, what worrying parent wouldn't want a child with a broad, flexible education that enables a shift to a new role or a whole new career?

But to AAC&U, "liberal education" does not necessarily mean study in a liberal-arts discipline. The association is "discipline agnostic," says Ashley Finley, AAC&U's vice president for research and senior advisor to the president.[12] Employers seem to agree with that. In *It Takes More Than a Major* and the next report, *Fulfilling the American Dream: Liberal Education and the Future of Work*, released in 2018, employers said that acquiring and being able to apply these human skills is far more important than the choice of major. Interestingly, in the 2018 report, these capacities and key learning outcomes were not tied to liberal education; they were called "college learning outcomes," seeming to mean that they could come from any program at a university. In fact, aside from in the title, liberal education was not mentioned in the 2018 survey at all.[13]

By the time AAC&U released *How College Contributes to Workforce Success* in 2021, this time based on a survey by Hanover Research, the disconnections between the liberal-arts disciplines and employer responses were glaring. The report contained a data point that would shock advocates of the liberal arts: when employers were asked which of the "attributes of a college education that combine breadth and depth of learning" they valued, "an emphasis on liberal arts disciplines" was listed dead last. Across the entirety of the report, employers assigned more value to exposure to fields in STEM (science, technology, engineering, and mathematics), involvement in work-study, practice with technical skills, and community engagement.[14]

With AAC&U's agnosticism toward liberal-arts disciplines, combined with findings like these, it's possible that the association gives administrators everything they need to cut liberal-arts departments or reduce them to general education and a smattering of electives in service to more technical or "vocational" majors. On financially stressed college campuses, where enrollments determine budgetary allocations and campus pecking order, enterprising deans of business or engineering schools could claim that their programs offer everything students need to get a liberal education. Why keep around philosophy or anthropology?

It's absolutely true that a student can get these transferable human skills from disciplines and activities well outside the liberal arts. Students at California State University Maritime Academy ostensibly train to work in the maritime industry, with a classroom curriculum that covers the breadth of maritime science, sustainability, engineering, technology, and business. That training involves boarding the *Golden Bear*, Cal-Maritime's ship, where students work together to solve complex technical problems and interpersonal conflicts as they sail to ports in other cities and countries. For safety and clarity on the sea, the students follow strict protocols and codes of conduct, which are opportunities to demonstrate responsibility and understand hierarchy. All the pieces are there: problem solving, group work, cultural exposure, communication skills, leadership skills, all applied in a real-world setting. From this training, Cal-Maritime students go on to work for (and even helm) tech companies, airports, amusement parks, and other complex organizations. They don't just become merchant marines.[15]

Students at the Culinary Institute of America, clearly not a liberal-arts institution, also get an education that challenges them to learn and demonstrate these capacities and key learning outcomes—and the training can be just as transferable. As students at the institute learn to braise beef or handle a chef's knife, they work in teams to turn out a full-course meal by lunchtime. They navigate around problems when the chicken doesn't arrive on the distribution truck or the pot of demi-glace goes crashing to the floor. They engage other cultures when they adapt recipes from Asia or South America or when working with local small farms. They are aware of how climate change and economic pressures might affect the demand for or availability of certain ingredients. They are trained in the culinary concept of *mise en place*—French for "everything in its place"—an organizational framework that allows chefs to manage the various ingredients coming into the kitchen and the food coming off the stovetop. "If you've ever seen some of the chefs graduate and go on to do other things—whether it's run their own businesses or run consumer-products companies—they take their *mise en place* with them, because it's now ingrained in them," says Dan Charnas, a New York University professor of journalism and author of *Work Clean: The Life-Changing Power of Mise-en-Place to Organize Your Life, Work, and Mind*.[16]

With this definition of liberal education, maybe the academic program doesn't even matter. Many of the skills that AAC&U assigns to liberal education could come from engagement in a student activity, an intramural club or sport, or even work-study. Under the definitions offered above, it's possible that you could get a liberal education without going to college at all. Enlist in the military or work your way from barista to manager at Starbucks: in either case, you'll get plenty of experience working in diverse teams, applying problem-solving skills, communicating with people from different cultural backgrounds, demonstrating digital and numerical literacy, and more. Noel Ginsburg, the former CEO of a plastics company and the founder of CareerWise USA, which helps students connect to apprenticeships, puts it bluntly: "Soft skills are actually better taught in a business environment than they are in a classroom."[17]

Indeed, most of AAC&U's own surveys indicated that employers didn't think they were getting these skills from college graduates. AAC&U saw it as a curricular problem. "While employers clearly value liberally educated graduates, their actual experience with job applicants and new hires has shown that not all recent graduates have, in fact, received a liberal education," wrote Lynn Pasquerella, the president of AAC&U, in the 2021 report.[18]

We have argued in this book that students acquire desired hard and soft skills in their courses when they understand *why* they are sitting in those courses and what relevance those courses have to their hidden intellectualism and goals beyond college. This is the core problem at the heart of the translation chasm.

Pasquerella attempts to bridge this chasm with a story about her son Pierce that appears in *What We Value: Public Health, Social Justice, and Educating for Democracy*—a story she also tells in her public appearances. Pierce wanted to go into television and film production, and like Isaiah from chapter 1, he "railed against what he saw as the hoops he had to jump through just to get behind a camera," Pasquerella writes. "They are just trying to get our money by making me take courses that I will never use, like Small Group Communication and Intercultural Competence," Pierce complained one day to his mother; to his father, an entomologist; and to his brother, who was getting a doctorate in African American studies.[19]

Pierce saw the value of his liberal-arts courses in graduate school, after he got a job working on the *Jerry Springer Show*. "Now I understand the value of a liberal education," he told his mother over the phone. "I had to run out and get ties and cigarettes for the talent and spent two hours in the green room with them. I finally get why I needed to take courses in small group communication and intercultural competence."

This anecdote comes off as shallow. Fetching cigarettes and ties, and talking with Jerry Springer's television guests, doesn't require the liberal arts—it just requires a little common sense. The real question is this: Why couldn't Pierce figure out the crystal-clear connection between taking courses in small-group communication and intercultural competence and making films and TV shows? These courses would have spelled out in their syllabi the *hard, analytical* skills that students would pick up and later be able to demonstrate in work and in other life settings. To cite some from a real small-group communication syllabus: comparing theories of small-group and team dynamics; developing effective team problem solving; cultivating communication skills to contribute to effective leadership; preparing, practicing, and delivering oral presentations in a team setting; and communicating ethically.

But here is the critical point: If Pierce, the son of a liberal-arts college president and an entomologist, can't bridge the translation chasm in courses like these, how would students without that kind of cultural capital figure it out?

While Pierce had a retrospective epiphany about the value of his communications courses, Isaiah, while still in his undergraduate program, had a series of conversations with people out in the work world (during his research investigative inquiry), who pointed to the skills and competencies he would need. Isaiah then knew why he picked his courses and what kinds of information and skills he should take from them. This is what John Dewey pointed to: students engage with their courses and are more likely to retain and later use the embedded skills if they can see their relevance.[20] Students see this relevance when those skills are tied to their vocational purpose or hidden intellectualism and when they can design those skills as part of their undergraduate studies.

Liberal-arts skills go far beyond bland "people skills" to something more. The concepts, theories, and methodologies that underlie study in liberal-arts disciplines like anthropology, English literature, and philosophy can be vocational, but we usually just draw a line from these disciplines to merely educational arenas, like teaching, research, or working for cultural institutions. In anthropology, for example, students pick up hard skills grounded in ethnography—learning how to use qualitative and quantitative techniques to analyze the cultural systems embedded in society and how, through these systems, people create meaning in politics, business, religion, and their own families. The work world is one of these cultural systems, too.

Depending on how anthropology majors want to use these skills, they can research other types of systems for good careers out in the world: by analyzing the labor market for government organizations, or a company's culture on behalf of a consulting firm or an interior-design company, or practices in the delivery of health care across race, ethnicity, or sexual orientation. All of this depends on how students learn to fill in the blanks.

Are advisors, career counselors, or even faculty prepared to help students see the hard skills in liberal-arts disciplines and how they might translate into roles across the job market? The survival of anthropology departments—and so many others in the liberal arts—depends on having these conversations. Yet students rarely have a chance to discuss how liberal-arts theories and methodologies, with their technical skill sets, readily transfer to other noneducational areas across the job market: to business and consulting, to innovations in health care, tech, finance, and more.

The Rift between Nonvocational and Vocational

Returning to Columbia College after a summer in New York City, Sarah planned her study-abroad experience: France in the spring and Spain the following fall. She researched the many cultural and career-relevant possibilities in Europe, approaching the experience differently from many of her peers, who tended to think of study abroad as simply about reading French literature and experiencing life in a different country. Sarah wanted a more practical experience. She discovered she could take courses that would grant her certification from the French and Spanish education ministries to use those languages in business practices. She could also take business classes that would give her a different perspective on a facet of Western European culture not found in simply studying literature.

Sarah aced those courses and came back certified to use French and Spanish in myriad commercial settings, from business negotiations to broadcasting for the media. But when she returned to Columbia College, Sarah was in for a shock: Her faculty advisor, the chair of the French department, would not accept her credits in business language or the French business courses as electives for the major. The department would only accept studies in French literature. Courses in business language and practices—taught in French and concerning current issues in France's economy and everyday economic life—didn't qualify as French culture and would not count toward her major requirements, Sarah was told.

Sarah ran headlong into a faction of higher education that views the study of liberal arts in college as mostly a personal exploration of the canon of humanistic knowledge, a faction that takes a skeptical view of college as career preparation. The liberal arts are not about arming students with the skill sets catered to a specific job, they say; in fact, these liberal-arts advocates often refer to those disciplines as "nonvocational." Instead, the liberal arts prepare students for a life of self-reflection, scholarship, and cultural engagement that leads them to ponder the "Big Questions," as John Churchill, the former executive director of Phi Beta Kappa and dean emeritus of Hendrix College, argues in *The Problem with Rules: Essays on the Meaning and Value of Liberal Education*. Those intellectual exercises gained through a liberal-arts education, he claims, are all students need to find a career path. For Churchill, the real value of a liberal-arts education is not in its career outcomes but in "the development of the skills of deliberation" so that students can craft their best sense of self.[21]

In *The Real World of College*, Wendy Fischman and Howard Gardner, both professors at Harvard University, argue that colleges and universities, focused as they are on career preparation, have lost their central mission. After having more than two thousand interviews with undergraduates at various colleges, they lament that most students take a transactional view of higher education, "preoccupied with issues of jobs and/or institutional reputation."[22] Colleges, they believe, should instead guide students to focus on intellectual development and engage the "big questions" that underlie the academic enterprise. Fischman and Gardner invent a metric—"higher-education capital," or HEDCAP—to evaluate each interviewed student's "ability to attend, analyze, connect, and communicate on issues of importance and interest."[23] From the sample interviews cited in the book, students who have a high HEDCAP score tend to be well spoken and display erudition, and they tend to downplay the career or financial outcomes of college.

Parents "should bracket the vocational theme song" of college and encourage their children to focus more on personal transformation, Fischman and Gardner suggest. "If you focus solely on 'employment' and 'jobs,' you will undermine your offspring's opportunity to become a broad and well-informed adult, worker, parent, and a citizen." They recommend that students and their parents soak up "*nonvocational* aspects of college" (their emphasis): art museums, performances, campus speakers, and "traveling adventures," local and abroad.[24]

Fischman and Gardner elaborated on the book's argument in an interview with *Inside Higher Ed*. "The institution of higher education gives mixed messages or the wrong message about what college is about," Fischman said. "In an effort to please the customers—the students and the parents—it speaks to what they want, which, again, is jobs, internships, study abroad, all these experiences off campus and in the future, rather than focusing on what is good about college itself." Gardner was even more dismissive of higher education's focus on helping undergraduates find career paths: "If you are a decent student," he said, "you will not have to worry about getting a job, no matter what campus you're at."[25]

All of this is infuriatingly privileged and out of touch. Most students do not have the luxury to ignore the potential career outcomes of a college investment—and those outcomes are far from assured, even for good students. Students who hope to engage in culture like museum exhibits and artistic performances need to have the disposable income and discretionary time to do so, which is provided by having a good job after college. In any case, pursuing these experiences while in college also consumes time and money, and the average student works more than twenty hours a week just to cover college costs.

In *The Evidence Liberal Arts Needs: Lives of Consequence, Inquiry, and Accomplishment*, Richard Detweiler, president emeritus of Hartwick College and former president of the Great Lakes Colleges Association, does not forget that students need to land jobs after graduation. But the solution he sees is less about what students choose to study and more about the college environment. For him, the ideal setting is the small liberal-arts college. Such institutions prepare students for lives of societal impact, inquiry, and accomplishment—the central purpose of a nonvocational education, he argues. Students might have to wait a while, though, for that payoff, as Detweiler says those habits of mind "may not emerge until well past middle age."[26]

Detweiler interviewed a thousand college graduates of various ages and found that students who prospered from their college education studied topics across a range of disciplines—a key point of his study that leads to an enigmatic formula: students who had success in the job market were more likely to have taken "more than half their courses outside their major."[27] But which courses or what combinations? He doesn't know. An analysis of the transcripts and course syllabi of his interview subjects is beyond his study's scope and "would likely give little insight into the degree to which interrelationships [between domains of knowledge] were examined."[28]

The content of what people studied is less important, he claims, than the fact that they ranged across disciplines, formed relationships with faculty members and the educational community outside classes, and declared a nonvocational major. Those factors, he argues, lead graduates to become organizational leaders, lifelong learners, culturally aware, fulfilled, altruistic, and successful.

Detweiler acknowledges that for the liberal arts, "the marketing challenge is a complicated one," but he argues that college leaders should sell those programs on the long-term outcomes of producing a "responsible and productive citizenry required for the success of our democracy," not on the prospects of landing that first job.[29]

Churchill, Fischman and Gardner, and Detweiler don't offer much help to parents and students trying to bridge the translation chasm. But with dense, academic prose, it's clear they aren't writing to parents and students. They are writing to their colleagues.

If their intent is to preserve liberal education, though, parents and students are the key audience. When colleges perform program reviews and select departments to eliminate, those decisions are often grounded in the demand for those programs, measured by the number of full-time equivalents (FTEs) they generate, the number of students who graduate in the major, and the ties to other programs and the mission of the campus.

FTE is the fundamental metric, meaning that students and parents, not fellow academics, decide the fate of academic programs. Arguments grounded in personal inner growth, deep thinking about big questions, and engaging with cultural institutions might work for families with ample income and workplace connections, but the average family wants something tangible from their higher-education investment: a job after graduation, with a decent income and good prospects for career advancement. Parents and students already hear loud, and often inaccurate, arguments that liberal-arts degrees are career dead ends. Given the choice between a "vocational" program, whose title appears to offer a short crosswalk from college to career, and a liberal-arts program, whose inherent values "may not emerge until well past middle age," their likely decision is obvious.

The Hard Skills of Personal Development

The notion that the liberal arts cultivates personal development—leading students to ponder big questions, think critically, engage culture—may not make an effective sales pitch to parents and students, but that doesn't mean we should dismiss it. The arts and humanities, in particular, offer windows into other cultures and even other mindsets. Stories and historical accounts of flawed heroes, hubristic military leaders, and doomed love affairs act as a form of virtual reality, allowing students to imaginatively experience different frames of mind and complicated problems they might never otherwise encounter. History, literature, philosophy, sociology, and other humanistic disciplines deliver a particular set of transferable skills that you can't find in fields like engineering, accounting, computer science, or even the sciences belonging to the liberal arts.

These skills of the arts and humanities are transferable across the job spectrum; they undergird employers' interest in qualities like empathy, effective leadership, and critical and creative thinking. But they are also useful in any setting that a student encounters, even in their personal lives. They provide a means for students to better understand themselves and the skills to think through their thoughts and actions.

Training in the liberal arts may indeed lead to the kind of personal reflection and development of social and cultural capital that Churchill, Detweiler, and Fischman and Gardner argue for. But the power of the liberal arts is not simply about introducing students to the broad swaths of art or culture that might lead them to visit a museum someday or read poetry in their spare time. It is also about—perhaps primarily about—providing pragmatic frames for understanding the continually changing social and cultural dynamics of the day-to-day world we live and work in.

William G. Perry Jr., someone we brought up in chapter 3, studied the process that students go through to become complex, independent thinkers and what liberal education contributes to that process. His work formed the foundations of student-development theory. In his classic book from 1968, *Forms of Ethical and Intellectual Development in the College Years*, Perry pointed out that being able to think is not in itself enough to distinguish a liberally educated individual. "Anti-intellectuals have been known to master mountains of data and technology," he writes. "The anti-intellectual cannot be passed off as one who refuses to think. Many think dangerously well." Still, the anti-intellectual refuses to think about one thing: thought. "Most particularly his *own* thought."[30]

"In contrast, the liberally educated man," Perry writes, "has learned to think about even his own thoughts to examine the way he orders his data and the assumptions he is making and to compare these with other thoughts that other men might have." According to Perry, "The characteristic of the liberal arts education of today . . . is its demand for a sophistication about one's own line of reasoning as contrasted with other possible lines of reasoning. In short, it demands metathinking." The liberal arts intentionally puts students in positions where they have to test their thinking against the thoughts of others.[31]

Perry chronicles how students move from looking at the world in black-and-white terms, shaped by the traditions in which they are raised, to a realization that there is a plurality of perspectives and values that challenge one another. For Perry, students demonstrate their liberal education when they learn how to develop their personal commitments within an ever-changing, ever-evolving global culture.

Perry found an analog to support his theory in Thomas Kuhn's *The Structure of Scientific Revolutions*, which discusses the nature of the "paradigm shift."[32] Through the liberal arts, students are faced with anomalies that challenge their "personal paradigms." The liberal arts provides students with pragmatic frames and skill sets they can use to examine their assumptions, make judgments about which assumptions are valid or invalid, and rebuild their personal paradigm to better interact with the new environment they are living in. This is an ongoing process as a lifelong learner develops the agility to negotiate a continually changing world. These skills apply not just to understanding traditional canons of literature, art, music, and history but to the interactions and artifacts of any culture—including the culture of work. The liberal arts helps us understand how cultures interact, mutate, and grow into new cultural statements, movements, and artifacts. A liberal education even applies to the dynamics of our daily personal perspectives, interactions, and relationships.

These pragmatic frames are especially necessary for historically underserved students in building their social and cultural capital. A background in this way of thinking, embedded in these pragmatic frames, is an unspoken, underappreciated form of wealth that students use to ascend the social-mobility ladder.

In 1997, Earl Shorris wrote in *Harper's Magazine* about the founding of the Clemente Course for the Humanities, an award-winning program that helps "individuals who have been denied access to economic, cultural and social opportunities" to "develop the critical, reflective and creative skills" that lead to empowerment and social mobility. While writing a book about poverty, Shorris had once concluded that the "surround of force" (hunger, police pressure, drugs, crime, etc.) kept the poor from being "political," as Thucydides would describe it: the engagement in everyday civic interactions among people in families, communities, and government. "The absence of politics in their lives is what kept them poor," he writes.[33]

His view changed, however, during a research visit to an Upstate New York prison. There he met Viniece Walker, an inmate who had studied philosophy while incarcerated and insisted that an antidote to poverty lay in taking people to "plays, museums, concerts, lectures, where they can learn the moral life of downtown." Shorris knew what she meant: the humanities was the key to learning Thucydides's concept of politics. Working with the Roberto Clemente Family Guidance Center, he recruited impoverished students for a humanities course to test the concept.

When Shorris pitched the course to students, he painted it as a pragmatic way to gain social and cultural capital: "If the political life was the way out of poverty, the humanities provided an entrance to reflection and the political life," he writes. "Rich people learn the humanities in private schools and expensive universities. And that's one of the ways in which they learn the political life. I think that is the real difference between the haves and have-nots in this country. If you want real power, legitimate power, the kind that comes from the people and belongs to the people, you must understand politics. The humanities will help."

The students were introduced to the *Epic of Gilgamesh*, the prehistoric art of the Lascaux caves, Confucius, Heisenberg, Plato—and transformations began. Shorris captured this in an anecdote about David Howell, a big man with a history of violence but an enthusiasm for the Clemente Course readings. One day, Howell called Shorris to say that he had some trouble with a coworker. "She made me so mad, I wanted to smack her up against the wall."

"What did you do?" Shorris asked him, fearing Howell was calling from jail after smacking her.

Howell replied: "I asked myself, 'What would Socrates do?'"

David Howell's liberal-arts training allowed him to enter a virtual reality, conduct a dialogue, and shift his personal paradigm to begin to live a political life. Howell used the Socratic method and the narrative imagination to engage in a comparative analysis about what he could do, versus what he *ought* to do, which is the grounds of ethical reasoning. He used hard-skill methodologies inherent to the humanities to navigate the politics of his workplace. The power of the liberal arts rests in negotiating the mundane events and pragmatic decisions of our lives, but students rarely encounter this value proposition of the liberal arts from parents, career counselors, or even their coursework.

Shorris was right that access to liberal-arts disciplines is an issue of equity. "The liberal arts are under attack. So why do the rich want their children to study them?" asks the headline of a 2019 *Washington Post* article.[34] "Studying humanities is a luxury only wealthy students can afford," declares a 2017 headline from MarketWatch.[35]

The liberal arts faces a hard reality, namely, that the values propounded above are difficult to measure in terms of income. Parents and students—hyper-focused on the financial returns of college and facing a translation chasm—make their choices about majors (and even liberal-arts institutions themselves) based on that simple, often erroneous formula of major-equals-job. With fewer students choosing many of the liberal-arts majors—and few people on campus tying these liberal-arts hard skills to roles and activities of the workplace and our daily lives—the outcomes are predictable: when a program review comes around, with its hard-nosed assessment of enrollment and tuition revenue, liberal arts programs go on the chopping block—except at elite schools with ample resources and students with financial safety nets.

As a result, what we are witnessing in higher education right now is a loss of programmatic biodiversity on many campuses, with consequences for students and the institutions themselves. If college is a kaleidoscope, each discipline is a particular lens through which a student can see the world. In addressing a question or problem, a theater major will bring a skill set and perspectives different from those of a math or music major. What's more, without theater, math, music, or other liberal-arts disciplines present on campus, the kaleidoscope produces fewer patterns, fewer possibilities from the combinations of different disciplines.

When a campus loses disciplines, students can experience (without even knowing it) a kind of diminishment in the daily conversations and encounters they have in dorm rooms, libraries, dining halls, and gyms. These serendipitous conversations are just as crucial to expanding perspectives, building cultural capital, and sparking new ideas as any course content.

Like in any environment, this loss of biodiversity threatens the ecology of an institution, even higher education itself, as a whole. Creativity and innovation—lauded so often by entrepreneurs and "disruptors"—exist in the spaces between disciplines. It's what happened when Steve Jobs matched his interests in typography and calligraphy with technology to influence the design of the Macintosh desktop, word-processing software, and the aesthetic of other Apple products.[36] It's how Don Seiden combined his expertise as an artist with his experiences working with psychiatric patients to develop the master's program in art therapy at the School of the Art Institute of Chicago, a pioneering program in psychotherapy.[37] It's what Arthur Koestler referred to in *The Act of Creation* as "bisociation," a blending of elements drawn from two previously unrelated patterns of thought to create a new pattern—a dynamic found in biophilic design, behavioral economics, sabermetrics, graphic novels, and hip-hop.[38]

Sarah Writes the End of Her Story

After Columbia College's French department told Sarah that her time living and studying language, culture, and business in France would not count as electives toward her French major, Sarah was enraged. To meet the department's requirements, she would have to spend another year at the college. But Sarah thought about her experience in New York City, where she had met people from the French studies department at New York University; she researched that program, which combined skills in French and business, and realized she could use it as a model to design her own major. She put together her work in France with her studies in Spain, added courses in marketing and statistics to flesh out her degree plan, and dropped her French major.

She needed an internship—and a lightbulb switched on when one of the peer mentors in the Center for Engaged Learning asked her, "Who sells South Carolina?" As it turned out, the South Carolina International Trade Association was heavily involved in luring businesses from France (and many other countries) to operate in the state and utilize the Port of Charleston for imports and exports to the world. Sarah set up a research investigative inquiry with the CEO of the trade association, who quickly hired her because of her language certifications and experience to conduct market research. "I was the only person with a bachelor's degree in the office," Sarah says. "I learned that others on the team were from the Masters of International Business program at the University of South Carolina—everybody was from a different country, from Italy, Germany, Austria, and China."

Eventually, Sarah felt a yearning to get back to Europe, particularly Barcelona, where she had fallen in love with the city (and someone she'd left behind there). She set her sights on enrolling at ESADE, an internationally ranked business school in Barcelona, and started another series of research interviews to find a scholarship. She came across one offered by Rotary International and talked to a local representative of Rotary, who gave her a tip for winning an award: at the welcome party, he said, "work the room," because the scholarships always went to people who impressed Rotary's board members. "I had identified the seven people on the board I needed to mingle with, looked them up on LinkedIn, and came up with something interesting to say to each of them," she says. "Something that's a bit outside the box."

Kathleen Duffy, of Arizona State University, rightly says that students need to be able to tell a story about their degree—for employers in interviews, for personal statements on graduate-school applications, for clarity in their own personal narrative. But in order to tell a story, you have to have a story to tell, and it's difficult to come up with that narrative if you're still struggling with a translation chasm.

Sarah, having created a narrative about her journey through Field of Study, had everything she needed to tell her story to the board members—how she consciously linked French and Spanish to business and contemporary culture. After the event, Sarah was one of the awardees.

She went off to ESADE, picked up Catalan, and did an internship with a start-up company that sharpened her skills in business intelligence and market research. She graduated and used her skills to land a position with a Barcelona-based start-up called AirDNA in 2016.

That same year, the French department at Columbia College closed, along with other departments with withering enrollments, including philosophy and history. (Spanish was reduced to a minor.) The French department could have found myriad ways to boost its enrollment numbers, given that South Carolina is now host to more than 1,200 international companies employing more than 170,000 people.[39] The French faculty could have worked with the career-services office to make connections with those companies and create partnerships with local high schools offering French, thereby showing students the inherent marketability of the language and setting up a pipeline into the college's French program. French, after all, is consistently listed as one of the most-useful business languages in the world, applicable not only in France but also in parts of Africa, Canada, the Caribbean, and Southeast Asia.[40] By showing how French could interact with the blank spaces present in almost any degree—without changing anything the French faculty were already doing in their courses—the department could have brought together the vocational and nonvocational to bridge the translation chasm and perhaps have fended off its demise.

Things turned out better, though, for Sarah. Several years after she started as one of four employees at AirDNA, the company grew and was bought out by a larger firm, and Sarah got a hefty payout from her vested shares. These days, she sharpens her French by getting together with francophone friends over good wine and cheese, talking the night away.

Part of Sarah's success comes from her tenacity and her refusal to take no for an answer. Another part comes from how she consciously arranged her interests, passions, skills, and her degree into a pattern that she and others could understand. "There really is a hidden job market for people who know how to just show up and say, 'Hey, I have this skill set, and this is how I can be beneficial to you,'" she says. "If you're good enough, they'll make space for you. Don't wait for somebody else to open an opportunity. Just go and open it yourself with what you want to go after and what your skill set is. And I do that every day. My job is made up."

6

The Need for Hacking

IN THE FALL OF 2019, Kaylan walked across a stage at Chicago State University's College of Pharmacy to a faculty member, who placed a white coat over her shoulders. It was a symbol of her acceptance into pharmacy school and her first major step toward becoming a doctor of pharmacy.

The white-coat ceremony is a common rite of passage across health-professions schools and an important moment for students who make it there. Family members and friends watching the pomp assume that these students succeeded simply through a combination of smarts and hard work; that they entered the pre-pharmacy program, excelled at the courses, put together the relevant experiences, did well on the GRE admissions test, and sailed right into pharmacy school on those credentials, as if on laid track.

The reality, of course, is more complicated—and in the case of Kaylan, far more complicated. Initially, Kaylan made misinformed college choices, and she stumbled along the way. Her profile under any predictive-analytics measure would indicate that she had little chance of doing well enough in college to move on to a graduate program, much less attend a white-coat ceremony for pharmacy school.

But Kaylan succeeded because she hacked the college game, utilizing its numerous routes, loopholes, and back doors. For Kaylan, that meant using a Field of Study approach to discover the critical information she needed. With that information, she would find the appropriate major that worked for her, build her professional contacts, and line up the experiential learning that paved her way to graduate school.

Kaylan's journey defies a conventional view about selective schools: the more elite the college, the more likely that college will open a student's way to graduate school, a prominent job, and the "good life"—at least as that life is defined by people who work at those elite colleges. In 2023, the economists Raj Chetty and David Deming at Harvard, along with John N. Friedman at Brown University, argued that people in high-level leadership positions in prestigious firms, health care, and government disproportionately came from Ivy-plus colleges (the eight Ivy League institutions, plus the University of Chicago, Duke, Massachusetts Institute of Technology, and Stanford). But Chetty and his colleagues aren't sure why elite colleges provide a pipeline to elite positions, even as they acknowledged that students at those schools largely come from elite families.[1]

"We're able to show the causal effect of attending one of these colleges and not directly unpack what these colleges are doing internally to generate those great outcomes that we see," Chetty said in a Brookings Institution webinar about the study. "We'd like to think maybe some of it is these great professors that you have at these institutions, but in reality, our sense is that there are lots of other things going on as well—likely the networks you form." So, he was asked, why not just encourage prestigious companies to change their hiring practices and consider people from various backgrounds and non-Ivy schools? Chetty suggested it would be easier to change the admission policies of institutions like Dartmouth, Harvard, and Stanford. Such a reform would find supporters in national conversations about banning legacy admissions, broadening affirmative action, and providing more financial resources for low-income students attending elite schools.[2]

But Chetty's suggestion runs against the reality of college practices:

colleges may officially end legacy admissions, but they're unlikely to change the underlying principles behind them—that is, providing access to wealthy and powerful families that contribute to the college's endowment and public profile, along with connections to elite corporate resources. As it stands, the number of low-income students attending elite colleges is already so low that even doubling the number of students at, say, Harvard, would have minimal impact on addressing the larger social issue of income inequity.[3] Even when they are enrolled, as Anthony Jack has pointed out in The Privileged Poor, low-income students still have a tough go at these institutions; they do not understand the "hidden curriculum," and they do not come with the social and cultural capital (or the financial resources) to take advantage of many of the social situations, prominent lectures, and other campus opportunities where one-percent-ism is formed.[4]

But why all the focus on moving from the bottom quintile to the top 1 percent, which doesn't capture the breadth of students out there? Chetty's own research from 2017 shows that a number of less-selective institutions—institutions like Glendale Community College, Stony Brook University, or the University of Texas at El Paso—are more successful than elites in helping low-income, first-generation students achieve upward mobility after graduation. Stony Brook, for example, was three times more effective than Columbia University at elevating students from the bottom to the top quintile. As with his research on Ivy-plus schools, Chetty doesn't know what drives the success of these affordable, high-access institutions either, noting only that they offer students something "value-added" to the standard college experience. Given, though, that these colleges have lower instructional costs, lower tuition, and easier access for low- and middle-income students, he and his colleagues claim that identifying the value-added could "provide a scalable model for increasing upward mobility for large numbers of students."[5]

Kaylan's approach—and the approach of many students who have used Field of Study—challenges the conventional view about higher education. It's not about the institution; it's how students take advantage of the opportunities at their college. The fact is that students like

Kaylan—along with students like Tony and Monique, whom you'll meet in this chapter—got that value-added from conversations that are different from what most students encounter on campus. They got help in learning to hack the higher-education system to get where they wanted to go.

Unfortunately, as any reader of this book knows by now, most students don't get those types of conversations. Instead, they are benignly shepherded through the rote patterns and conventional pathways set up by the institution—guidance that leads too many students down the proverbial garden path. With that kind of conventional advice, the college journeys for Kaylan, Tony, and Monique—all of them transfer students, who are particularly vulnerable—would have ended in stumbling blocks, stopping out, and perhaps failure. But by looking at their academic programs through a Field of Study lens, we see how these students found the hacker's tool that helped them discover the hidden job market and utilize the blank spaces to design their undergraduate experience.

A Societal Fix in Hacking

The concept of hacking is not confined to the tech industry. It's everywhere. People hack structures and systems—like tax codes, legislative processes, or administrative regulations—to find advantages that benefit them. Bruce Schneier, a renowned cybersecurity expert and author of *A Hacker's Mind*, says that hacking seizes on loopholes in the rules "to force the system to behave in a way it shouldn't, in order to do something it shouldn't be able to do"—and so gain an advantage from that maneuvering. Schneier points out that society's hackers are often wealthy and connected. "A hacker is more likely to be working for a hedge fund, finding a loophole in financial regulations that lets her siphon extra profits out of the system," he writes. "Hacking is how the rich and powerful subvert the rules to increase both their wealth and power. They work to find novel hacks, and also to make sure their hacks remain so they can continue to profit from them."[6]

Wealthy people hack college, too. Just consider the role of private admissions counselors, who use their background in college administration and personal relationships with enrollment officers to help high schoolers game standardized tests or craft the perfect college essay. Think of the power of legacy admissions, or the promise of family donations, or the advantages of high-cost resume fodder, like intensive summer academic programs connected to elite universities or service-learning opportunities abroad. Once in college, wealthy students can fall back on their parents' connections and basic knowledge of the higher education game to line up internships and get advice on majors. In desperate cases, when they get in trouble or find that they're on the verge of failing out, they can ask a parent to intervene with a meeting with a college administrator.

Hacking is also an effective tool for changing societal structures for the better, particularly for a system as hidebound as higher education, Schneier says: "It's one of the ways systems can evolve and improve. It's how society advances. Or, more specifically, it's how people advance society without having to completely destroy what came before." Students like Kaylan, Tony, and Monique can succeed in college and achieve lofty goals, despite various disadvantages, if they have people teaching them how to hack higher education.

Kaylan typifies that first-generation student who isn't particularly academically gifted but has a strong work ethic that helped her earn good grades and succeed in her part-time cashier job at Target. The daughter of a career military man, she was raised in a lower-middle-class community in the Chicago Southlands. Her high school was a study in contradictions: it offered Advanced Placement and boasted a 92 percent graduation rate, but it passed students through—only 21 percent were proficient in reading and only 13 percent proficient in math at graduation. Kaylan was one of about 30 percent of the students who took advantage of a dual-enrollment program with a local two-year institution of higher education.

Initially, Kaylan hadn't planned to go to college. She thought that if she worked hard in high school, she could graduate, secure a decent job that didn't require a degree, and move up the career ladder from there. Believing college would give Kaylan more opportunities in life, her parents pushed her to apply to the University of Mississippi, the flagship university of the state they were both from, and to pursue pharmacy, simply because it was one of the few professional roles they could see in their community. Since her parents had no experience with college and her high school was of little help, Kaylan was on her own to navigate the college game—picking up pamphlets and watching YouTube videos on how to fill out financial-aid forms, take standardized tests, and apply to Ole Miss. The university accepted her, despite an ACT score that fell below the 25 percent threshold for admission.

Because she had college credits from dual enrollment in high school, she was allowed to skip orientation; but as a first-generation student lacking college literacy, she had no idea how to buy books or navigate the college environment. She picked chemistry as her major, guessing that it might have some relevance to the work in pharmacies, and she found herself one of the few African American students in the classes. Soon, the rigors of the sciences, her lacking a sense of belonging, and her father's loss of his job made her lonely for home, and she dropped out after her second semester to help the family save money. It was a fate that predictive analytics might have anticipated.

Kaylan drifted for a while back home in Chicago, working again as a cashier at Target, before her aunt suggested that she take another shot at pharmacy at Governors State University. Kaylan was tracked into a biology major with a full slate of STEM courses for the fall semester, including precalculus, chemistry, and a biology course, along with a couple of general-education courses. It would be a daunting schedule for any student, but it was particularly intimidating for someone who had been out of college for more than a year, had already struggled in the sciences, and now had to work to cover her expenses.

Kaylan was understandably worried about her chances of getting through the semester. She went to the Student Success Commons to ask for help and was referred to the Center for the Junior Year, where Kaylan started to learn how to hack the college system and take agency in her undergraduate experience.

When Higher Education Benefits from a Hack

Higher-education institutions like to broadcast their commitment to student success. In reality, though, colleges set up all kinds of barriers with their rules, procedures, and traditions—barriers that persist because of bureaucratic inertia and institutional self-interest. Just think of the lack of transparency around college costs: the difference between sticker price and discounting, the fees that hide in the paperwork, or the rules that require students to live on campuses where, perhaps not coincidentally, room-and-board revenue also happens to be a significant income stream for the institution.

Or consider the many ways that transfer students get snagged on bureaucratic processes and institutional culture when transitioning between colleges. If a student starts at a community college, completes thirty credit hours, then transfers before earning an associate's degree, that student would not count as completing a degree according to metrics of the US Department of Education, in a policy that disincentivizes helping students transfer early, even when those students might benefit by staying in sequence with the timing of course offerings at the four-year college. Transferring students also often encounter discrepancies in common course names and numbers, which may block those students from transferring credits earned at community college into a major, forcing them to take more upper-division courses at the new institution. That situation persists, in part, because academic departments get financial support based on the number of students they enroll in upper-division courses.[7]

Experts note that the best approach to transferring would start at the beginning of a student's college journey and design an undergraduate curriculum backwards from that student's end goal—ideally with the help of "success coaches" who have an understanding of the hidden job market and its relationship to the college curriculum. That's not, however, the interaction that community-college students typically have. Instead, conversations with transfer students tend to start in the second year and focus on procedures at the two-year institution (like completing pathway requirements) before processing the student for the handoff to the next institution. "The hot thing is to develop these success coaches," says Janet Marling, executive director of the National Institute for the Study of Transfer Students at the University of North Georgia, "but we're not equipping the success coaches with the right information to have those meaningful conversations with the students."[8]

Usually transfer students from underserved backgrounds don't possess the social and cultural capital to push for a personalized approach, either. "When you're working with community college students, so many of them are just thrilled to be in college, and they can't get any further than that—to think about a time horizon that's four years away feels very overwhelming and impractical," says Marling. "Too often when you're looking at first-generation students, low-income students, students of color . . . they're not culturally encouraged to buck any system, especially a system they do not understand."

Most of the time, the procedures and regulations at institutions are neutral, neither working for nor against students; they are simply there. They become problematic when staff members at an institution follow them unthinkingly, simply because following institutional rules and guidelines is an easy way of doing business within an institution. Think for a moment: As we have said already, there is no required major for medical school, and any number of ways can lead to medical school based on a student's strengths and interests. But when students who want to go to medical school are routinely directed to the premed advisor housed in the life sciences, is it any wonder why biology becomes the standard premed major?

For students to think outside disciplinary boxes and set pathways—for them to consider hacking college—they need someone who can teach them to ask questions that will help them discover the details, rules, and possibilities in the system and figure out how to shape those elements to reach their goals. Like any good tax accountant who helps a client find the hidden deductions, an advisor or mentor has to understand the granularity of college procedures and ask the questions that get students to work the system.

Here's a common scenario: A student has to drop a course to accommodate a shifting work schedule, thus falling below full-time status. That student gets a frightening automated message from the financial-aid office: *Our records show you are not making "satisfactory academic progress" under US Department of Education regulations, which may affect your financial aid.* Anyone who understands the rules of satisfactory academic progress knows, though, that the regulations offer wiggle room and that students can always appeal—but it helps if they have coaching. Students can work in concert with financial aid and advising to hammer out course scheduling over the span of a year (including summer sessions) to reduce their academic load, remain within the rules, and find a balance with life issues. (Proactive mentors would even help a student anticipate the need to make some of these plans and maneuvers ahead of time.)

Even when navigating an academic program full-time, students can learn hacks to serve their academic needs, while playing to their financial limitations and harried schedules. For example, instead of declaring a minor, which can add unnecessary requirements, students could be taught to use the blank spaces to create course clusters in the skill and content areas they need. First-generation students could be coached more frequently on how to strategically use standard academic policies—like using pass/fail options for electives distant from a student's area of study, giving that student exposure to critical skills without risking their grade point average.

The very notion of creating an independent-study course seems complicated to first-generation students (if they even know it's possible), but with good coaching, the process is pretty straightforward: Teach a student to identify faculty members as field-of-study specialists; those faculty members could be at another institution. Coach that student on how to connect their hidden intellectualism with a faculty member's research focus, creating a conversation where "passion meets passion." If the faculty member agrees to supervise the research project, the student then needs to submit a course proposal to the department for approval. In many instances, students can get templates for those proposals from academic departments, making coaching a student through that process even easier.

Students arriving on campus with college literacy and a wealth of social and cultural capital may already know how to negotiate the system—or simply may know that bending the rules is possible. First-generation, low-income students can pull off similar hacks if they find people who help them discover the levers in the system and pull them in making informed choices.

Initially, Kaylan wasn't so lucky. When she enrolled again in college and mentioned an interest in pharmacy to the admissions office, she was tracked into the standard pathway: biology, regardless of whether that major fit her particular strengths or interests, primarily because the university's premed advisor at the time was a faculty member in the biology department.

Imagine what could have happened to Kaylan if she had continued down this road, never being challenged to question the conventional route to pharmacy school. The science and math courses in the fall semester would have overwhelmed her, and odds are that her grades would have suffered. If she got anything less than a B in those courses, that would have knocked her out of the running for pharmacy graduate programs, which require a high grade point average, especially in STEM courses. In the worst-case scenario, Kaylan might have decided she couldn't handle college altogether and then dropped out of Governors State to return to a low-level retail job.

Kaylan's Hack

Instead, something else happened. When Kaylan came to the Center for the Junior Year, the peer mentor she met with asked her a question she didn't anticipate—one of those questions in the Field of Study approach that shakes up a student's preconceived notions of the work world they hope to enter: *We have no idea what pharmacists actually do. Do you?* To get a clearer picture, Kaylan started a research investigative inquiry that drove her hack.

Her first step was to talk to pharmacists in the working world. The pharmacists at her own Target store wouldn't give her time for a research interview, so a peer mentor suggested that Kaylan reach out to half a dozen other big-chain pharmacies in her neighborhood, which yielded three interviews. The mentors at the center helped Kaylan come up with a set of interview questions that focused on the problems pharmacists face when dealing with low-income populations, such as the high cost of medicine and the complications of insurance policies—all areas that interested Kaylan. The mentors helped her practice for the interviews.

Kaylan's conversations with the pharmacists provided some unexpected information: They told her that the industry is evolving, as pharmacies are becoming more like mini-clinics and the profession is leaning toward a public-health role. A biology major would not introduce her to the public-health issues that pharmacists deal with every day, they said. This was a crucial piece of information that contradicted what she was hearing from the university's advisors. She needed skills that would come from programs in public health, intercultural communication, and the social sciences.

When Kaylan asked about the importance of hands-on experience, her contact at a CVS Pharmacy told her about that corporation's program to recruit and train pharmacy technicians. Kaylan immediately expressed interest in that program, and the pharmacist, seeing her drive and commitment, offered her a position right there in the interview. This opportunity changed Kaylan's situation completely. Now her job to cover the costs of college would also be her experiential-learning opportunity.

After she brought this information back to her mentors at Governors State, her next step was to research the prerequisites for pharmacy school. She would need various science and math courses, she learned, but she did not need to be a biology major. In fact, most of the pharmacy programs she researched required only nine science and math courses outside the standard general-education requirements—in other words, only about a quarter of the courses the typical student takes in an undergraduate program. She could spread those STEM courses over the course of her undergraduate career so that she never had to face a killer semester like the one she had originally lined up for fall.

Working with the peer mentors, she began to learn how to use the blank spaces to redesign her college plan. She dropped the biology major and enrolled in Governors State's program of interdisciplinary studies, where she plotted out semester course schedules. She would never have more than two science or math courses per semester, and she could plan tutoring support ahead of those semesters. She filled in the blank spaces with courses in public health, economics, psychology, and health administration, all selected to develop the skill sets that the pharmacists emphasized were important in her research interviews.

For Kaylan, hacking college started to generate its own momentum, yielding unexpected opportunities, ones she never would have known about had she followed the conventional path. Her network of professors in her community-health courses knew of her work at CVS and told her about a collaborative summer research program, between Governors State and the University of Illinois at Chicago's medical school, to study health-care disparities in the Chicago Southlands, specifically focused on breast-cancer awareness among low-income women of color. Everyone in Kaylan's professional network encouraged her to apply, and she was accepted on the strength of her work at CVS with underserved populations. Working with faculty from UIC Medical School during her senior year, Kaylan submitted a proposal and presented her research on Black women and cancer screening at the New England Science Symposium, hosted by Harvard Medical School.

"It was all so surreal," Kaylan says, reflecting on her hack of her undergraduate education. There she was, rubbing elbows with students and faculty at Harvard. "At that point, I gained the confidence to do whatever I put my mind to and work hard for."[9]

Tony's Hack

There is more to a successful undergraduate career than picking the right courses. Embedded in the transfer game, for instance, are administrative processes that can either be hidden opportunities or procedural pitfalls. For first-generation and low-income students, avoiding the pitfalls is challenging enough, because they aren't always found among the usual problems with transferring credits and financial aid. Sometimes avoiding a procedural pitfall requires students to pause and reconsider a planned pathway or a timeline imposed by their college, which may regard its statistics for degree completion more than it considers the life circumstances of its students. Many low-income college students perform a high-wire act in balancing their academic and extramural lives, and they need to design a plan that gives themselves the best chances to succeed.

This was Tony's situation when he arrived at the Center for the Junior Year at Governors State; he was eager to finally transfer to a four-year institution and get on with his college journey. If he had rushed his transfer, however, he would have dashed his dreams and missed out on crucial opportunities that would set him up for success in the future.

Tony was driven and smart, and he would be a dream recruit for many colleges and universities. In high school he had enrolled in the honors program, taking honors courses in English, biology, mathematics, and chemistry, and he carried a weighted grade point average of 4.0. He aspired to go to medical school.

But he came with a major limitation. He had been born in Mexico and was undocumented. His high-school counselor saw his potential and helped him enroll in honors courses, but after she learned of his citizenship status, all she could talk about were the barriers he faced. He would get no financial aid and might not even get in-state tuition, she warned. "I kind of lost hope," Tony says. "I didn't feel like I tried as hard as I should have in my senior year."

He started out at Joliet Junior College, in Illinois, where his part-time jobs could cover tuition. Looking for help, he met with an advisor who merely reviewed the basic requirements Tony would need to graduate but did not refer him to the honors program (even given his excellent high school grades) or to any sources of financial help. "They just said, 'OK, look into scholarships and just find my own way,'" Tony says.

He believed a biology major would get him into medical school and plotted his schedule with the courses he thought he needed for the major. He wanted to get through the two-year program as fast as possible, to move on to the upper division, but it was a grind balancing his work hours with study time. He would get up in the morning, go to class for most of the day, then go to one of his menial jobs for the afternoon and much of the evening, then later cram in his studies. Under this workload, his grades in chemistry suffered. Feeling pressure to finish his associate's degree and get on with his life, he figured he would graduate from Joliet Junior College and retake chemistry at a four-year institution to raise his GPA.

In the middle of the spring semester of his last year at Joliet, he attended an admissions event at Governors State University and told the staff there about his intent to major in biology for premed. Since there was no premed advisor at Governors State at the time, the staff sent Tony to the Center for the Junior Year to talk about his interests and to figure it out.

There, Tony started learning how to hack the college game. When he walked in, the center staff talked with him about his goals and asked to look at his transcript. Those poor grades in chemistry stood out—and would prove to be yet another barrier to medical school for Tony. If he transferred to Governors State, the center staff explained, he would slam into a procedural barrier: Joliet Junior College would lock up his entire transcript, including his grades in chemistry. Retaking chemistry at Governors State would not replace those grades; instead, the grades from the two institutions would be averaged, and the grades for all the courses, good and bad, would show up on his medical-school applications. This could kill his chances of getting in.

Talking with Tony, the center found out that he didn't know about Joliet Junior College's honors program, which could provide resources that would benefit his applications to medical school. The center also learned that Tony didn't know that he should be looking for experiential-learning opportunities, which are a key piece of any medical-school application. His current jobs, which provided no relevant experience, would get in the way of finding one of those learning opportunities. The center staff encouraged Tony to look into Joliet's program for emergency medical technicians, which would give him all the qualifications he needed to get hired in a health field, along with a significantly higher income and invaluable experience for medical school.

Tony, still enrolled at Joliet, resisted the advice. Wouldn't this just add up to an extra year at a college he never wanted to attend in the first place? But the staff laid it out: If Tony went to medical school, he would be in school for many years to come. If one more year at Joliet could significantly raise his chances of reaching his goal, wouldn't it be worth it?

The center explained to Tony the Field of Study process and helped him devise a plan for researching his options at Joliet. First, he would meet with the registrar and ask about Joliet's course-repeat policy. Second, he would meet with staff in the EMT program to find out what it is, what it requires, and where it might lead. Third, he would visit the honors program and introduce himself.

Tony left the office and sent an email later that week to say he had set up the meetings. The center never saw Tony again.

Let's ponder what could have happened to Tony if he had continued along his college path with no intervention. His grades in chemistry might have been better at Governors State, provided that he also figured out a more forgiving work schedule. Even with his improved performance in chemistry, though, those higher grades from Governors State would be averaged with his lower grades from Joliet, which would decrease his overall GPA and weaken his medical-school application. He would also have struggled to find relevant hands-on experience that would let him write a compelling narrative for the application's personal statement. But after two years at Joliet, Tony had found no leads (and no time) for experiential learning. Despite his smarts and drive, Tony's chances for medical school would likely not look promising. He might wind up as just another student caught up in the college bureaucracy, trying to complete an undergraduate degree while spread too thin.

Fortunately, that's not how things turned out for Tony. Through three research interviews he lined up, he found ways to hack his college journey. First of all, from the registrar, Tony learned that repeating the chemistry courses at Joliet would replace the poor grades he had earned earlier, so he delayed graduation and elected to retake chemistry.

Then he met with people in the EMT program and told them he wanted to go to medical school. The program director told Tony that starting out as an EMT was one of the smartest moves he could make to raise his chances of getting in medical school. This was a nugget of information Tony wasn't expecting. He applied and was accepted to the program, which he finished while he was retaking the chemistry courses. Soon, Tony was working for a private ambulance company—a job that not only paid significantly better than the menial jobs he had held before, but it also provided front-line experience in health care and volunteer opportunities in the emergency room of a local hospital, where Tony could shadow doctors.

When Tony met with staff members in Joliet's honors program, they asked him why he took so long to find them. When Tony explained his interest in going to medical school and his plan to enroll at Governors State, staff members told him to aim higher; they outlined the relationship between Joliet's honors program and the honors program at the University of Illinois at Chicago. Tony started meeting with a staff member in the honors program twice a week, who helped him with his application to UIC and in finding scholarship money at the university.

Once enrolled at UIC, Tony worked as a bilingual tutor for microbiology courses, a job that boosted his confidence in his abilities. His professors noticed his intelligence and motivation, and they offered to write reference letters for his application to medical school. One professor took Tony under his wing, asking him to help with research on irritable bowel syndrome and crediting Tony in the resulting paper.

Tony's hack—which started with researching policies for repeating courses and seeking out some unnoticed resources—opened up a range of possibilities for him, boosted his motivation, and led to some unexpected realizations.

The most jarring realization was that he didn't want to become a doctor, after all. Tony was admitted to UIC's medical school. But during the pandemic, prior to starting his graduate program, Tony worked as a patient-care technician at Rush University hospital, where he saw intense stress put on the doctors. What's more, he noticed that the doctors would breeze in and out of the examination rooms, asking only a few questions before moving on to the next patient. It was the nurses and physician assistants who spent the most time with patients, listening to their stories and unpacking their problems. One physician assistant in particular, named Michael, called on Tony to help him with a woman who spoke only Spanish. She had lost her husband to COVID-19 a few weeks earlier, and now she was sick. Michael "was very kind, very empathetic," Tony says. He didn't just prescribe medicines but actually listened to the patient to find the root problems.

Through working with people like Michael, Tony had found his passion, his *why*: "I want to be able to interact with the patients. This is exactly why I got into health care. Talking to different types of people from diverse backgrounds was just very appealing to me."

He decided to pass on his acceptance to medical school. Using the principles of the research investigative inquiry, he contacted faculty in various physician-assistant programs, looking for the right people to study with. He is now completing a physician-assistant program at Northwestern College.

Tony's story reveals a few lessons that should inform any student-success effort. First, note that although Tony worked with the Center for the Junior Year at Governors State to retool his college plan, he never ended up matriculating at that university. Many administrators, who want to capture and hold on to students for enrollment numbers, might look askance at this outcome. But working successfully with a student doesn't always mean that the student will matriculate at your institution. That is the real student-centered approach—one that helps students get to their goal, no matter where that takes them.

Second, bailing on a college plan is not the same as giving up on a dream, particularly when that dream gets prematurely tied to an occupation that the student doesn't fully understand. Many students—especially smart, driven students like Tony—barrel through an undergraduate degree toward hazy and untested aspirations, only later to find out those aspirations weren't what they wanted after all. Through his research interviews and the experiential opportunities that came from them, Tony saw clearly what becoming a doctor was really all about, and the experience opened his eyes to other options that would provide him a better chance of realizing his dream.

Third, by showing students how to play the college game—testing ideas and finding opportunities through a research investigative inquiry—students develop lifelong skills that not only help them navigate the rest of their undergraduate education but that also show them how to navigate later moments in their life and career. Once Tony learned how to work with the college structures and to network with people who could help him line up relevant experiences, he acquired the tools that would allow him to create opportunities where none had existed. He built out his college know-how and his social capital and crafted experiential-learning opportunities that positioned him to succeed. "The ball started rolling," he says, looking back on his college experience, "and just kept rolling."

Monique's Hack

Monique was a typical community-college student. She was locked into her college choice by finances and geography, under pressure to pick something practical over a potentially risky passion. She had started out on a pathway program, figuring that it would eventually lead somewhere in the work world. Like a lot of community-college students, she was getting "point-to-point" advising: instead of looking at Monique's end goals and working backwards to help her craft an undergraduate education, her advisors focused mostly on satisfying the immediate requirements that would get Monique to the stage of transferring.

Monique came from a middling high school, is biracial and first-generation, and worked hard in high school to earn a weighted GPA above 4.0 and high ACT scores. She was driven to have a better life than her parents, who were older than average, needed some caretaking, and earned wages that put them in a lower-middle-class bracket. They didn't need Monique's financial help now, but they likely would someday. In any case, Monique was on her own in paying for college—and in figuring out the college game.

Monique's worries about taking on debt dictated all of her college choices. After high school, she enrolled at a local community college on a straightforward calculation that her Pell Grant would cover most of the tuition and fees and that the college's proximity would allow her to live at home.

She entered college with an unusual diversity of Advanced Placement credits, in English, psychology, and studio art. She loved art and thought that if she pursued graphic design, she could make a decent living in a creative field. She quickly realized, however, that she loved getting her hands dirty by drawing, painting, sculpting—a tactile type of art that isn't mediated by a computer and rendered on a screen. Looking for a path away from graphic design, she took psychology courses and found them interesting enough, so she decided to pursue psychology, since the discipline sounded vaguely like a career path.

Monique discovered that Governors State University offered a grant for students enrolled in one of its dual-degree programs, with guaranteed admission, tuition frozen at the date of enrollment, a promise of financial support until graduation, and a meeting with a transfer specialist, who would slot Monique's courses into the requirements for a major in psychology. Monique saw how the dual-degree program would expedite her clearing a number of bureaucratic and financial hurdles, and soon she found herself as a psychology major at Governors State.

Monique then went looking for a work-study job and found an opening in the Center for the Junior Year as a peer mentor, which she thought would make for good counseling experience. Monique quickly discovered this job would not ask her to be a typical mentor, focused on the emotional needs of her peers and making referrals to student-support services. Rather, the center's peer mentors learned all about the university's little-known rules and procedures, and they themselves had to go through the Field of Study process—including conducting a research investigative inquiry—as part of their training. The rationale was simple: peer mentors couldn't properly coach students with this method if they hadn't first taken on their own wicked problem in designing a personally meaningful and marketable undergraduate experience. Monique, like the other mentors, soon discovered the challenge at the heart of the process: helping someone clarify their hidden intellectualism and vocational purpose is a far cry from casually asking, "What are you interested in?"

This is where Monique started hacking her own college experience. In reflecting on her life aspirations, Monique mentioned that she wanted to continue her interests in art while she finished her degree in psychology. That led to a driving question for her research investigative inquiry: Are there people who combine art and psychology in their work? People in the center already knew the answer to that question, but Monique had to learn the answer for herself as part of the training, especially if she planned to help other students discover their own hidden intellectualism and vocational purpose.

During her research, Monique came across the website for the American Art Therapy Association, which provided contact information for association staff members as well as practicing art therapists across the country. She reached out to three therapists in the area and researched the field to come up with engaging interview questions, where passion could meet passion: Is there an advantage to using art in therapy as opposed to talk therapy? Can art therapy be used to address a broad range of afflictions, from anxiety and depression to severe trauma? Can art therapy work in group settings?

The prospect of interviewing someone intimidated Monique, who was reserved, never drawing attention to herself. She practiced making a cold call with the center's staff, getting comfortable with creating a conversation through her questions—a skill she would use later as a peer mentor. After a week of practice, she went out into the world to talk to art therapists.

Monique came back from the interviews elated. She had found people who made a good living combining studio art with psychology in art therapy, a validating and motivating discovery. She also learned that she didn't need to be an art major to be an art therapist; that eighteen hours of electives in two- and three-dimensional studio art, including painting, drawing, and ceramics, would serve as prerequisites for graduate school. Monique learned that there are many ways to use art in therapeutic settings, but she focused on two options: becoming a certified art therapist or becoming a licensed professional counselor who uses art. She could use the blank spaces in her undergraduate program to simultaneously prepare for both routes.

What's more, Monique discovered how easily she could build a network through the research investigative inquiry. All the therapists she contacted offered to help her make connections in the field, and one therapist—an adjunct faculty member who worked at Governors State's Family Development Center, a community-focused early childhood program—offered to let Monique shadow her every week.

Monique wondered if her shadowing gig could become an independent-study course. Through her mentorship training, she was learning how to hack the system by researching the rules and procedures of her own institution—yet another skill she would later share with her mentees. Creating an independent-study course, she found out, involved no more than pitching the idea to the chair of the psychology department. Because Monique's mentor in art therapy was an adjunct college instructor, the department chair agreed to let her turn the shadowing experience into a course with credit.

The capstone of her undergraduate experience was her field placement in a psychoeducational program helping veterans with posttraumatic stress disorder. She landed this placement through a referral from the adjunct instructor she had shadowed. There, she had her first opportunity to incorporate art into a group therapy session. She handed out unpainted masks to the veterans and played a clip from *The Avengers*, where Bruce Banner, haunted by the Hulk hiding inside him, reveals his secret to the team of superheroes: "I'm always angry." Monique instructed the former soldiers to paint their inner Hulk on the mask. The veterans loved how the art project helped them reflect on and express their emotions, and Monique got high praise from the program director, which sparked her interest in working with survivors of trauma.

The annual conference for the Midwestern Psychological Association was held near Chicago that year, and the center's staff told Monique that she could hack her way into the conference to network with faculty members from other colleges. By now, Monique was comfortable with making cold calls. She contacted the conference organizers, offering volunteer work in exchange for free admission, and they agreed. Between the panels and sessions, when she wasn't checking in attendees at the registration booth, Monique met with faculty and directors of various graduate counseling-psychology programs and showed them her work. All of them talked up their own program and encouraged her to apply. Following up on those connections, Monique was eventually accepted to five reputable programs in the Chicago area.

Again, however, money limited Monique's choices. She enrolled instead in the master's program in mental-health counseling at Governors State, where she could get a good scholarship and a teaching assistantship that would cover most of her costs and let her graduate without debt.

When it came time for Monique to set up another field placement, she drew on all the research and networking skills she had learned in her college career. One of her contacts told her about upcoming field-placement openings at the University of Chicago's hospital that fit her growing interest in trauma therapy. People in Monique's network knew staff members in the hospital program who sent reference letters in support of her. She landed a spot. Evidently, her work there was excellent, because the hospital hired her as a therapist in the emergency department upon graduation. Today, she is a licensed clinical professional counselor and is considering doctoral programs in the field.

Monique's hack drew on the various techniques of Field of Study, driven by the research investigative inquiry. Notice again how this process snowballs, particularly once the student has the knowledge and agency to work the system. Monique's ability to make connections and her contemplation of what she truly wanted, unhindered by her preconceived notions of a job, led to her discovery of multiple hidden job worlds: in art therapy, trauma psychology, and psychology in emergency medicine. Armed with the ability to steer conversations and connect with people, she navigated her way into once-hidden jobs that melded her talents and interests. Those abilities will continue to pay dividends in years to come, as Monique contemplates moves in her career.

What might have happened to Monique, though, had she not learned how to hack her college education? Ever limited by her finances, she could have found herself on the degree-competition treadmill. Given that students typically lack deep engagement with advisors or career services, she likely would have never had conversations that challenged her to clarify her hidden intellectualism or vocational purpose—conversations that led her to discover the connections between psychology and art. Because Governors State had no program or courses in art therapy, she would not have found the field in the course catalog, nor would she have been pushed to conduct a research investigative inquiry, where she did discover the field, met practitioners in it, and availed herself of the experiential learning they could offer.

Like many students, Monique might have just followed a standard degree map, picking courses to satisfy requirements and her natural curiosity but not moving toward the goal of creating an integrated, marketable degree. She certainly would not have had a referral that led to her capstone at the veterans program, which unlocked graduate school and the final field placement that opened the door to her first job.

In all likelihood, Monique would have been just another psych major casting around for a career direction and could have wound up working a job disconnected from her degree, like at a bank or a retail store.

As it stands, though, Monique herself can hardly believe where her college journey has taken her. We reached out to Monique and asked her if she thought she would be where she is now when she started her Field of Study. She texted back emphatically: "No fucking way!"

College Is Not Destiny

You might be tempted to categorize Kaylan, Tony, and Monique as remarkable outliers, driven students and go-getters who would have succeeded regardless of any intervention. But putting in hard work at an American college doesn't necessarily lead students to succeed, especially when they are hammering away at a system they don't understand.

In the college-to-career game, success depends not just on how hard you toil on coursework but on how you work the institutional rules and uncover opportunities. For low-income students, learning those aspects of the college game unlocks their ability to climb the social-mobility ladder. Despite their diligence, Kaylan, Tony, and Monique each hit stumbling blocks that threatened to derail their aspirations and might have ended their college careers entirely. They faltered along the ways that students are typically routed through the system. Kaylan's misstep was getting tracked into a science-heavy major; Tony's was rushing headlong through the transfer process; Monique's was declaring a major with little sense of how she could apply her degree to the work world after graduation.

Though they suffered misdirection, each of these students encountered conversations that encouraged them to stop, to examine the granularity of the work world they sought to enter, and to get outside perspectives and build relationships that would set them on a different path, circumventing the barriers in their way.

Absent those conversations, these three students would have continued to be blindered by their major and to follow one of the well-trodden pathways through their institution. They would never have seen the various resources they could take advantage of or how their interests could open opportunities and lead to professional relationships in the hidden job market.

Consider Levi, a transfer student much like Kaylan, Tony, or Monique, whom we met at the University of Illinois at Springfield in May 2023. Levi loved studio art and had taken most of his classes in art at Lincoln Land Community College. But when he transferred, he felt pressured to pick something more practical, so he majored in business—a move he saw as starting over in his undergraduate education. "I wanted to be able to provide for myself in the future and have a stable job," Levi told us. "So I thought if I had a business degree, that would open more doors in the future." But he didn't quite know what those doors were or how to look for them.

What Levi did not understand is that any degree can lead into the hidden worlds in business, just as any major can become a premed or prelaw degree. There are many different ways to put together an undergraduate program that fits a student's academic strengths and sense of purpose. No one at his community college or at the university, however, had helped Levi see these connections. Most of his experiences with advisors had been transactional, so eventually Levi stopped going to see them. "Usually, they're assigned to you based on your department or major," he said. "No one provided that strong insight for me." If the advisors were just going to talk about meeting degree requirements, Levi said, he could figure out how to do that himself.[10]

Much of the national conversation about the game of college in relation to social mobility zeroes in on admissions. It aligns with the views of Raj Chetty and others, who contend that, if we expand access to elite institutions for more students who are historically underserved and low-income, we can improve their outcomes and mend a broken social-mobility ladder. That view drives some of the hand-wringing over the Supreme Court's 2023 decision to end affirmative action in college admissions.

But a name-brand college—or, for that matter, any college—offers no assurances for a graduate's outcome, and neither does the name of a major. "Access" may be one of the buzzwords for addressing social mobility, but we have to think about access in a different way. When students matriculate at any college, they have access to resources, but that doesn't mean they have a sense of what those resources are or how they could leverage them.

The fact is that the vast majority of first-generation and low-income students will never attend an elite institution—and even if they could get in and secure ample financial aid, there's no guarantee they will find their way through the social barriers and bureaucratic hurdles of the institution to reach their aspirations. After all, even wealthy students lose their way at Harvard, Stanford, and Duke, falling back on their wealth and family connections to make sense out of the degree.

Fixing the broken ladder of social mobility must focus on the plenitude of non-elite institutions—community colleges, regional publics, and less-selective privates—that already accept low-income students in numbers that dwarf the enrollment of elite colleges. Most students are like Kaylan, Monique, or Tony, bound by financial constraints to attend an institution that's close to home, no matter how it ranks on social-mobility scales. Those institutions should teach students a process that makes *any* institution a prime launching pad for a career and a life. The conversations that happen through a Field of Study approach give us examples of what that process might look like: clarify one's hidden intellectualism and vocational purpose; find the hidden job market attached to those interests and aspirations; create a network of people within that hidden job market; and use the blank spaces to design an undergraduate plan that integrates learning across the curriculum with experiential opportunities that students themselves can create. To facilitate Field of Study, institutions should reorient their support services and resources toward clearing away the bureaucratic roadblocks.

It's not where you go to college but how you *do college* that matters. When you talk to students about how college really works, you see them light up as they realize how they can assemble the disparate pieces of their undergraduate career into something personally and professionally meaningful—and in the process, they bridge the social and cultural divides in their lives. These students will return to these techniques, again and again, as they navigate to new jobs, new careers, and new learning opportunities throughout life.

7

Visible Students and Agile Institutions

YOU'VE SEEN YOUNG PEOPLE like Diana Vega working—maybe tending bar at your favorite restaurant or folding clothes at The Gap—and wondered if they were college students paying their way through school. Or maybe you assumed those young employees had taken a run at college, couldn't hack it, and dropped out—and that explains why they're pouring your beer or taking your Visa to ring up a sweater. Or maybe you didn't think about their lives at all.

Ned had never considered Diana's background when he saw her every Saturday for several years, working the register at the Jewel-Osco grocery store two blocks from his house in Evanston. Her hair and nails were always different colors from week to week, her demeanor always friendly and attentive—until one Saturday in August 2018, when her face carried a look of frustration and exhaustion. A look that said: What the hell am I doing here?

That expression prompted Ned to start a conversation with a simple question: "So, are you a college student?"

Diana was not a college student, nor was she a college dropout. She had graduated from DePaul University with a degree in psychology, with minors in Spanish translation and Latinx studies. Ned asked Diana what her GPA was. "Three point nine," she said, as she handed Ned his receipt and bag of groceries before moving on to the next customer.

The following Saturday, Ned saw Diana at the register again. "Did you know you graduated magna cum laude?" he asked. Diana nodded. After assuring her he wasn't a stalker, Ned asked her to share her resume with him; she followed up with an email later that day. Her resume, about a page and a half long, focused on her work at Jewel-Osco, and all her references were from the grocery store. It did not list her status as magna cum laude or her other qualifications that Ned would discover in time: her certification in Spanish translation, her membership in the National Society of Collegiate Scholars, her public service working with refugee populations and community organizations, or her research experience with Latinx and immigrant families. Nor did it give a hint of what barriers she had surmounted to reach these achievements. Her parents, both Mexican immigrants, spoke little English and worked minimum-wage jobs, and Diana often helped her parents and siblings navigate the social-service system.

Back in line at the grocery store the next Saturday, Ned asked Diana why she hadn't listed magna cum laude on the resume. "Is that important?" she replied.

Over the course of the next year, Diana and Ned would continue these checkout-line conversations, five minutes at a time, as Diana learned how to make sense of her undergraduate degree retroactively and use a research investigative inquiry to open up possibilities in her hidden job market.

To graduate magna cum laude, Diana must have crushed it in her courses, earning grades that put her on the dean's list. Wouldn't at least one of her professors, or perhaps her advisor, have paused long enough, out of curiosity, to find out more about the goals and dreams of this remarkable student? Someone, at least, should have pointed Diana to the university's honors program. Yet Diana had no idea she could have joined the honors program, no idea what doors her grades would open on campus or in the workplace, no idea how to broker her undergraduate education—and she blamed herself for not knowing.

"I was sort of invisible," she says now.

The Invisible Student

It's not just Diana. Most students who walk America's college campuses are invisible. You come across these students everywhere. They get middling-to-great grades, dutifully declare majors, and sign up each semester for a full slate of courses—perhaps not understanding, or even caring, what they are signing up for, so long as they tick the boxes on their degree audit. And they move through the system smoothly, with one major drawback: they are building empty college degrees, with no plan for how to connect that degree to the life that comes after.

Organizations like the University Innovation Alliance, a collective of seventeen institutions, are set up to help colleges figure out how to solve problems like empty degrees, by providing an arena for institutions to share "best practices." But the big institutions in the alliance consistently take an administrative, top-down perspective on what it means to operationalize those best practices at scale: Use guided pathways for undeclared students. Set up four-year degree maps for majors. Mine institutional data to identify what course combinations could be troublesome. Work across the silos in the organization to coordinate student support, social-service needs, and financial assistance. Match course learning outcomes to the career competencies promoted by the National Association of Colleges and Employers. And the like.[1]

These top-down solutions didn't help Diana or the other students we've profiled in this book. Predictive analytics and early-alert systems—the software that flags struggling students—have become the focus of student-success initiatives. This software can be a great tool for capturing students who are sinking to the bottom or in danger of stopping out, but it will not help an institution identify students who don't trip its preset alarms but who nonetheless are adrift for any number of reasons. These invisible students—students like Diana—are the majority of students on campus, regardless of whether they are high-performing or just getting by.

These systemized approaches miss the crucial factors that drive real educational success: conversations and relationships. Analytics, early alerts, degree maps, and pathways merely help advising offices monitor students toward degree completion; they tend to reinforce the transactional interactions that many students experience in advising. With these technocratic mechanisms in the driver's seat, there is no discussion of how to think beyond the major, to fill in the blank spaces in a degree meaningfully, and to create experiential-learning opportunities that integrate a student's degree planning with their hidden intellectualism and vocational purpose. And these mechanisms do not illuminate what's missing or misunderstood in a student's worldview about college programs and how those programs can connect to the granularity of the hidden job market.

Either by luck or by intuition, Diana had actually taken a Field of Study approach to her undergraduate education, just without knowing it. Many of her choices in college were driven by her personal lived experience. Diana focused her major on community psychology, which appealed to her when she saw her siblings and friends dealing with the trauma of the streets and dropping out of school. She earned a minor in Spanish translation because of her experiences in helping her mother speak to doctors after she got breast cancer in 2015. She added Latinx studies to sharpen her understanding of the challenges faced by her community on the north side of Chicago. She even picked up a research-project course during her last term that focused on the mental health of immigrant bilingual high-schoolers. Her advisor, who did not know what the focus of the research was, had suggested the course only because Diana needed more credits to keep her financial aid.

All of these pieces should have easily created an integrated undergraduate experience. By now, readers of this book could probably help Diana fit the pieces together. But on her own, she couldn't. Even her advisor at DePaul, it seems, did not. As Diana put it, all her advisor told her about getting a psychology degree was that it was a flexible major. "Well, you can do so much with it," she recalls her advisor saying. "It's a lot of jobs—like, anything—you can do with it." But what jobs are those exactly? Diana had no firm idea what her options with a psychology degree were. She would scan job boards, looking for positions that asked for a psych degree, but found nothing.

After graduation, Diana turned back to the only thing she knew, which was her minimum-wage job at Jewel-Osco: "I almost felt like, 'Is it just me, or am I not really prepared to get a job that's higher than Jewel?' Did I miss something?" While her parents and siblings lavished praise on her for being the first in her family to graduate from college, Diana lived with a sense of low self-esteem. "Everybody's like, 'You did it!' And I'm like, 'Did I really do it?' Because I feel like I'm still in the same spot of feeling lost."

Making Any Institution Work for Students

Consider this: Diana went to a relatively selective university, got excellent grades, and intuitively took advantage of relevant experiential-learning opportunities. But without the crucial conversations she needed to make sense of her undergraduate degree, she wound up after graduation exactly where she had started, with no increase in her family's intergenerational social mobility. If this is happening to students like Diana, it surely is happening to many other students who manage their way through their degree audit and never set off an alarm in the system. (Given the statistics around underemployment, Diana's postgraduation job outcome wouldn't be shocking if she had been merely an average student.)[2]

It might be tempting to say that if Diana had gone to an even more exclusive university, things might have turned out differently. As we laid out in the last chapter, many have argued that enrolling more lower-income students in elite institutions will propel those needy students into high-paying jobs and prominent positions.

But amid the dissolving confidence in higher education and its outcomes, college leaders at mainstream institutions need to broadcast a different story—and back it up with results: *any institution* can be an engine of social mobility if students learn how to make that institution and its offerings work for them. Field of Study models one way to teach students how to do that. With college staff acting as Socratic interrogators, students engage in that crucial discovery process that helps them make sense of their undergraduate experience, the nature of college learning, and its relationship to a vocational purpose.

Diana's story shows how simple this can be. Ned continued to see Diana at the Jewel-Osco on Saturdays, spending only around five minutes talking each time, over the course of about a year—a commitment that adds up to about four hours. But those short conversations were enough to put Diana back on a path toward upward mobility.

Here's how she did it: She knew that she had a desire to help kids who grew up in situations similar to hers, kids who struggled with poverty, language barriers, fitting in as immigrants, and the psychological stresses that come with all of that. She wanted to help adolescents who were falling into the cracks. All she needed to do was take advantage of what she had already set up as an undergraduate.

Diana set out on a modified research investigative inquiry, focused on clarifying her vocational purpose and the career space that she wanted to fit into. The three organizations she had worked with in college had focused on different facets of helping struggling adolescents: RefugeeOne provides support for immigrants in finding apartments, jobs, education, and services from the moment they arrive in the country;[3] Centro Romero offers education and support to help immigrant families enter mainstream American society and culture;[4] and the Culture and Evidence-Based Practice Lab at DePaul University studies anxiety, depression, and other mental-health challenges among immigrant youth, particularly Latinx youth.[5] She reconnected with her former colleagues at these organizations and asked them probing questions about what had called them to their particular work in the world of immigration. Through those conversations, Diana learned about the power of her network and began to clarify her own sense of purpose.

Diana also spoke with the social worker whom she knew from her time at Evanston Township High School. To pursue work in counseling and therapy, the social worker said, Diana would have to go to graduate school, and she should investigate two paths: a master's program in counseling or a master's program in licensed clinical social work.

She identified counseling and LCSW programs in the Chicago area, compared their curricula, and researched the career paths that follow degrees in each. She discovered, as many students don't know, that both programs lead to careers in clinical therapy. She had thought social work was just case management.

In one of those checkout-line conversations, she discovered that applying to graduate school should focus on finding faculty members who align with her area of interest, not on the brand name of the college. After perusing faculty bios on departmental websites, she identified half a dozen professors whose research and hands-on work cut across immigration, adolescents, and mental health. She was worried they wouldn't bother talking to her, but in another five-minute session at Jewel-Osco, Ned told her how to lead with her honors status: "Hi, I graduated magna cum laude in psychology from DePaul University, and I would like to set up a meeting about studying with you in grad school."

Everyone replied. It was Diana's first experience in understanding how magna cum laude opened doors. She clicked with a faculty member at Loyola University Chicago and enrolled there. When she needed a field placement, she sought advice from behind the register once again and was reminded to lean into her networks and her contacts from Evanston Township, where she ultimately landed a paid position.

After graduation, she was hired at a therapeutic day school in the same school district, where she works with immigrant adolescents who have been in and out of the foster-care system, who skip school and start fights. "I mean, it's a hard population," she says. "I'm not going to lie." But she loves the work and sees it as a trial by fire in her first job in what will be a long career. Since leaving Jewel-Osco, Diana has more than doubled her salary, with benefits, and she is in the process of completing the supervisory hours she needs to sit for the certification exam that will give her a counseling license. After that, she could go into private practice and double her salary once again.

"Maybe I can go to that ten-year high-school reunion, now that I have not just a simple job," she says. Among her former classmates, "you know, there are people that didn't make it that far."

Diana's journey might seem obvious to savvy readers of this book, but it was never obvious to her. "People assume that this should be common sense, that people should know these things," she says. "But it's like a whole new thing. There are so many questions. I definitely wouldn't have made it that far if I didn't have the guidance."

Diana needed crucial conversations to make sense of her undergraduate degree. Why did they happen in the checkout line of a Jewel-Osco?

Turn Students into Orienteers

In helping students acclimate to college, institutions often use the vocabulary of wayfinding: degree maps, pathways, orientation. But as we have pointed out in this book, the methods used aren't about real orienteering at all. Institutional advising and career counseling are more often about giving students prepared trails and predetermined destinations, which may or may not be where a student wants to go on the college journey.

The true skills of orienteering involve no trails at all. You make them. Orienteers are given topographical maps and compasses, taught the meaning of the elevation contour lines and water features, and instructed to chart their own paths to destinations, while avoiding hazards along the way.

If we want our students to become orienteers, to be self-directed designers of their undergraduate experiences and of their lives, we need to redefine what we mean by orientation—to make it an opportunity for students to discover the relationship among their personal, educational, and professional goals and the breadth of the learning opportunities on their campus. Think of the wasted opportunity that orientation represents on many campuses: it typically covers the ground rules of college life (don't cheat, drink in moderation), the locations of campus offices and resources (the library, the rec center), and the campus venues where students can build a social life. After this introduction, students are moved through a perfunctory advising session, where they register for their first classes.

Karnell McConnell-Black, the vice president for student life at Reed College in Oregon and a past president of the National Orientation Directors Association, told *Inside Higher Ed* that students should not focus on career planning during orientation. Instead, they should "start thinking about their passions and their purpose, about their mental health and physical wellness, and about community norms and values."[6]

Maybe that works for high-achieving, connected undergraduates at Reed, but low-income, underrepresented students need something more. They can't make good academic decisions in a career-development vacuum, yet they are asked to make academic decisions from the moment they arrive. Orientation should be about starting students in a process of clarifying their vocational purpose and making the best use of the resources their college has to offer. Typically, though, in orientation programs there is no discussion about how to find and meet faculty sharing a student's research interests (apart from relying on a department's name), how the reputed "crosswalks" between majors and careers may be mythical, how professional aspirations are accessible by many different academic routes, and how to begin thinking all of this through.

Orientation could introduce students to the important mapmaking skills that they will use throughout their years at college and beyond. Besides encouraging students' engagement with the campus community, orientation could encourage their engagement with the academic nature of campus. Introducing students to the Field of Study concept is one way to encourage that academic engagement in a more personal way for students.

What if a college introduced the Field of Study concept in an orientation session for a randomly selected group of students, similar to the session that Amanda Beleu experienced when she arrived at Columbia College, as related in chapter 4? A college could test the impact of the presentation, comparing those students' responses to those of other students who attended more conventional orientation sessions. Would they have a different sense of the landscape of college and of how to connect their goals to the opportunities the college offers? Would they have a different view of why they want to connect to faculty and what they ought to look for in a professor's background and interests? Most important of all, would they emerge with a new, nascent perspective on how their interests could fit into the granularity of the hidden job market, a perspective that goes beyond the formula of major-equals-job?

If that trial of Field of Study at orientation is met with interest among students and their parents, a college might consider broader comparative testing that could involve an orientation-to-college course or a freshman seminar or formal academic advising.

We're not naïve, though. Colleges are bureaucratically hidebound and slow to make wholesale changes. We are not arguing that colleges should drop everything they're doing or that Field of Study is the right approach for *all* students. What we do know is that various groups of students on any campus would benefit from having a different kind of conversation about college—and these conversations can be incorporated, with little disruption, into existing services and institutional structures, and at little cost.

After all, Raj Chetty has already called for finding and testing those "value-added" processes that help launch students from non-elite institutions. We argue that Field of Study, and the research investigative inquiry that drives it, is one of those processes. Because Field of Study has a curricular structure, it could be tested in a variety of different settings and be easily assessed. Campuses can decide where the approach fits best and which students it could help most profoundly.[7]

Elements of Testing Field of Study

As you are preparing to pilot-test the Field of Study approach on your campus, you'll need to consider some questions, which we answer below. The key is to utilize existing personnel and programmatic resources on campus; this keeps costs down and demonstrates that, if the test points to success, Field of Study can be implemented and scaled up at modest cost.

Which group of students do you want to test this with? We have focused in this book on first-generation, low-income students who came to college with aspirations and a commitment to learning but with no clear sense of how to realize those aspirations through the college curriculum. They could not make out a path from their college major to a postgraduation career.

We think that testing Field of Study with students who share these traits can provide a college with insights into how better to help this population on campus. A college might have various ways of identifying this group of students. For example, a college may choose matriculating students who are likely to struggle, according to the metrics tracked by a predictive-analytics system. A test group might consist of students who qualify for Pell Grants or those who arrive at college undeclared. Given the pressure to connect careers to liberal-arts majors, a college might select students declared in the liberal arts. (We believe students in preprofessional programs benefit just as much from the Field of Study approach, but college officials might see more dramatic results from students in majors without a clear career path.)

Field of Study is essentially problem-based learning and has a curriculum. So it may be worthwhile to test it as an enrolled course with expectations and deadlines, because the process involves assignments that are much like homework. And making Field of Study into a course would ensure that students return, week after week, and report their progress toward solving an individual wicked problem: how to design their undergraduate program.

A variety of venues lend themselves to testing the method, even beyond a summer orientation. Many colleges have summer bridge programs, first-year one-credit orientation courses, or "mastering college" courses—all of which are designed to help students make sense of the college experience.

Colleges also offer, for example, first-year composition courses, where a student's wicked problem of designing an undergraduate education can become the theme of the course. The Field of Study process lends itself to the types of essays that composition courses cover: self-reflection, critical analysis, description, evaluation, and a research proposal. A student's reflective essay assignment, for example, could have them explore their hidden intellectualism and vocational purpose. A research proposal could be their proposed design for their undergraduate experience.

As another example, Field of Study could be tested in a traditional first-year seminar. A third of the course's curriculum could be devoted to the tenets of the method and team-taught with a peer mentor. Or a college could incorporate lessons on the Field of Study approach in its residential programming.

Of course, the process could also be tested in advising or career services. Pick two advisors and assign each advisor a cohort of students. One cohort would participate in advising as it is currently offered, using the standard advising syllabus; the other cohort would go through the process of Field of Study. Both advisors should be connected to their student cohort through the institution's learning management system (LMS), not a typical practice in advising. Because Field of Study follows a curriculum, the advisor could plot out the steps for students, with various activities to engage in over the course of a semester and with deadlines for completing them. Plus, the advisor and students would have more of a direct line of communication to each other, similar to what students experience with professors in their courses. The students could use the LMS to share with their peers their experiences in research interviews, the hidden jobs they have discovered, faculty they have identified by their field of study, and the procedural hacks they are using. The experiment might show an institution how an LMS could produce efficiencies in advising and how advisors can become as vital of a teacher as other instructors on campus.

The spine of the curriculum covers a dozen steps:

1. **Set up the wicked problem.** Help students see the difference between their hidden intellectualism and vocational purpose

and the downside of merely declaring a major that sounds like a job. Help them discover the need for multidisciplinarity and the opportunities in the blank spaces.
2. **Understand how to see faculty as Field of Study specialists.** Students discover the granular interests of faculty members and determine how those interests intersect with their own.
3. **Understand the hidden job market.** Students come to appreciate the granularity of the world of work and how their interests might connect to opportunities there.
4. **Find their space in the hidden job market.** This is the personalization of the process. Students work on discovering the positions that correspond to their hidden intellectualism and vocational purpose. These niches exist even in traditional corporate settings.
5. **Identify the people working in that hidden job market.** Students look for people who are doing what they could see themselves doing in the professional world. These people may become part of a student's social network.
6. **Prepare for and conduct research investigative inquiry interviews.** Students collect the inside information they need to fill out their undergraduate program, explore the possibilities for experiential learning with interviewees, and build their social network.
7. **Translate the gathered information into learning opportunities.** Students are shown that learning opportunities can exist on campus not just in the form of courses but also in student activities and jobs at the institution. Additional learning opportunities might be found in off-campus organizations, summer opportunities, or one-off courses at other institutions.
8. **Share what they learned with the group.** Students can help one another by sharing the information they have found while researching the hidden world of work. They can also share tips about what approaches worked best in their interviews.
9. **Propose a design for an undergraduate education.** Students

design their education backwards from their goal. They assemble the learning opportunities in general education, their major, and electives to plan an integrated undergraduate experience. Students should incorporate out-of-classroom and off-campus experiences as part of the design. A student's design has to go beyond merely picking a major. It has to show how the student made informed decisions in filling in the blank spaces.

10. **Devise a plan for creating experiential-learning opportunities.** A student's research interviews might have yielded leads for an experiential-learning opportunity. Students should not overlook unpaid experiences if those experiences will provide them access to insiders, skills applicable to their areas of interest, or chances to build cultural and social capital.
11. **Present their undergraduate design to peers.** Students present their design for their undergraduate education to their peers, who get to ask questions about it or make suggestions.
12. **Let the plan evolve.** A student's plan is continually tested through the research investigative inquiry and always subject to revision.

What kind of people should guide the students when testing Field of Study? We propose having two layers of people who guide students through Field of Study: supervisors from the faculty or staff and peers who come from the student body. On every campus, there are people who are already thinking along the lines of what we've laid out in this book. They come from the faculty, student affairs, advising, career development, athletics, residence life, and more. They might realize intuitively that the undergraduate degree could be more integrated, going beyond pushing students to pick a practical major, and they might already be trying to have deeper conversations with students to explore these possibilities. What they may lack are the vocabulary and framework to undertake Field of Study. Many have never considered, for example, how the blank spaces on a degree audit can become a vehicle for integrating learning across the curriculum. The staff or faculty members who trial Field of Study should ideally come from those who desire to try something new.

Training in Field of Study for faculty and staff should be grounded in the kinds of case studies that we discuss in this book. Challenge these faculty and staff members to think differently about majors and the learning opportunities across the curriculum. The case studies must provide examples that lead faculty and staff to recognize that there is no set program for prelaw or premed and that there are numerous ways to get into business that do not involve majoring in business. They need to discover for themselves how marketable a degree in fine arts or German really is—and how using the blank spaces drives much of that marketability.

Faculty and staff also need to learn to see the hidden experiential-learning opportunities both on campus and off. Part of this learning process is about seeing the granularity of the hidden job market and realizing how that granularity can open up opportunities. A useful exercise: start to build out asset maps of unusual and underutilized resources in and around campus. An asset map should include the often-overlooked talents and interests of staff members on campus.

A final preparation for testing Field of Study is to train peer advisors, those who will help fellow students through the process. As we mentioned in Monique's story, peers are trained by going through the Field of Study process themselves, while reflecting on the methods and rationale behind the various steps.

Where on campus should the conversations of Field of Study take place? New programs often occupy a spot on campus that allows easy access to students and to resources those students can use. And programs that hope to demonstrate their usefulness to the institution and generate campus-wide support need to be in a visible space.

One suitable place to house Field of Study operations would be the library or information commons. We know that various campus offices fiercely compete for space in library buildings (particularly if those buildings are new), but any office that occupies a library space should be aligned with the mission of the library. Field of Study, as a research process, fits within the library's mission as a research space and a repository of cultural capital. For a student seeking to clarify hidden intellectualism or vocational purpose, or to begin exploring the world of a hidden job market, the library is an underutilized place of discovery. Many students see the library as simply a quiet spot to study or nap, or as a social space, or the place they have to go to check out reserved material for class assignments.[8]

Situating Field of Study in the library reinforces the role of faculty, staff, and peer mentors as people who ask challenging questions, knowing they don't have the answers but directing students to those who can find answers. For example, a student like Shay might walk into a Field of Study office and express an interest in the world of spoken word and underserved youth—an aspiration that might befuddle traditionally minded career counselors and advisors. But that student, if sent to a reference librarian and databases, would find a wealth of resources that start to open up that world. Librarians can show students various ways to conduct their research.

Locating Field of Study activities within the library serves an additional logistical purpose: it reduces the chance that students will get lost along the way in carrying out Field of Study research. One of the risks for students in advising and career counseling comes after they leave an appointment. Sent away with an assignment to look into something, they may get waylaid by life's interruptions and demands and never complete the task. If housed in the library or information commons, Field of Study faculty, staff, and peer mentors can walk students over to reference librarians to immediately begin the research.

The Field of Study office itself should be a repository of incoming information, one that breaks down office walls and encourages continual conversation among the people there—because that's what makes the office a learning organization. Newspapers, magazines, public radio, information about local events and organizations—all should be circulated daily in the office and relayed among the staff and students. Anything a student or staffer sees, reads about, stumbles across at a yoga class, or overhears at a coffee shop can be useful information to open up new possibilities in the hidden job market.

What sort of assessment can test the outcomes of piloting Field

of Study? We imagine a simple pre- and post-pilot comparative assessment. An administrator in charge of undergraduate studies can confer with institutional research to identify the learning outcomes that the institution wants to see and then develop a pre-assessment and a post-assessment for those students who participate in the pilot.

Final Thoughts: Talent Development, Meaningful Degrees, Fulfilling Lives

Over the months we worked toward finishing this book, higher education seemed to be poised on a precipice. Prior to the COVID pandemic, many institutions faced unsteady finances and growing questions about their value propositions.[9] Robert M. Zemsky, a leading scholar of higher education at the University of Pennsylvania, had released a book outlining a formula to measure a college's level of financial stress.[10] One company had devised its own process for identifying colleges likely to close but decided to keep secret its list of wobbly colleges after various institutions threatened to sue.[11]

Then COVID-19 abruptly closed campuses, followed by the murder of George Floyd, the insurrection on January 6, and other social unrest that fractured the nation. This period of tumult put enormous stresses on colleges, communities, and students. Yet it also offered an opportunity for reflection and reinvention. The pandemic relief funds from the federal government briefly alleviated some of the financial pressure on many institutions. For desperate colleges, the money was mere life support. But those institutions with resources could use the moment to face changing demographic realities, fix their finances, establish partnerships, and reexamine what they offer and why.

No doubt, many students and parents, with schools and workplaces in lockdown, were also examining their lives and daily patterns and questioning the direction they were pursuing, both personally and professionally: *Do I really have to commute to the office and sit at a desk when I can do my work from anywhere? Is school for learning, or is it for day care and hoop-jumping? I hate what I am doing; do I need a change? Am I really happy with my life?*

Pandemics have a tendency to alter societies, forcing a redistribution of wealth and a jumbling of social hierarchies and values. COVID-19 illuminated fractures in how we live, work, shop, learn, and govern. What this all means for students and their relationship to college isn't entirely clear. But it is clearly changing.

Coming out of the pandemic, three salient trends in higher education emerged. The first has been a wave of closures and financial restructuring at the kinds of institutions that serve students like those featured in this book: modest private colleges and regional public universities. Among them are some colleges with recognizable names, like the College of Saint Rose. Some, it seems, used the federal relief money to delay difficult decisions—and once that money dried up, the fissures in their operations started showing.

To add to the troubles, a narrative doubting the value of college took hold in mainstream newspapers and dinner-table conversations.[12] With a shortage of workers in key industries during the pandemic and in the months that followed, employers (including some state governments) issued announcements saying that they would look past degree requirements and hire people with no college degree.[13] That policy move—along with the advocacy of organizations pushing skills-based hiring and college alternatives—reopened a national discussion about the value of the college degree, the skills it delivers (or doesn't deliver) to the workplace, and the baccalaureate as a barrier to people who have the experience and skills but don't have a diploma. Higher education's critics and political foes found yet more fodder in data showing that 45 percent of graduates are underemployed ten years later.[14]

In the private lives of students and their families, a crisis in mental health emerged, around what students believe is possible for themselves in life and how secure they feel about their future. One study from Harvard found that 56 percent of young adults struggled with financial worries and a significant share harbored "a general 'sense that things are falling apart'" in society, the environment, and politics. The authors said that the financial worries and mental-health challenges differed by gender, class, and race; rich kids struggle to maintain the trappings of achievement and high-status jobs, while poor kids "contend daily with the deprivations and degradations of poverty." Worries of some kind, however, were consistent across the board. Most striking in the Harvard study was that half of the survey's young respondents "reported that their mental health was negatively influenced by 'not knowing what to do with my life,'" and nearly 60 percent said they felt a lack of meaning, purpose, and a sense of direction. The study noted that nearly none of the respondents listed school or work as a source of meaning or purpose and that many simply felt pressure to achieve. "Disconnected from meaning," the authors wrote, "achievement is a particularly frantic, hellish hamster wheel."[15]

This vortex of criticism about higher education makes sense in the context of empty college degrees. Against the backdrop of the widening wealth gap and the relentless conversation about majors and average salaries, it's no wonder that students feel anxious over the tension between a need to feel financially secure and a desire to find a meaningful pursuit in life. Students are deeply interested in tackling the problems that ignite them, that resonate with their background, but are frightened of pursuing those interests because everyone tells them the pursuit will lead to a hand-to-mouth existence. Sadly, many are consequently pushed into something perceived as "marketable" or "in demand" but ultimately personally empty.

Those empty college degrees drive the conversation about underemployment and the value of college, too. The student who is unable to tell a story about her degree, or is unclear about its possibilities and opportunities, finds herself stuck at The Gap, or tending bar, or behind the cash register at Jewel-Osco; and if she doesn't blame herself, as Diana did, she may well blame the college "scam." The negative narrative even comes from those students who earn empty college degrees and then, by luck or family connections, stumble into decent jobs, which have little to do with the major they declared. If they don't use much from their college studies in their work, they might conclude that college is just another rubber stamp—so why pay for those years of electives and general education? If a workplace can teach you the day-to-day duties, why go to college at all?

College leaders, professors, and staff across the country have anxiously watched the growing public doubt over the value of the college degree, wondering what will become of their jobs, their institutions, and the American system of higher education.

The truth is that the American higher-education system has created these problems itself, mostly as a result of its inward focus. Colleges value research over teaching, even at institutions that claim to have a teaching mission. "Student success" initiatives, upon closer look, largely focus on processing students through degree requirements, with little regard for what makes up a quality undergraduate education. Over the years, institutions' inconsistency in leadership, jockeying with institutional peers, short shrift to advising and mentorship, and lavish capital spending on vanity projects, nonacademic frills, and high-profile but underachieving centers have only added to the sector's difficulties. Most damaging of all, many colleges have not created a coherent and integrated educational mission that brings together the various units that make up a college campus. Instead, in this pressured environment, the siloed academic departments and colleges, student-affairs offices, and other units are jockeying for the largesse of campus administration.

Let's not kid ourselves. First-generation, low-income, and underrepresented students are the ones who bear the brunt of the consequences of this flawed system, as they often enroll at second- or third-tier universities that aren't prepared to accommodate them. These institutions may not have the staff to interact with students individually, so their success initiatives appear to focus on damage control. After early-alert systems raise red flags that a major isn't working for a student, college staff tend to redirect that student to something less challenging, perhaps with lower-level career prospects. Or they create curricular "gadgets"—badges, certificates, and other add-ons—that students can paste into their transcripts to signal they are "business-ready." These badges and certificates lean on industry skill sets, such as data analytics, coding, and digital marketing, to give students *at least something* for prospective employers to latch on to, since the student can't tell a coherent story about their degree. What's more important for these institutions than a student's career prospects or personal goals is how that student contributes to the institution's graduation metrics. And for the most part, first-generation, low-income students do not even know how these underlying structures and institutional motives are influencing the trajectory of their lives.

These are the dynamics behind the dispensing of empty college degrees. Empty college degrees are what drive the national conversation about the value of higher education and the lack of skills that employers say college graduates bring to the job. And many of these institutional motives are largely about propping up the current structures and systems, at a time when institutions need to be more agile.

What if a college responded to these challenges not by launching a glitzy new initiative or by changing the direction of the institution but by changing the conversations students have? Change the conversations, by helping students locate and better utilize the resources on and around campus, and you can change the way students perceive themselves and their institutions, and how they interact with those institutions.

A college's academic agility is already found in the vast learning resources on campus, where faculty adjust their research interests to address wicked problems that cut across sectors of the work world and many aspects of our lives. In this vibrant campus learning environment, colleges can rethink how they prepare students for "industry needs" in a world where those needs are highly varied and continually evolving. The true challenges and opportunities lie in wicked problems, which demand a human touch: a multidisciplinary, synthetic approach that accounts for multiple perspectives on the issues.

The challenge for colleges is to break down the bureaucratic view of the undergraduate degree, taking off the blinders of the major and introducing students to the notion that their own interests and personal convictions exist as wicked problems waiting to be solved. This is how institutions become agile: they help students see all of these options and opportunities as a way to prepare for any field, any area of interest, and as an opening to a vast hidden job market. Those badges and certificates that colleges push on students are a gimmick; on many campuses, the learning opportunities already exist in courses. When colleges bundle courses to create badges and certificates, they demonstrate how students could create *their own* course clusters by availing themselves of the blank spaces. All Field of Study does is expand this concept across the bachelor's degree.

If students have the right conversations, they learn how blank spaces can become a vehicle to integrate their undergraduate plan. The power is not in the badges—it's in the conversations.

Conversations are the key piece of talent development and should have a critical role in higher education for the future. Find the drive and talent in individual students, and teach the students how to turn the college kaleidoscope, to customize and manipulate the undergraduate program while still fitting within the degree-requirement framework of majors.

Let's make something clear: Field of Study does not mean getting rid of the major-minor system or overhauling anything structural about the curriculum at all. It seeks to enhance the effectiveness of the system by leveraging the flexibility inherent to the blank spaces, ditching the major as the guiding principle, and teaching students to look for the relationships among learning opportunities on campus. This challenges students to engage with diverse learning possibilities and better prepares them for addressing complex problems.

The major-oriented view of the undergraduate degree is killing the humanities and the fine arts, and they aren't helped by the advocates who want to yoke them to soft human skills. "Each intersection defines a new type of job," writes George Anders in *You Can Do Anything*. "Curiosity + data science = market research. Empathy + gene sequencing = genetic counseling. Creativity + information networks = social media manager."[16] No, it's the intersections found among the *hard skills* in sociology and history combined with data science that can lead to market research. It's philosophy, psychology, and biology, maybe with some training in gene sequencing, that opens a door to genetic counseling. And as Carla showed us, it's Spanish and communications studies, combined with technical courses, that engaged her intellectual interests to seek a career in social media.

Students need to rediscover the power of a discipline as a lens on the world and start to see their professors as field-of-study specialists who can help them discover those worlds in detail. This is how faculty demonstrate to students that disciplines can accommodate any number of major-and-blank-space combinations, leading in any direction—but only if students have the conversations that teach them how to discover and assemble the pieces to play to their strengths and interests.

Zachary Stein, a Harvard-trained education futurist, would call this relationship between faculty and students an authentic version of "teacherly authority," where the student acknowledges the teacher for the wisdom, knowledge, skills, and other qualities that can help that student someday rise to the level of the teacher. Stein contrasts this with the bureaucratic form of teacherly authority, where students see their professors and other staff as gatekeepers to grades and credits, to be earned by regurgitating information they might see as irrelevant.

Stein believes education is now "in a time between worlds," when the complexity and granularity of world problems can no longer be addressed by the current approaches to education. "Do we really know what kinds of skills are needed in perpetually volatile labor markets and technology intensive workplaces? Who are we to tell future generations what to think, feel, or do with this world we are leaving them? Despite some superficial answers from corporate think tanks and academics: *twenty-first century education is an unknown entity.* It is still a future unrealized. Twenty-first century education is beyond what anyone can yet imagine, let alone implement."[17]

To us, this means that colleges shouldn't focus solely on preparing students for job slots and current industry needs but on how those students see their interests and skills in relation to the wicked problems that pervade every sector of the hidden job market. When students learn to design their undergraduate program, they can employ those same design skills to see the connections to other things. This gives them the ability to shift—the way that all the students profiled in this book shifted personally and professionally. Shifting is a developmental process, a lifelong tool that will allow these students to adapt to a fluid job market and changing life circumstances.

Nobody knows all the job slots out there. Students may hear the motto "We're preparing you for jobs that don't yet exist," but most of the world of work is already invisible to students, essentially nonexistent. Majors are not generic, and neither are jobs, and the name of a major does not offer any insight into the variety of paths that students can create if they make use of the blank spaces.

Take Diana, for instance, who graduated as a psychology major. As a label, that major fails to encapsulate her actual field of study: community psychology, focusing on the challenges faced by immigrant youth in school systems. Diana's undergraduate education was vastly different, for example, from how Monique expressed her hidden intellectualism through a psychology degree.

But Diana didn't have the social and cultural capital necessary to see the connections between her academic program, the skills it offered, and the world of her hidden job market—and she wasn't helped to see those connections, beyond being guided through the turnstiles to graduation. Until Diana learned to frame all of these pieces through a Field of Study process, not the major she graduated with, it was an empty psychology degree, with an outcome in underemployment. When she started to see how the pieces integrated with her vocational purpose and connected to a hidden job, Diana began to realize where her talents could fit, and she started to become an agile learner. Most of all, she built out these skills in a personally meaningful sector of society that needs her, one that will provide her a comfortable living.

Many students arrive at college wanting to work on civic, social, and environmental problems. For first-generation, low-income, and underrepresented students, especially, these wicked problems have been part of their lived experience. Even students in job-oriented majors bring personal convictions that drive them to use the skills of business or law to transform their neighborhoods and the lives of people like themselves. The opportunities lie in that drive.

Zachary Stein points out that technological, economic, and political developments now change so rapidly that even society's "elders" have "no idea, really, what to tell the kids about what tomorrow is going to be like." The answer, he believes, is to help younger generations "listen to the future and then give them the help that they realize that they need" to navigate the road ahead. Stein believes that educational leaders "need to re-ground education of the youth in the communities that they live [in] and in the concrete problems of those communities."[18]

The present and the future will be shaped by wicked problems—and it's not just about big global issues. It's about the wicked problems that people deal with every day, like how localities decide which books the public library should circulate or how neighborhoods get bike lanes installed on their streets. It is about how people negotiate the day-to-day dynamics that arise in any workplace or community setting they are in. These complex issues proliferate across employment and civic sectors at rates that outpace any college's efforts to build academic programs to tackle them. Wicked problems need an unconventional approach to education. Despite all the attention paid to data analytics and artificial intelligence as tools to solve industry problems, much of the real work in problem solving will continue to be done by people who can synthesize competing perspectives, work across disciplinary boundaries, ask good questions, and negotiate solutions that can flex and change. That talent development begins when a student starts designing an undergraduate education to meet her future.

ACKNOWLEDGMENTS

First of all, a big thank-you to Dan Berrett, Evan Goldstein, and Brock Read, who gave Scott space apart from his day-to-day duties at the *Chronicle of Higher Education* to write the manuscript. Thanks, too, to Jennifer Ruark, the deputy managing editor at the *Chronicle of Higher Education*, who assigned and oversaw "A Crusade against Terrible Advising," the story that kicked off this project. Greg Britton, of Johns Hopkins University Press, first suggested turning the article into a book and offered guidance along the way.

Both Dan and Jenny read early versions of this book and offered invaluable comments, critiques, and validation. We are also indebted to a number of other people in higher education who read the draft and came back with similar suggestions and support: Chuck Ambrose, a former president of Pfeiffer College, the University of Central Missouri, and Henderson State University; John Barnshaw, the managing director at STRATA9; Jonathan Brand, the president of Cornell College; Matthew Cooney, an associate professor of education and the director of the Interdisciplinary Leadership Doctoral Program in the College of Education and Human Development at Governors State University; Michael J. Lansing, a professor of history at Augsburg College in Minneapolis; Jamie Opdyke, the associate director for Learning Support Services at Linfield University; Robin Rosenthal, the former provost of Columbia College; Mark Salisbury, the cofounder and CEO of TuitionFit; Scott Smallwood, the cofounder and CEO of Open Campus; and Martin Van Der Werf, the director of editorial and education policy at Georgetown University's Center on Education and the Workforce.

Special thanks to Tom Fisher, the director of the Minnesota Design

Center and Dayton Hudson Chair in Urban Design in the College of Design at the University of Minnesota; and Teresa Spaeth, the director of strategic initiatives at the University of Minnesota, who read an early draft of the book and invited us to the university to meet with system leaders and staff to discuss how to implement Field of Study at scale.

A heartfelt offering of remembrance for the late Joyce Fields, a former professor of child and family studies, who adopted and supported the Field of Study method at Columbia College. Her mentorship helped dozens of students transform their lives.

Ned thanks Chris, his "spousal unit," as his daughters fondly call her. "She kept reminding me of what this project was for when I had my doubts and kept reminding me of what called me to this work when I wanted to quit. I thank her for walking this path with me."

Scott sends love and gratitude to Kim, who brought meals on trays on long writing days and offered a beacon of light in a dark time.

Lastly, we want to acknowledge the students who let us share their stories in this book and the scores of students over thirty-five years who trusted the Field of Study process.

NOTES

Introduction

1. Scott Carlson, "The Transfer Maze," *Chronicle of Higher Education*, August 4, 2023, https://www.chronicle.com/article/the-transfer-maze.

2. Scott Carlson, "What Gets Forgotten in the Debates about Liberal Arts," *Chronicle of Higher Education*, March 5, 2018, https://www.chronicle.com/article/what-gets-forgotten-in-debates-about-the-liberal-arts/.

3. Scott Carlson, "Graduates Are Told They Can Do Anything with Their Degrees. Is That Why They Feel Lost?," *Chronicle of Higher Education*, October 2, 2018, https://www.chronicle.com/newsletter/the-edge/2018-10-02.

4. We struggled with "Field of Study" as a name for the process we describe in the book, and a few early readers questioned the use of the term, for various reasons. Many people already use the terms "major" and "field of study" interchangeably, and some readers thought this would be confusing. We decided to keep "Field of Study" because we think it gets at the notion of something bigger than a major—an area of interest that integrates learning across the curriculum—and we failed to come up with an alternative that didn't sound inflated.

5. Aurélio Valente, Darcie Campos, Ned Laff, and Maristela Zell, "Building an Equity-Minded Pathway for Transfer Student," *A Vision for Equity* (Washington, DC: American Association of Colleges and Universities, March 22, 2018), 30, https://www.aacu.org/publication/a-vision-for-equity.

6. Scott Carlson, "A Crusade against Terrible Advising," *Chronicle of Higher Education*, August 4, 2020, https://www.chronicle.com/article/a-crusade-against-terrible-advising.

7. Gerald Graff, *Clueless in Academe: How Schooling Obscures the Life of the Mind* (New Haven, CT: Yale University Press, 2003): 211–31.

8. According to the 1983–85 catalog of undergraduate programs at the University of Illinois at Urbana-Champaign, students interested in the IPS program had to fulfill certain criteria: candidates had to prepare a proposal that included a rationale for their program of study; an explanation for how they had researched the parameters of their program (a stage that later influenced the development of what we call a "research investigative inquiry"); a drafted curricular plan that identified courses across the curriculum and illustrated how they fit together; a plan for finding an experiential-learning component; and a statement of how all

of this would integrate with their postgraduate goals. The catalog is archived digitally at https://www.ideals.illinois.edu/items/34434; see pages 258–59.

9. Pierre Bourdieu, "Forms of Capital," in *Handbook for the Sociology of Education*, ed. John Richardson (Westport, CT: Greenwood, 1985), 1–29.

Chapter 1. The Blank Spaces

1. Ember Smith, Ariel Gelrud Shiro, Christopher Pulliam, and Richard V. Reeves, "Stuck on the Ladder: Wealth Mobility Is Low and Decreases with Age," Brookings Institution, June 30, 2022, https://www.brookings.edu/articles/stuck-on-the-ladder-wealth-mobility-is-low-and-decreases-with-age/.

2. Neil Irwin, "To Understand Rising Inequality, Consider the Janitors at Two Top Companies, Then and Now," *New York Times*, September 3, 2017, https://www.nytimes.com/2017/09/03/upshot/to-understand-rising-inequality-consider-the-janitors-at-two-top-companies-then-and-now.html.

3. Rick Wartzman, "College for All Has Failed America. Can It Be Fixed?," *Capital & Main*, December 14, 2023, https://capitalandmain.com/college-for-all-has-failed-america-can-it-be-fixed.

4. "The Rising Cost of Not Going to College," Pew Research Center's Social & Demographic Trends Project, February 11, 2014, https://www.pewresearch.org/social-trends/2014/02/11/the-rising-cost-of-not-going-to-college/.

5. Andrew Hanson, Carlo Salerno, Matt Sigelman, Mels de Zeeuw, Stephen Moret, Amy Wimmer Schwarb, Brian Hendrickson, et al. *Talent Disrupted: College Graduates, Underemployment, and the Way Forward*, Burning Glass Institute and Strada Education Foundation, February 2024, https://static1.squarespace.com/static/6197797102be715f55c0e0a1/t/65fb306bc81e0c239fb4f6a9/1710960749260/Talent+Disrupted+03052024.pdf.

6. "Price-to-Earnings Premium for Four-Year College: A New Way of Measuring Return on Investment in Higher Ed," Third Way, September 28, 2023, https://www.thirdway.org/report/price-to-earnings-premium-a-new-way-of-measuring-return-on-investment-in-higher-ed.

7. Zachary Bleemer, Mukul Kumar, Aashish Mehta, Chris Muellerleile, and Christopher Newfield, *Metrics That Matter: Counting What's Really Important to College Students* (Baltimore: Johns Hopkins University Press, 2023).

8. Anthony P. Carnevale and Ban Cheah, *Five Rules of the College and Career Game*, Georgetown University Center on Education and the Workforce, 2018, https://cew.georgetown.edu/wp-content/uploads/Fiverules.pdf.

9. Jeffrey J. Selingo, *There Is Life after College: What Parents and Students Should Know about Navigating School to Prepare for the Jobs of Tomorrow* (New York: William Morrow, 2016).

10. George Anders, *You Can Do Anything: The Surprising Power of a "Useless" Liberal Arts Education* (New York: Little, Brown, 2017).

11. Gallup, "Strada-Gallup 2017 College Student Survey," Gallup.com, January, 2018, https://news.gallup.com/reports/225161/2017-strada-gallup-college-student-survey.aspx.

12. Michael T. Nietzel, "Has the Time for Three-Year College Degrees Finally Arrived?," *Forbes*, January 21, 2024, https://www.forbes.com/sites/michaeltnietzel/2024/01/02/has-the-time-for-three-year-college-degrees-finally-arrived/?sh=4c12f1ed7054; Emma Whitford, "Colleges Explore a New Three-Year Bachelor's Degree Program," *Inside Higher Ed*, November 9, 2021, https://www.insidehighered.com/news/2021/11/09/colleges-explore-new-three-year-bachelor%E2%80%99s-degree-program.

13. *Integrity in the College Curriculum: A Report to the Academic Community; the Findings and Recommendations of the Project on Redefining the Meaning and Purpose of Baccalaureate Degrees* (Washington, DC: American Association of Colleges, 1985), 2.

14. Carol Geary Schneider, "Challenge and Response: Integrity and AAC&U's Reform Initiatives, 1985-1994," *Liberal Education* 100, no. 4 (1995): 28-37.

15. Daniel F. Chambliss and Christopher George Takacs, *How College Works* (Cambridge, MA: Harvard University Press, 2018), 40-46.

16. A number of people we spoke to while writing this book—including the president of a Research I institution—seem surprised to learn that you don't have to be a biology or chemistry major to go to medical school. Geoffrey Young, a senior director at the Association of American Medical Colleges, who has served on multiple admissions committees, confirmed for us that as long as a student demonstrates an ability to handle the science courses, choice of major does not matter. "Medical schools are going to be looking for diversity, and diversity of education and experience is just as important," Young said. "Ideally, when you think about the type of physician that you would like caring for you or your loved one, you want someone who is an excellent communicator, who listens carefully, who understands the science, but also understands the context you, as a patient, come from—your home, your culture, your environment, and be willing and open to learn and listen to that perspective." Interview with Geoffrey Young, November 28, 2023.

17. Selingo, *There Is Life after College*, xi-xv.

18. Camron Hardesty bio, Poppy website, https://www.poppyflowers.com/about.

19. Jane Dunlap Sathe, "Charlottesville-Based Flower Firm Poppy, the Fastest-Growing Florist in the Country, Closes $6.5M Funding Round," *Daily Progress*, December 26, 2023; Elana Lyn Gross, "How to Turn Your Side Hustle into Your Dream Job," *Forbes*, July 28, 2018, https://www.forbes.com/sites/elanagross/2017/02/10/how-to-turn-your-side-hustle-into-your-dream-job/; Christine Hall, "Poppy Says 'I Do' to New Capital for Digital Booking, Fulfillment of Wedding Flowers," TechCrunch, December 6, 2023, https://techcrunch.com/2023/12/06/poppy-digital-booking-wedding-flowers/.

20. Leo M. Lambert, "The Importance of Helping Students Find a Mentor in College," Gallup.com blog, November 29, 2018, https://news.gallup.com/opinion/gallup/245048/importance-helping-students-find-mentors-college.aspx.

21. Richard J. Light, *Making the Most of College: Students Speak Their Minds* (Cambridge, MA: Harvard University Press, 2004), 81-91.

22. Gerald Graff, *Clueless in Academe: How Schooling Obscures the Life of the Mind* (New Haven, CT: Yale University Press, 2003), 27.

23. *The 2014 Gallup-Purdue Index Report*, Gallup, December, 30, 2019, https://www.gallup.com/services/176768/2014-gallup-purdue-index-report.aspx. Similar findings came out of the National Alumni Career Mobility Survey, which notes that students who had significant career mobility and success after graduation said that their institutions helped them to understand career opportunities, create a career plan, and make professional connections. Lightcast, *National Alumni Career Mobility Annual Report*, 2023, https://www.datocms-assets.com/62658/1698163616-nacm-annual-report-2023.pdf.

Chapter 2. The Curricular Maze

1. Ned Laff, "Revisiting Guided Pathways" (presentation, Thrive Chicago, Chicago, IL, July, 2017).

2. Mike Peel, "The Rise of the Modern Disciplines and Interdisciplinarity," chap. 2 in *Introduction to Interdisciplinary Studies*, 2nd ed., ed. Allen F. Repko, Rick Szostak, and Michelle Phillips Buchberger (Los Angeles: Sage, 2020), 26–55.

3. In a handout to students, for example, the Santa Barbara City College Transfer Center says that declaring a major early "can help you graduate in 4 years" and that "choosing a major takes the guesswork out of choosing what courses to take." https://www.sbcc.edu/transfercenter/files/AdvantagesofDeclaringaMajorasEarlyasPossible.pdf.

4. Carl Straumsheim, "Decision Time," *Inside Higher Ed*, August 23, 2016, https://www.insidehighered.com/news/2016/08/24/study-finds-students-benefit-waiting-declare-major; David B. Spite, "Simply Declaring a Major Equals Timely Graduation Right?," Voices of the Global Community (blog), National Academic Advising Association, February 19, 2013, https://nacada.ksu.edu/Resources/Academic-Advising-Today/View-Articles/Simply-Declaring-a-Major-Early-Equals-Timely-Graduation-Right.aspx.

5. College Board, *Book of Majors 2018* (New York: College Board, 2017).

6. "T-Shaped Professional," Collegiate Employment Research Institute, Michigan State University," n.d., https://ceri.msu.edu/publication-collection/t-shaped-professional.html.

7. Ned Laff first presented "The Myth of the Academic Major" at the National Conference on the First Year Experience, Columbia, SC, in fall 1986.

8. Thomas R. Bailey, Shanna Smith Jaggers, and Davis Jenkins, *Redesigning America's Community Colleges: A Clearer Path to Student Success* (Cambridge, MA: Harvard University Press, 2015), 15–60.

9. Bailey, Jaggers, and Jenkins, *Redesigning America's Community Colleges*, 22.

10. Bailey, Jaggers, and Jenkins, *Redesigning America's Community Colleges*, 68–69.

11. Skyline College, "Interest Areas," https://skylinecollege.edu/interestareas/.

12. Connecticut State Community College, Naugatuck Valley, "Areas of Study," https://nv.edu/academics/academic-programs/areas-of-study.

13. Skyline College, Arts, Languages & Communication, https://skylinecollege.edu/interestareas/artlanguageandcommunication.php.

14. "What Is Guided Pathways—And Why Are We Still Talking about It?," EAB blog, April 24, 2019, https://eab.com/resources/blog/community-college-blog/what-is-guided-pathways-and-why-are-we-still-talking-about-it/.

15. Davis Jenkins, Hana Lahr, and Amy Mazzariello, *How to Achieve More Equitable Community College Student Outcomes: Lessons from Six Years of CCRC Research on Guided Pathways*, Community College Research Center, September 2021, pp. 2–3, https://ccrc.tc.columbia.edu/media/k2/attachments/equitable-community-college-student-outcomes-guided-pathways.pdf.

16. Jenkins, Lahr, and Mazzariello, *How to Achieve More Equitable Community College Student Outcomes*, 3.

17. Berkeley Career Engagement, https://career.berkeley.edu/start-exploring/informational-interviews/questions/.

18. Berkeley Career Engagement, https://career.berkeley.edu/start-exploring/informational-interviews/.

19. Bailey, Jenkins, and Jenkins, *Redesigning America's Community Colleges*, 182–84.

20. See examples of advising syllabi: Kansas State University, https://engg.k-state.edu/docs/asc/academic_advising_syllabus.pdf; University of California at San Diego, https://warren.ucsd.edu/academics/PDF--NFRS-Advising-Syllabus-2022.pdf; University of Louisville, https://louisville.edu/education/undergrad-advising-student-development/files/advising-syllabus.pdf.

21. Median salary in Maryland, $50,272, ZipRecruiter, https://www.ziprecruiter.com/Salaries/Academic-Advisor-Salary--in-Maryland; average advisor salary, $53,677, Salary.com, https://www.salary.com/research/salary/benchmark/academic-advisor-salary.

22. "Why Are Academic Advisors Leaving the Field?," Reddit post, October 11, 2022, https://www.reddit.com/r/studentaffairs/comments/y102c9/why_are_academic_advisors_leaving_the_field/; "Student Affairs salary makes me doubt staying long-term," Reddit post, June 12, 2023, https://www.reddit.com/r/studentaffairs/comments/147nug0/student_affairs_salary_makes_me_doubt_staying/.

23. Scott Carlson, "Tenure's Broken Promise," *Chronicle of Higher Education*, March 11, 2021, https://www.chronicle.com/article/tenures-broken-promise.

24. John T. McGreevy, "The Great Disappearing Teaching Load," *Chronicle of Higher Education*, February 3, 2019, https://www.chronicle.com/article/the-great-disappearing-teaching-load/.

25. Zac Auter and Stephanie Marken, "Professors Provide Most Valued Career Advice to Grads," Gallup, November 16, 2018, https://news.gallup.com/poll/244811/professors-provide-valued-career-advice-grads.aspx.

26. What Can I Do with This Major, University of Tennessee at Knoxville, 2023, https://whatcanidowiththismajor.com/about/.

Chapter 3. The Wicked Problem

1. Shelby Bowers, "South Carolina's Corridor of Shame," April 19, 2021, https://storymaps.arcgis.com/stories/a57474f36c7144b3a42932a4e37abd6c.

2. Horst Rittel and Melvin Webber, "Dilemmas in a General Theory of Planning," *Policy Sciences* 4, no. 2 (June 1973): 155–69, https://www.sympoetic.net/Managing_Complexity/complexity_files/1973%20Rittel%20and%20Webber%20Wicked%20Problems.pdf.

3. Mark C. Taylor, "Opinion | End the University as We Know It," *New York Times*, April 27, 2009, https://www.nytimes.com/2009/04/27/opinion/27taylor.html.

4. Scott Carlson, "How the Coronavirus Tests Higher Ed's Disciplinary Fault Lines," *Chronicle of Higher Education*, March 24, 2020, https://www.chronicle.com/article/how-the-coronavirus-tests-higher-eds-disciplinary-fault-lines/.

5. "Columbia | Year of Water," Columbia University, https://yearofwater.columbia.edu/.

6. Scott Carlson, "A Tiny College Nurtures Big Ideas," *Chronicle of Higher Education*, October 29, 2012, https://www.chronicle.com/article/a-tiny-college-nurtures-big-ideas/.

7. "Cluster Hiring Initiative," Office of the Provost, University of Wisconsin at Madison, https://facstaff.provost.wisc.edu/cluster-hiring-initiative/.

8. "Integrative Learning and Signature Work," American Association of Colleges and Universities, https://www.aacu.org/office-of-global-citizenship-for-campus-community-and-careers/integrative-learning.

9. Julia Lang and Dustin Liu, "The Case for ChatGPT as the Ultimate Educator's Toolkit," eSchool News, December 11, 2023, https://www.eschoolnews.com/digital-learning/2023/09/20/generative-ai-tools-educators/.

10. "Career Quiz," of the College Board, BigFuture, https://bigfuture.collegeboard.org/career-search/career-quiz; Texas Career Check, https://texascareercheck.com/.

11. Rooted and Radical, https://youngchicagoauthors.org/rnr.

12. MAPP career assessment, https://www.assessment.com.

13. William G. Perry Jr., *Forms of Intellectual and Ethical Development in the College Years: A Scheme* (New York: Holt, Reinhart, and Winston, 1970), 56.

14. Split This Rock, https://www.splitthisrock.org.

Chapter 4. The Hidden Job Market

1. Donald Asher, *Cracking the Hidden Job Market: How to Find Opportunity in Any Economy* (Berkeley, CA: Ten Speed Press, 2011).

2. Positions confirmed with staff and human resources at the Walters Art Museum, https://thewalters.org.

3. "Ralph Rinzler: Bluegrass Music Hall of Fame & Museum," Bluegrass Music Hall of Fame & Museum, December 30, 2019, https://www.bluegrasshall.org/inductees/ralph-rinzler/.

4. Beth Akers, *Making College Pay: An Economist Explains How to Make a Smart Bet on Higher Education* (New York: Currency, 2021), 70.

5. Akers, *Making College Pay*, 61.

6. Akers, *Making College Pay*, 70.

7. Akers, *Making College Pay*, 61.

8. Akers, *Making College Pay*, ix–x.

9. Akers, *Making College Pay*, x–xi.

10. Email exchanges between the authors and Beth Akers, January 17 and 30, 2023.

11. Anthony Jack, *The Privileged Poor: How Elite Colleges Are Failing Disadvantaged Students* (Cambridge, MA: Harvard University Press, 2019).

12. NameLab, https://www.namelab.com.

13. John Rampton, "Mark Cuban Says 'Follow Your Passion' Is the Worst Career Advice You Can Get. Here's Why," *Entrepreneur*, March 16, 2023, https://www.entrepreneur.com/living/mark-cuban-says-follow-your-passion-is-the-worst-career/447293.

14. Cal Newport, *So Good They Can't Ignore You: Why Skills Trump Passion in the Quest for Work You Love* (New York: Hachette Book Group, 2012).

15. Julia Korn, "'Follow Your Passion' Is the Worst Career Advice—Here's Why," *Forbes*, November 9, 2022, https://www.forbes.com/sites/juliawuench/2021/05/19/follow-your-passion-is-the-worst-career-advice-heres-why/?sh=695e2e6622d4.

16. Newport, *So Good They Can't Ignore You*, 32.

17. Scott Galloway, *The Algebra of Happiness: Notes on the Pursuit of Success, Love, and Meaning* (New York: Portfolio, 2019); "Professor Scott Galloway: Why Following Your Passion Is Only for the Rich + What to Do Instead," YouTube, August 1, 2023, https://www.youtube.com/watch?v=3EsJhjBm6g8; video-recorded episode of *Habits and Hustle*, a podcast hosted by Jennifer Cohen.

18. Galloway, *Algebra of Happiness*, 37.

19. Jennifer Cohen, *Bigger, Bolder, Better: Live the Life You Want, Not the Life You Get* (New York: Hachette Books, 2022).

20. Jennifer Cohen, "The Secret to Getting Anything You Want in Life," TEDx Talks, November 21, 2019, posted on YouTube, https://www.youtube.com/watch?v=wM82hE6oimw.

21. Cohen, "Secret to Getting Anything You Want in Life."

Chapter 5. The Liberal Arts and Field of Study

1. Vacation Rental World Summit, "VRWS 2022 Agenda," September 15, 2022, https://vacationrentalworldsummit.com/agenda-2022/.

2. Natalia Lusin, Terri Peterson, Christine Sulewski, and Rizwana Zafer, *Enrollments in Languages Other Than English in US Institutions of Higher Education, Fall 2021*, Modern Language Association, 2023, https://www.mla.org/content/download/191324/file/Enrollments-in-Languages-Other-Than-English-in-US-Institutions-of-Higher-Education-Fall-2021.pdf; Ryan Quinn, "Foreign Language Enrollment Sees Steepest Decline on Record," *Inside Higher Ed*, November 16, 2023,

https://www.insidehighered.com/news/faculty-issues/curriculum/2023/11/16/foreign-language-enrollment-sees-steepest-decline-record.

3. Anemona Hartocollis, "Can Humanities Survive the Budget Cuts?," *New York Times*, November 3, 2023, https://www.nytimes.com/2023/11/03/us/liberal-arts-college-degree-humanities.html.

4. *Robot-Ready: Human+ Skills for the Future of Work*, Strada Education Foundation, November 13, 2018, https://stradaeducation.org/press-release/robot-ready-labor-market-analysis-finds-human-skills-in-high-demand/.

5. George Anders, *You Can Do Anything: The Surprising Power of a "Useless" Liberal Arts Education* (New York: Little, Brown, 2017).

6. Interview with Kathleen Duffy, July 14, 2022.

7. Sanford J. Ungar, "7 Major Misperceptions about the Liberal Arts," *Chronicle of Higher Education*, February 28, 2010, https://www.chronicle.com/article/7-major-misperceptions-about-the-liberal-arts/.

8. "From Physics to Finance," California Institute of Technology, February 15, 2018, https://www.caltech.edu/about/news/physics-finance-81407.

9. Interview with Thomas Luke, December 5, 2023.

10. Christina Tkacik, "Maryland's Goucher College Is Eliminating Several Majors, Including Math," *Washington Post*, August 16, 2018, https://www.washingtonpost.com/local/education/marylands-goucher-college-is-eliminating-several-majors-including-math/2018/08/16/31c62228-a173-11e8-8e87-c869fe70a721_story.html; Colleen Flaherty, "Cuts to Liberal Arts at Goucher," *Inside Higher Ed*, August 16, 2018, https://www.insidehighered.com/news/2018/08/17/goucher-college-says-its-eliminating-liberal-arts-programs-such-math-physics-and.

11. Hart Research Associates, *It Takes More Than a Major: Employers Priorities for College Learning and Student Success*, American Association of Colleges and Universities, April, 2013, https://www.aacu.org/research/it-takes-more-than-a-major-employer-priorities-for-college-learning-and-student-success.

12. Interview with Ashley Finley, December 1, 2022.

13. Hart Research Associates, *Fulfilling the American Dream: Liberal Education and the Future of Work*, American Association of Colleges and Universities, 2018, https://www.aacu.org/research/fulfilling-the-american-dream-liberal-education-and-the-future-of-work.

14. Ashley Finley, *How College Contributes to Workforce Success*, American Association of Colleges and Universities, 2021, https://www.aacu.org/research/how-college-contributes-to-workforce-success.

15. Scott Carlson, "A New Liberal Art," *Chronicle of Higher Education*, September 24, 2017, https://www.chronicle.com/article/a-new-liberal-art/.

16. Carlson, "New Liberal Art"; Dan Charnas, *Work Clean: The Life-Changing Power of Mise-en-Place to Organize Your Life, Work and Mind* (New York: Rodale, 2016).

17. Scott Carlson, "Why Colleges Need to Embrace the Apprenticeship," *Chronicle of Higher Education*, June 4, 2017, https://www.chronicle.com/article/why-colleges-need-to-embrace-the-apprenticeship/.

18. Finley, *How College Contributes to Work Force Success*, iv.

19. Lynn Pasquerella, *What We Value: Public Health, Social Justice, and Educating for Democracy* (Charlottesville: University of Virginia Press, 2022), 118–19.

20. John Dewey, *Experience and Education* (New York: Macmillan, 1938).

21. John Churchill, *The Problem with Rules: Essays on the Meaning and Value of Liberal Education* (Charlottesville: University of Virginia Press, 2021), 53.

22. Wendy Fischman and Howard Gardner, *The Real World of College: What Higher Education Is and What It Can Be* (Cambridge, MA: MIT Press, 2022), xii.

23. Fischman and Gardner, *Real World of College*, 67.

24. Fischman and Gardner, *Real World of College*, 296–97.

25. Susan Greenberg, "Earning Is More Important than Learning," *Inside Higher Ed*, March 7, 2022, https://www.insidehighered.com/news/2022/03/08/authors-discuss-how-higher-education-has-lost-its-way.

26. Richard A. Detweiler, *The Evidence Liberal Arts Needs: Lives of Consequence, Inquiry, and Accomplishment* (Cambridge, MA: MIT Press, 2021), 100.

27. Detweiler, *Evidence Liberal Arts Needs*, 168.

28. Detweiler, *Evidence Liberal Arts Needs*, 85.

29. Detweiler, *Evidence Liberal Arts Needs*, 214–15.

30. William G. Perry Jr., *Forms of Ethical and Intellectual Development in the College Years: A Scheme* (New York: Holt, Reinhart, and Winston, 1970), 39.

31. Perry, *Forms of Ethical and Intellectual Development*, 39, 33.

32. Perry makes a brief and commonly overlooked reference to Thomas S. Kuhn deep in his *Forms of Ethical and Intellectual Development*: "This form of revolutionary restructuring has been revealed as a characteristic of the evolution of scientific theory (Kuhn, 1962). Strangely enough we have found no explicit description of this kind of transformation as a phenomenon in human personal development" (109–10). Perry's analogy suggests that personal development is akin to the "paradigm shift" in science that Kuhn outlined in his *The Structure of Scientific Revolutions* (Chicago: University of Chicago Press, 1962). In 2005, Ned wrote about the similarities between Perry and Kuhn, arguing that the skills of academic inquiry could drive personal development. Through liberal education, students encounter "anomalies" that challenge their "personal paradigms" and foster their personal development. Part of the reason Field of Study mentors are instructed to ask students disruptive questions ("I have no idea what you mean when you say you're a business major. Can you explain it?") is to throw anomalies at students and challenge their conventional thinking about majors and marketability. See Ned Scott Laff, "Setting the Stage for Identity, Learning, and the Liberal Arts," *New Directions for Teaching and Learning* 103 (Fall 2005): 3–22.

33. Earl Shorris, "Liberal Learning: As a Weapon in the Hands of the Restless Poor," *Harper's Magazine*, September 1997, 50–59.

34. Valerie Strauss, "The Liberal Arts Are under Attack. So Why Do the Rich Want Their Children to Study Them?," *Washington Post*, May 26, 2019, https://www.washingtonpost.com/education/2019/05/26/liberal-arts-are-under-attack-so-why-do-rich-want-their-children-study-them/.

35. Jillian Berman, "Studying Humanities Is a Luxury Only Wealthy Students

Can Afford," MarketWatch, November 26, 2017, https://www.marketwatch.com/story/why-studying-humanities-is-a-luxury-only-wealthy-college-students-can-now-afford-2017-11-21.

36. Jon Robinson, "Steve Jobs, Typographer," UX Planet, December 14, 2021, https://uxplanet.org/steve-jobs-typographer-2e450a356437.

37. Don Seiden biography, http://www.donseiden.com/bio.htm.

38. Arthur Koestler, *The Act of Creation* (London: Hutchinson, 1964).

39. "Expand to the US," South Carolina Department of Commerce, https://www.sccommerce.com/international/international-business.

40. "The Top Languages to Learn for International Business," Thunderbird School of Global Management, https://thunderbird.asu.edu/thought-leadership/insights/foreign-languages-business; "The 12 Most Important Languages to Learn for Success in 2021," University of the People, February 21, 2024, https://www.uopeople.edu/blog/most-important-languages-to-learn/.

Chapter 6. The Need for Hacking

1. Raj Chetty, David J. Deming, and John Friedman, "Diversifying Society's Leaders? The Determinants and Causal Effects of Admission to Highly Selective Private Colleges," working paper 31492, National Bureau of Economic Research, July 2023, https://www.nber.org/papers/w31492.

2. Brookings Institution, "Who Gets into College and Why Does It Matter?," recorded presentation, July 26, 2023, https://www.brookings.edu/events/who-gets-into-college-and-why-does-it-matter/.

3. "Increasing Economic Diversity at Ivy League Schools Shouldn't Be That Hard," HEA Group, September, 2023, https://www.theheagroup.com/blog/ivy-league-pell.

4. Anthony Jack, *The Privileged Poor: How Elite Colleges Are Failing Disadvantaged Students* (Cambridge, MA: Harvard University Press, 2019).

5. Raj Chetty, John N. Friedman, Emmanuel Saez, Nicholas Turner, and Danny Yagan, "Mobility Report Cards: The Role of Colleges in Intergenerational Mobility," working paper 23618, National Bureau of Economic Research, July 2017, http://www.nber.org/papers/w23618.

6. Bruce Schneier, *A Hacker's Mind: How the Powerful Bend Society's Rules, and How to Bend Them Back* (New York: W. W. Norton, 2023), 1–28.

7. Scott Carlson, "The Transfer Maze," *Chronicle of Higher Education*, August 4, 2023, https://www.chronicle.com/article/the-transfer-maze.

8. Interview with Janet Marling, May 12, 2023.

9. Late in writing this book, we learned that Kaylan had decided to make yet another shift in her academic and professional identity. While in pharmacy school, Kaylan became fascinated with the practice of basic research on pharmaceuticals, and she realized she wanted to use a position in academe to help more women of color pursue STEM subjects and fields, both in high school and college. She is now in a doctoral track in biology at Purdue University.

10. Interview with Levi, May 2, 2023.

Chapter 7. Visible Students and Agile Institutions

1. *Proactive Advising: A Playbook for Higher Education Innovators*, University Innovative Alliance, n.d., https://proactiveadvising.theuia.org.

2. Andrew Hanson, Carlo Salerno, Matt Sigelman, Mels de Zeeuw, Stephen Moret, et al. *Talent Disrupted: College Graduates, Underemployment, and the Way Forward*, Burning Glass Institute and Strada Education Foundation, February 2024, https://static1.squarespace.com/static/6197797102be715f55c0e0a1/t/65fb306bc81e0c239fb4f6a9/1710960749260/Talent+Disrupted+03052024.pdf.

3. RefugeeOne, https://refugeeone.org.

4. Centro Romero, https://centroromero.org.

5. Culture and Evidence-Based Practice Lab, DePaul University, https://www.cebplab.com.

6. Colleen Flaherty, "Orientation for 'Gen P,'" *Inside Higher Ed*, September 7, 2023, https://www.insidehighered.com/news/student-success/college-experience/2023/09/07/why-colleges-are-paring-down-new-student.

7. Raj Chetty, John N. Friedman, Emmanuel Saez, Nicholas Turner, and Danny Yagan, "Mobility Report Cards: The Role of Colleges in Intergenerational Mobility," working paper 23618, National Bureau of Economic Research, July 2017, http://www.nber.org/papers/w23618.

8. Scott Carlson, "The Library of the Future," *Chronicle of Higher Education*, March 2022.

9. Scott Carlson, "The Oddsmakers of the College Death Watch," *Chronicle of Higher Education*, January 31, 2020, https://www.chronicle.com/article/the-oddsmakers-of-the-college-deathwatch/.

10. Robert M. Zemsky, Susan Shaman, and Susan Campbell Baldridge, *The College Stress Test: Tracking Institutional Futures across a Crowded Market* (Baltimore: Johns Hopkins University Press, 2020).

11. Jack Stripling, "A Doomsday List of Possible College Closures Inspired Panic and Legal Threats. That's Telling," *Chronicle of Higher Education*, November 22, 2019, https://www.chronicle.com/article/a-doomsday-list-of-possible-college-closures-inspired-panic-and-legal-threats-thats-telling/.

12. Scott Carlson, "What's Really behind the View That Higher Ed Isn't Worth It?," *Chronicle of Higher Education*, February 6, 2024. https://www.chronicle.com/article/whats-really-behind-the-view-that-higher-ed-isnt-worth-it.

13. "College Degrees No Longer Essential for Some State Jobs," GovTech, January 29, 2024, https://www.govtech.com/workforce/college-degrees-no-longer-essential-for-some-state-jobs; Andrew Smalley, "States Consider Elimination of Degree Requirements," National Council of State Legislatures, October 4, 2023, https://www.ncsl.org/education/states-consider-elimination-of-degree-requirements.

14. Hanson et al., *Talent Disrupted*.

15. Richard Weissbourd, Milena Batanova, Joseph McIntyre, and Eric Torres with Shanae Irving, Sawsan Eskander, and Kiran Bhai, *On Edge: Understanding and Preventing Young Adults' Mental Health Challenges*—Making Caring Common, Making

Caring Common Project, Harvard Graduate School of Education, October 24, 2023, https://mcc.gse.harvard.edu/reports/on-edge.

16. George Anders, *You Can Do Anything: The Surprising Power of a "Useless" Liberal Arts Education.* (New York: Little, Brown, 2017), 4.

17. Zachary Stein, *Education in a Time between Worlds: Essays on the Future of Schools, Technology, and Society* (Bright Alliance, 2019).

18. "Zak Stein—Why All Global Crises Are Crises of Education," a video-recorded episode of the podcast *Global Governance Future*, YouTube, posted July 6, 2021, https://www.youtube.com/watch?v=4yC9D1ce4xo.

INDEX

academic advising: bureaucracy and, 64-65; caseloads, 50, 64; conflict of interest in, 64; criticism of, 2, 6-7; faculty role in, 65-66; vs. Field of Study approach, 4-5, 13; focus on return on investment, 28-29, 109; "guided pathways" model, 51; hiring practices, 63; institutional expenses on, 50, 62; major-oriented approach of, 3, 199-200; purpose of, 50-51, 61-62, 185-86; salaries in, 64; students' experience with, 5, 57, 62-63, 73, 164, 169, 181-82, 185; training in, 63
academic departments, 46
accounting training, 104
Act of Creation, The (Koestler), 148
ACT score, 157, 170
actuarial science, 127
Acura, 113
Adler Planetarium, 108
advanced courses, 86
Advanced Placement credits, 156, 170
Airbnb, 122
AirDNA, 122, 150
Air Force Academy High School, 15
Akers, Beth: career trajectory, 111, 121; idea of following the passion, 110, 117; *Making College Pay*, 109; pathway through college, 109-10, 111, 112
Alcorn Middle School, 90, 91, 93, 94
Algebra of Happiness, The (Galloway), 118, 119
American Art Therapy Association, 171
American Association of Colleges (AAC), 23-24
American Association of Colleges and Universities (AAC&U): agnosticism toward liberal-arts disciplines, 135; report on academic advising, 5; survey of employers, 134-35, 136-37; view of integrative learning, 76
American Association of Community Colleges, 55
American Economic Association, 24
American Enterprise Institute, 109
AmeriCorps, 95
Anders, George: *You Can Do Anything*, 23, 124, 199
anthropology majors, 138-39
appreciative advising, 7
apprenticeship programs, 3, 136
Arizona State University (ASU), 127, 149
artificial intelligence, 80
arts programs, 21, 90, 170, 171, 172-73
art therapy, 171, 172-73
Asch, Moses, 107

badges, 22, 25, 197-98, 199
Bailey, Thomas R., et al.: *Redesigning America's Community Colleges*, 49, 51, 55
Bard College, 124
Bigger, Bolder, Better (Cohen), 119
biology major, 157
bisociation, 148
blank spaces, 8, 26-28
Blumenstyk, Goldie, 7
Book of Majors 2018, 46
bootcamps, 22
Bourdieu, Pierre, 12
boutique "homestay" industry, 122
Brookings Institution, 153
Brown University, 153

California Institute of Technology (Caltech), 129, 130
California State University Maritime Academy (Cal Maritime), 135

capstone courses, 48, 76, 77–78, 92, 93, 172, 174
career-assessment tests, 80
career centers, 3, 4, 66, 67–68
career paths: networking and, 113, 114, 116–17; parents' role in choosing, 98, 110; personal interests and, 8–9, 107–8, 109–10, 117–18, 119–20
Center for Engaged Learning: advice on choice of major, 125–26; networking opportunities, 115–16; organization of interviews at, 99–100, 106; peer mentors in, 105, 131, 149; student placement at, 90, 93, 115–16
Center for the Junior Year at Governors State University: peer mentors in, 57, 161, 170–71; students' experience with, 25, 28, 31, 57, 61, 157, 164, 165, 168
Centro Romero, 183
certificate programs, 49–50, 52, 139, 149, 179, 197–98, 199
Chai Folk Ensemble, 119
Charnas, Dan: *Work Clean*, 136
chemistry major, 157, 165, 166, 167
Chetty, Raj, 153, 154, 187
Chicago Scholars Foundation, 6, 15–16, 28
Chicago's Mercy Home for Boys and Girls, 95
child-and-family-studies program, 93
Chronicle of Higher Education, 1, 3, 4, 7, 129
Churchill, John, 142; *The Problem with Rules*, 140
city politics, 30–31, 32
Clemente Course for the Humanities, 145, 146
Clueless in Academe: How Schooling Obscures the Life of the Mind (Graff), 8, 39
Cohen, Jennifer, 118, 119–20, 121; *Bigger, Bolder, Better*, 119
college graduates: competencies of, 133–34, 136–37, 138; readiness for job market, 24–25, 34, 197–98; underemployment of, 4, 20, 178–79, 182, 185, 196
College of Liberal Arts and Sciences at ASU, 127
College of Pharmacy at Chicago State University, 152
College of Saint Rose, 195
College of the Atlantic, 75

College of Urban Planning and Policy, University of Illinois at Chicago, 33
colleges: admission practices of, 153–54, 155–56, 176; bureaucratism of, 187, 198–99; cluster hiring initiative, 76; competition for resources, 46; COVID-19 pandemic and, 194–95; financial restructuring of, 195; focus on research, 197, 198; full-time equivalents, 143; institutional bureaucracy, 158; as kaleidoscope, 91–92; loss of programmatic biodiversity, 147–48; organizational structure, 45, 46; prestige of, 153; program reviews, 142–43; ranking of, 20–21; reorganization of, 74–75; social mobility and, 183; student success initiatives, 158–59, 160, 197; teaching mission, 197–98; "zones of inquiry," 74, 76
College Scorecard, 18, 20
college staff, as student advisors, 191–92
College Summit organization, 72
college-to-career trajectory: books on, 11, 34; conditions for success, 175; discussion about, 12; example of, 34, 108; Field of Study elements in, 10; networking and, 116; rules of, 22; social and cultural capital in, 124, 132; vocational aim of, 28–29
Columbia Art Museum, 91
Columbia College in South Carolina: advisory services at, 115, 116; courses offered at, 93; elementary-education program at, 125; exchange programs, 105; experiential learning options, 139; language programs at, 131, 148, 150; political science classes, 72–73; recruiting event at, 99; scholarships, 72, 94
Columbia University: Community College Research Center at, 49, 55, 62; economics faculty at, 111; "Year of Water" at, 75
communications programs, 53, 55, 68, 127, 138, 200
community-based learning, 87, 92
Community College Research Center (CCRC), 49–50, 55, 62
community college students, 1, 2–3, 169
Compaq, 113
Complete College America, 55
composition courses, 188, 189

Confucius, 146
conversations, 38–39, 199
counseling programs, 184
COVID-19 pandemic, 194–95
craftsman mindset, 117
credit policies, 139–40, 148, 157, 158
critical-thinking skills, 19, 128
"Crusade against Terrible Advising, A" (Carlson), 6–7
Cuban, Mark, 117
Culinary Institute of America, 135–36
cultural capital: concept of, 12; importance of building of, 31, 38, 113, 124, 132, 145–46, 161, 201
Cultural Services of the French Embassy, 131
Culture and Evidence-Based Practice Lab at DePaul University, 183
curricular "gadgets," 197–98
curriculum: criticism of, 24; first-year composition courses, 188–89; in four-year institutions, 55; student use of, 25; in two-year institutions, 49–50, 51
CVS Pharmacy, 162, 163

dance majors, 127–28
Dartmouth College, 124, 153
data-crunching companies, 122
Davidson College: liberal-arts education at, 37; preparation of foundational skills at, 34–36
Deming, David, 153
DePaul University: academic advisors, 181; Culture and Evidence-Based Practice Lab at, 183; psychology program, 178, 184; public policy program, 16, 29, 30
Detweiler, Richard, 142; *The Evidence Liberal Arts Needs*, 141
Deutsche Bank, 129
Dewey, John, 138
Dowling, Laura, 36
dual-degree programs, 132, 156, 157, 170
Duffy, Kathleen, 127, 128, 149
Duffy Group, 127
Duke University, 153, 177
Dylan, Bob, 107

EAB (education company), 55
early-alert systems, 13, 180, 197
economics majors, 110, 111
employers: AAC&U survey of, 133, 134–35, 136–37; assumption about liberal arts, 126–27, 128; desired skills in college graduates, 133–34
empty college degrees: debates over, 8, 13; definition of, 7, 18, 23; employment prospects and, 66, 180, 196, 201; root causes of, 26, 27, 45; value of higher education and, 198
Emsi (labor market analytics firm), 124
EMT programs, 166, 167
engineering major, 21, 108
Epic of Gilgamesh, 146
ESADE (business school), 149, 150
Etsy, 124
Evanston Township High School, 184
Evergreen College, 75
Evidence Liberal Arts Needs, The (Detweiler), 141
experiential learning: benefits of, 36, 169, 182; blank space of, 26; career prospects and, 10, 69; educational plan and, 87; medical schools and, 165–66; mentors and, 39, 58, 85; options, 27, 61, 62, 131

faculty: as academic advisors, 65–66, 191–92; as field specialists, 86; professional development of, 65; research interests, 48, 198; responsibilities of, 65; students and, 85, 86, 96; tenured, 65
Far Horizons Lab, 108
Field of Study approach: benefits of, 32, 166, 177, 181, 183, 184–85, 199–200, 201; clarification of hidden intellectualism and vocational purpose, 29–31, 58, 79–80, 121; *vs.* conventional advising, 4–5; cultural capital and, 12; exploration of the world outside academe, 25, 31; faculty and, 184; focus on student interest, 25, 58; incorporation into curriculum, 79, 186–87, 188; intrinsic strength of, 87; IPS elements in, 10, 11; notion of, 205n4; as pedagogical activity, 87; peer mentors training in, 171; principles of, 4, 9, 99; steps of, 40–41, 79–87; students' experience with, 5–6, 12, 33, 37, 79, 96–97, 130, 148–50; techniques of, 173–74; training of faculty and staff in, 191–92; wicked problem and, 78–79, 81

Field of Study, pilot-testing of, 13, 187–94; in advising or career services, 189; assessments for, 193–94; elements of, 187–94; locations on campus for, 192–93; in residential programs, 189; targeted groups, 188; in traditional first-year seminar, 189; training of peer advisors for, 191–92
field placement, 184
Fields, Joyce, 89
finance programs, 129
fine arts majors, 109–10, 128, 199
Fischman, Wendy, 141, 142; *The Real World of College*, 140
Five Rules of the College and Career Game (report), 21
Florida Atlantic University, 7
Focus2Career test, 80
Folklife Center, 105–6
Forbes, 117
foreign-language major, 67
Forms of Ethical and Intellectual Development (Perry), 144, 213n32
French language major: career path, 125–26; in commercial settings, 132, 139, 148, 149–50; courses in, 139–40; studies abroad, 130, 131
Friedman, John N., 153
full-time equivalents (FTEs), 143

Galloway, Scott: *The Algebra of Happiness*, 118, 119
Gallup-Strada College Student Survey, 23
Gardner, Howard, 141, 142; *The Real World of College*, 140
general education, 17, 18, 23, 26
Georgetown University, 21
George Washington University, 114
Glendale Community College, 154
Golden Bear (ship), 135
Goldman Sachs, 129
Goucher College, 129, 130
Governors State University: admissions event at, 165; advising services at, 4, 25, 161, 162, 164, 167, 168; art programs, 174; collaborative summer research program, 163; dual-degree programs, 170; Family Development Center, 172; general education requirements, 30; interdisciplinary studies, 163; mental-health counseling program, 173; pharmacy studies at, 157; quality of education, 16–17, 166; survey of students, 5
grade point average (GPA), 165, 166, 170, 179
graduate studies, 96, 105
Graff, Gerald, 9; *Clueless in Academe: How Schooling Obscures the Life of the Mind*, 8, 39
Great Recession of 2008, 128–29
guided pathways, 51, 52–53, 55–56
Guthrie, Woody, 107

Habits and Hustle (podcast), 118
Hacker's Mind, A (Schneier), 155
hacking, concept of, 155
hacking college: benefits from, 157, 158–61, 165; strategies, 153, 156–57, 163, 167, 171, 172, 173; as tool for changing societal structures, 156; by wealthy people, 155–56
Hager Sharp (public-relations firm), 117
Hampshire College, 75
Handshake recruiting platform, 100
Hardesty, Cameron, 34, 35, 36, 37
Harper's Magazine, 145
Hartocollis, Anemona, 123
Hart Research Associates, 133
Harvard Medical School, 163
Harvard University, 140, 153, 154, 177, 195, 196
Heisenberg, Werner Karl, 146
Hendrix College, 140
hidden intellectualism: career trajectory and, 28; clarification of, 29–31, 38, 58, 63, 88, 105, 107–8, 121; college curriculum and, 8–9; cultural capital and, 12; definition of, 104; discovery of, 120; hidden job market and, 4, 104–5, 106, 117; interdisciplinarity of, 48–49; passion and, 120; practicality and, 120; students' representation of, 82
hidden job market: college degree and, 176; definition of, 9–10, 100–101; employment opportunities in, 67, 101–3; granularity of, 113; hidden intellectualism and, 4, 104–5, 106, 117; investigation of, 109, 174; in museums, 101–2; pathways into, 58, 80
higher education: choice of institution of, 23; conflicting interests in, 38; debates on value of, 195, 196–98; as employment

requirement, 17–18, 20, 195; financial barriers to, 19, 20; "five rules" of, 21–22; general-education requirements, 17, 23; goal of, 140, 200–201; holistic vs. linear thinking in, 29; importance of conversation in, 38, 39; misperceptions about, 15, 17, 18–19, 44–45; professional advancement and, 114; resistance to change, 75; return on investment, 109; social mobility and, 19, 176–77, 182–83; studies of, 39; talent development, 199
higher-education capital (HEDCAP), 140–41
high-school counselors, 44
Holmes, Roland "Rollie," 10, 11
honors programs, 164, 165, 166, 167, 178–79, 184
Hospital for Special Surgery in New York City, 129–30
Howell, David, 146–47
human ecology major, 75
humanities programs, 21, 22, 123, 199

Illinois Institute of Technology, 108
Illinois State Museum, 2
Indeed recruiting platform, 100
independent-study courses, 160, 172
Individual Plan of Study (IPS), 10, 11, 78, 205n8
informational interview, 59–60
Inside Higher Ed (news source), 141, 186
integrative learning, 76–77
Integrity in the College Curriculum: A Report to the Academic Community, 23, 24
interdisciplinary programs, 10, 48, 74–76, 78, 163, 167
international business program, 149
internships, 105, 106–7, 149, 150
invisible students, 180–82
Ithaca College, 110
It Takes More Than a Major: Employer Priorities for College Learning and Student Success survey, 133
Ivy League institutions, 153

Jack, Anthony: *The Privileged Poor*, 112, 154
Jerry Springer Show, 137
Jobs, Steve, 117, 148
Joliet Junior College, 164, 165, 166, 167
journalism major, 22, 52, 53, 54

K–12 curriculum, 107
Kirk, James T. (character), 7
Koestler, Arthur: *The Act of Creation*, 148
Korn, Julia, 117
Kuhn, Thomas S., 145, 213n32

Laff, Ned, 1, 4–5, 6, 7, 11, 178–79, 183
Lambert, Leo M., 37
language programs, 123, 124, 131–32, 149
Lascaux caves, 146
Latinx studies, 179, 181
law schools, 64–65
Lazear, Eddie, 111–12
learning, as interpretive experience, 92
learning management system (LMS), 189
legacy admissions, 156
liberal arts: academic debate on, 123, 140–42; cutback of, 123, 130, 135; earning bracket and, 22; elitist view of, 141, 147; employers' assumption about, 126–27, 128, 134–35, 136–37; enrollment in, 123; job market and, 10, 123–25, 127–29, 136, 137–38, 143; personal development and, 137, 143–45, 146–47; value of, 137, 147; vs. vocational programs, 128, 140
Liberal Education (periodical), 24
licensed clinical social worker (LCSW) programs, 184
Light, Richard J.: *Making the Most of College: Students Speak Their Minds*, 39
Lightcast (labor market analytics firm), 124
Lincoln Land Community College, 1–2, 3, 13–14, 176
linguistics programs, 113–14
LinkedIn, 117, 120
Lofton, Fiona, 99
Louder Than a Bomb slam-poetry competition, 88, 89, 94
low-income students: academic advising for, 164, 181–82; challenges of, 44, 56–57, 154, 157, 158, 159–60, 173, 182; citizenship status of, 164; in elite institutions, 154, 177, 182; Field of Study approach used by, 181; field placements, 184; financial aid for, 160, 164, 181; institutional bureaucracy and, 158–59; interests and passion of, 121, 183; minimum-wage jobs and, 178, 182; networking and, 112–13; possibilities

low-income students (*cont.*)
  in hidden job market, 179; programs and resources for, 43–44; research investigative inquiry of, 183; social and cultural capital of, 145, 159; success coaches for, 158–59, 160; vocational purpose of, 183; work and study balance, 164, 165
Loyola University Chicago, 184
L'SPACE Mission Concept Academy, 108
Luke, Thomas, 129, 130

MAC Alpha Capital Management, 129
MacArthur Foundation, 43
magna cum laude, 179–80, 184
major-equals-job mentality, 18, 45–46, 47–48, 124–25, 128, 199–200, 201
majors: AAC report on, 23–24; act of choosing, 2, 3, 47, 56, 108, 109–10; career trajectory and, 8, 9, 45–47, 67, 108–9; conventional college guidance for choosing, 3, 4, 8, 26, 57–58, 126; core courses, 27, 46; earning bracket and, 21–22; job market and, 8, 9, 17, 47–48; myth of, 45; return on investment, 9; translation into skills, 127. *See also* meta-majors; *and individual majors*
Making College Pay (Akers), 109
Making the Most of College: Students Speak Their Minds (Light), 39
MAPP (Motivational Appraisal of Personal Potential) career assessment, 90
marketing, 57, 113–14
MarketWatch, 147
Marling, Janet, 159
Martin, Steve, 117, 118
Massachusetts Institute of Technology (MIT), 129, 130, 153
McConnell-Black, Karnell, 186
McKissick Museum, 116
media-relations offices, 85
medical schools: conventional path to, 164, 165, 167; diversity of education and, 207n16; EMT program and, 166, 167; experiential-learning opportunities in, 165–66
mental-health counseling program, 173
mentors, 15–16, 37, 39, 57, 58, 105, 131, 149, 161, 170–71
Merrill Lynch, 129

meta-majors: creation of, 51–52; criticism of, 56; examples of, 52–53, 54–55
Miami University, 123
microcredentials, 22
Midwestern Psychological Association conference, 173
Milken Center for Advancing the American Dream, 116–17
Millennial Trains Project, 34
minors (electives): act of choosing, 6, 181; blank spaces, 26, 27; core courses, 27
mise en place concept, 136
Modern Language Association (MLA), 123
Monster.com, 120
Montás, Roosevelt, 123
Moore, Isaiah, 15
Morehouse College, 16
Morningstar (company), 124
Mullenix, Elizabeth Reitz, 123
museums: college programs, 114; communities and, 114–15; curation of collections, 99–100; hidden job market in, 101–3, 104; internship in, 106–7; professional opportunities in, 98, 99–100, 104, 105
Myers-Briggs test, 80

name-brand institutions, 130
NameLab, 113, 114
NASA, 108
National Alumni Career Mobility Survey, 208n23
National Association of Colleges and Employers, 180
National Institute for the Study of Transfer Students, University of North Georgia, 159
National Orientation Directors Association, 186
National Society of Collegiate Scholars, 179
Naugatuck Valley Community College, 52
networking, 106, 112–14, 115–16
New England Science Symposium, 163
Newport, Cal, 117, 118
New York Times, 123, 124
New York University, 148
Northwestern College, 168

orientation sessions, 185, 186–87

paradox of choice, 27–28, 49, 51, 54
Pasquerella, Lynn: *What We Value*, 137
Pasquerella, Pierce, 137, 138
passion: clarification of, 107–8, 120, 165, 168; definition of, 105; idea of following, 110, 117–18, 119–20; vs. income, 107–12
PayPal, 124
"people skills," 138
Perry, William G., Jr., 92, 145; *Forms of Ethical and Intellectual Development*, 144, 213n32
personal development, 143–45, 202, 213n32
personal interests: career paths and, 28; clarification of, 30
pharmacy schools, 161–62, 214n9
Phi Beta Kappa, 140
philosophy major, 127
physics programs, 129, 130
Plato, 126, 146
political science major, 16, 30
Porto, Portugal, 122
Posse Foundation, 6
predictive analytics system, 180, 188
President's Council of Economic Advisors, 111, 112
"Price to Earnings Premium" (PEP), 20
Privileged Poor, The (Jack), 112, 154
Problem with Rules, The (Churchill), 140
project management skills, 128
psychology major, 170, 171, 178; arts therapy and, 172–73; job options, 181–82, 201
public school system, 20, 125, 164

Ralph Rinzler Folklife Archives and Collections, 106
Real World of College, The (Fischman and Gardner), 140
recruiting events, 98–99
Redesigning America's Community Colleges (Bailey, Jaggers, and Jenkins), 49, 51, 55
Reed College, 186
Reeves, Keanu, 119
RefugeeOne, 183
religious-studies majors, 128
rental sector, 122
research interview, 60, 61
research investigative inquiry (RII): benefits of, 187; as "blue ocean" strategy, 114; college-to-career path and, 169, 179–80; components of, 83; design of educational plan, 49, 87, 104, 174; faculty involvement in, 85; for foreign-language programs, 131; goals of, 58–59, 113, 120, 168; initial stage of, 83; interviews with professionals, 138, 149, 171–72; modification of, 183; personal interviews, 84–85; for pharmacy program, 161–62; questions for, 60–61; resources beyond academe and, 99, 108; as student assignment, 86
return on investment (ROI), 109, 112, 129
Rinzler, Ralph, 106
Rittel, Horst, 73
Roberto Clemente Family Guidance Center, 146
Robot-Ready: Human+ Skills for the Future of Work report, 124
Rooted and Radical Youth Poetry Festival, 88
Rotary International, 149
Rush, Bobby, 32

Santa Barbara City College Transfer Center, 208n3
satisfactory academic progress, 160
Schneider, Carole Geary, 24, 26
Schneier, Bruce, 7, 156; *A Hacker's Mind*, 155
science major, 129–30
Seeger, Pete, 107
Seiden, Don, 148
Selingo, Jeffrey J., 34–35, 37; *There Is Life after College*, 22, 34
service-learning projects, 87, 90–91
Shallal, Andy, 94
Shark Tank, 117
Shorris, Earl, 145, 146, 147
Silicon Valley start-ups, 132–33
simplehuman, 113
Skyline College: guided pathways at, 52; meta-majors at, 52, 54–55
slam-poetry competitions, 88, 89, 90, 94–95
small-group communication syllabus, 137–38
Smithsonian Folklife Festival, 106
Smithsonian Institution, internship opportunities, 105, 106
social capital: college-to-career path and, 124; concept of, 12; importance of, 28, 112, 146, 161, 201; networking and, 113

social media: networking economy and, 112; professional use of, 58, 61, 68
social mobility: broken ladder of, 177; college education and, 154, 176-77, 182-83; concept of, 12; involvement in politics and, 145-46
social work, 183-84
Socrates, 146
soft skills, 132-33, 136-37
South Carolina International Trade Association, 149
South Carolina's Corridor of Shame, 71
South Carolina State Museum, 99-100, 105
Spanish language specialization, 123, 125, 126, 139, 149-50, 179, 200
Spanish translation minor, 181
Split This Rock organization, 93-94
"sprinter" students, 22
Stanford University, 153, 177
Star Trek franchise, 7
start-ups, 36-37
Stein, Zachary, 200, 202
STEM (science, technology, engineering, and mathematics) disciplines, 134-35
St. Leo High School, 33
Stony Brook University, 154
Stovall, David, 96
Strada Institute for the Future of Work, 124
"straggler" students, 22
Straus, Jessica, 34, 35
Strong-Campbell test, 80
students: academic advising experience, 5, 57, 62-63, 73, 164, 169, 181-82, 185; backgrounds of, 11, 34, 44, 71-72, 125, 156; career aspirations, 34, 35, 98, 99, 104, 121, 156-57; categories of, 22; challenges of, 57, 69; choice of major, 47, 62, 70, 126, 130-31, 148; conversations on campus, 38; course selection, 43, 56-57, 68-69; creation of opportunities for themselves, 121; cultural and social capital of, 88, 132; curriculum building, 42; debt of, 111; dropout rates, 38; educational plans, 205n8; faculty and, 39, 85-86, 96, 200; Field of Study approach used by, 12, 37, 73, 81, 88, 92, 94, 95, 96-97, 108, 154-55, 181; graduate studies, 96, 105; hidden intellectualism of, 36, 39, 40, 82, 88, 105, 106; honors programs, 178-79; inequality, 38; integrative learning, 76-77; internship opportunities, 105, 106-7, 150; learning experiences of, 40, 92-93; mental-health challenges, 195-96; mentors of, 37, 50, 57, 58, 163; misinformed college choices, 152-53; navigation of college environment, 42, 49, 50, 51, 52, 67, 157; off-campus opportunities, 90, 93-95; orientation sessions, 186; passions and interests, 72, 73, 88-89, 125, 131; readiness for job market, 20, 41, 200, 201; at recruiting events, 98-99; research investigative inquiry, 40, 161-62; scholarships, 72; skills development, 36, 41, 89-91; social connections, 40, 94, 95-96, 115-16; study-abroad experience, 36, 139; success stories, 11-12, 150-51; ultimate goal of, 70; "undecided," 81; upper-division courses, 86; vocational purpose of, 36-37, 40, 82; and wicked problems, 73, 78, 201-2; work experience, 100, 105, 117. *See also* low-income students
Student Success Commons, 157
success coaches, 158-59, 160
summer bridge programs, 188
Syracuse University, 109, 110

Target store pharmacy, 161
Taylor, Mark C., 74, 75, 78
teacherly authority, 200
telecommunication internships, 108
Texas Career Check, 80
There Is Life after College (Selingo), 22, 34
Third Way (think tank), 20
Thrive Chicago, 43, 56, 57, 58, 69
Thucydides, 145, 146
Tice, Jordan, 117
transfer students, 155, 158-59, 164, 170, 175
translation chasm, 124, 130, 137, 138, 142, 147, 148, 149, 150
T-shaped professional, 48, 55, 134

undergraduate education: basic components, 26; blank spaces in, 26-28; career trajectory and, 41; design of, 40-41; publications on, 38
Ungar, Sanford J.: *Chronicle of Higher Education* essay, 129

UnitedHealthcare, 127
university, notion of, 48
University Innovation Alliance, 180
University of Angers, 125
University of California, Berkeley, 59
University of Chicago, 124, 153
University of Chicago hospital, 173
University of Illinois at Chicago (UIC), 33, 108, 163, 167
University of Illinois at Springfield (UIS), 1–3, 16, 176
University of Illinois at Urbana-Champaign, 16; Individual Plans of Study program, 10, 76, 205n8
University of Mary Washington, 22
University of Mississippi, 157
University of North Georgia, 159
University of Pennsylvania, 194
University of Salamanca, 125
University of South Carolina, 116, 149
University of Tennessee, 67
University of Texas at El Paso, 154
University of the Arts, Philadelphia, 115
University of Wisconsin at Madison, 76
U.S. News and World Report rankings, 109

Vacation Rental World Summit, 122
vocational education, 128, 135, 139–41
vocational purpose: career trajectory and, 9, 28–29; clarification of, 29–30, 40, 58, 63, 88, 107–8, 121; definition of, 104; development of skill set for, 36–37; discovery of, 120; interdisciplinarity of, 48–49; students' representation of, 82
Vrbo, 122

wage premium, 20
Walker, Viniece, 146
Walters Art Museum, 101, 102–3, 114
"wanderer" students, 22, 27
Washington Center, 32
Washington Post, 147
Webber, Melvin, 73
What Can I Do with This Major? (website), 67
What We Value (Pasquerella), 137
White, Shad, 123
white-coat ceremony, 152
White House Office for Drug Policy, 36
wicked problem, 9, 25, 73–74, 76, 78, 198, 201, 202
Work Clean (Charnas), 136

You Can Do Anything (Anders), 23, 124, 199
Young, Geoffrey, 207n16
Young Chicago Authors, 88, 89, 93, 95

Zemsky, Robert M., 194

Explore other books from HOPKINS PRESS

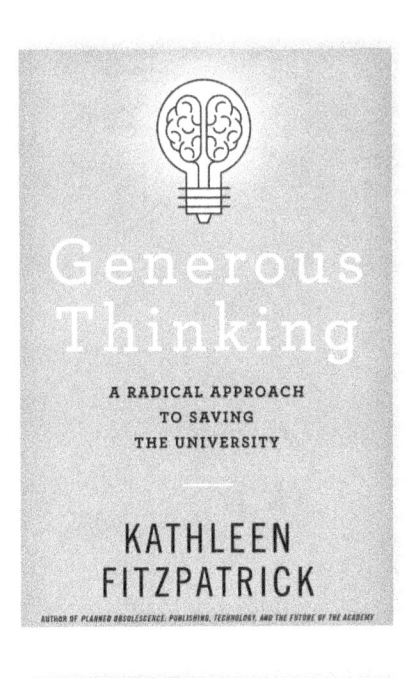

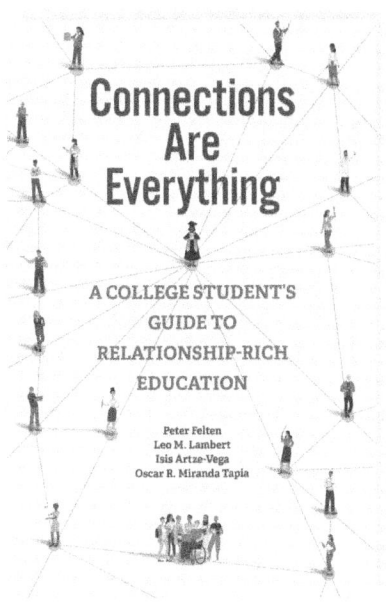

Generous Thinking
A RADICAL APPROACH TO SAVING THE UNIVERSITY

KATHLEEN FITZPATRICK

AUTHOR OF PLANNED OBSOLESCENCE: PUBLISHING, TECHNOLOGY, AND THE FUTURE OF THE ACADEMY

Teaching Change
How to Develop Independent Thinkers Using
- ✓ Relationships,
- ✓ Resilience, and
- ✓ Reflection

José Antonio Bowen
Author of *Teaching Naked*

Cultivating Inquiry-Driven Learners: The Purpose of a College Education for the Twenty-First Century
Clifton Conrad & Laura Dunek

second edition

Connections Are Everything
A COLLEGE STUDENT'S GUIDE TO RELATIONSHIP-RICH EDUCATION

Peter Felten
Leo M. Lambert
Isis Artze-Vega
Oscar R. Miranda Tapia

JOHNS HOPKINS UNIVERSITY PRESS | PRESS.JHU.EDU